*Roni Berger, PhD, CSW*

# Stepfamilies
## *A Multi-Dimensional Perspective*

"**T**his book reflects what is known about stepfamilies while adding a novel dimension based on postmodern thinking. The author's unmistakable message is that stepfamilies are a 'unique breed' and not a 'deficit model' of the non-stepfamily.

Dr. Berger interviewed a wide range of non-clinical stepfamilies and she demonstrates convincingly the unique characteristics of these complex, multiple, and interactive systems with their diversified and ambiguous roles that may be conflictual, but can also lead to enrichment and versatility. One of the great merits of this book is that the author challenges the existing negative myths and also develops a novel category that focuses on the family's own perception. By giving this category a new name, Berger honors the need for new language as she calls these types 'integrated, invented, and imported families.' In the chapter on culture, Dr. Berger's wide view includes such topics as immigration as well as gay and lesbian families, all of which have a different view and tolerance for stepfamilies.

The book is enriched by excellent and poignant case examples in which the members' own voices are heard. A brief section on clinical approaches provides a thoughtful bridge for clinicians working with these increasingly predominant families. Altogether, this book should serve as an excellent source for training groups (universities) and any other interested group dealing with this population. I enthusiastically recommend it."

**Gerda L. Schulman, MS, LLD**
*Family Therapist
in Private Practice,
Riverdale, NY*

"**I**n *Stepfamilies: A Multi-Dimensional Perspective* Roni Berger presents a comprehensive, rich, well-conceptualized, and innovative classification of stepfamilies. The volume is particularly useful in its attention to practice issues and to the variety of stepfamily profiles, cultural diversity, and the changing social context of the stepfamily.

This solid volume is well-constructed and packed with interesting, relevant, theoretical, and clinical material. Filled with excellent case illustrations and lucid commentary, this book is extremely important and useful for all clinicians, regardless of their discipline."

**Yael Geron, PhD**
*Senior teacher,
Bob Shapell School of Social Work,
Tel Aviv University, Israel*

The Haworth Press
New York • London

# Stepfamilies
## *A Multi-Dimensional Perspective*

# *HAWORTH* Marriage and the Family
## Terry S. Trepper, PhD
## Executive Editor

# Stepfamilies
## *A Multi-Dimensional Perspective*

Roni Berger, PhD, CSW

The Haworth Press
New York • London

The Haworth Press, Inc., 10 Alice Street, Binghamton, NY 13904-1580

Cover design by Monica L. Seifert.

**Library of Congress Cataloging-in-Publication Data**

Berger, Roni.
    Stepfamilies : a multi-dimensional perspective / Roni Berger.
        p.   cm.
    Includes bibliographical references and index.
    ISBN 0-7890-0281-7 (alk. paper)
    1. Stepfamilies.  2. Family social work.  I. Title.
HQ759.92.B465  1998
306.874—dc21
                                                                    98-6171
                                                                    CIP

# ABOUT THE AUTHOR

**Roni Berger, PhD, CSW,** is Assistant Professor at the Adelphi University School of Social Work in Garden City, Long Island. She is also the Supervisor of Group Work in the Russian Adolescent Program of JBFCS. Dr. Berger serves on the Advisory Boards of International Conferences of Family Therapy and is a member of the Association for the Advancement of Social Work with Groups, the Council on Social Work Education, and the Adelphi University Senate. She is the author or co-author of five books, numerous journal articles, and has spoken at several conferences on social work with families and with groups. Her current research interests include cross-cultural aspects of stepfamilies, immigrant stepfamilies, and adolescent immigrants.

# CONTENTS

# Acknowledgments

This book is the work of many individuals. Without Dr. Florence Kaslow, who initiated the writing and who guided, supported, and helped me in every possible way, this book would not have been written. My friend, teacher, and colleague, Jona M. Rosenfeld of Jerusalem accompanied and guided me in my professional education and career and in my search for understanding stepfamilies. I want to thank the stepfamilies who opened their homes and their hearts to me, taught me invaluable lessons about the life, struggles, and strengths of stepfamilies, and were always cooperative and patient with my intrusive questions. My students and supervisees helped me to collect data, contributed clarifying questions, and were never tired of listening to my endless preoccupation with stepfamilies. And, thanks to all my colleagues in Adelphi University School of Social Work and in the Jewish Board of Families and Children Services who accompanied and supported me in the long journey of writing this book. Special thanks to Beverly Diamond, Lois Stein, and Lynn Marie Cervo for their help in processing data for different chapters. Last, sincere thanks to my own stepfamily—my husband Howard and my son Dan who encouraged me to go on, tolerated my ups and downs, and always strongly believed in me.

# Foreword

Dr. Roni Berger succeeds admirably in this book in presenting a multi-dimensional perspective on stepfamilies in keeping with her intended objectives. Heretofore, many writers on this topic, as well as clinicians and organizations that work with remarriage families, have tended to lump them all together. The myriad variations were muted, leading to a lack of clarity about and awareness of the different kinds of stepfamilies and of the idiosyncratic characteristics that typify families in each category.

In this volume Berger clearly delineates the separate but overlapping structural, dynamic, and developmental characteristics of stepfamilies. Certainly anyone observing and/or treating blended families should not be unaware of the stark differences between a stepfamily that had been in existence only three months and one with a longevity of thirteen years; or a stepfamily with parents age thirty and one in which they are newly married but in their early fifties, with each having college-age children. Her accurate description of these different groups of characteristics offers a vivid portrayal of their main features.

The classification system Berger elucidates is long overdue in the field, and marks a major leap forward. The case examples given for integrated, invented, and imported stepfamilies, respectively, are quite illuminating. No doubt clinician readers who have treated stepfamilies will experience some "instant recognition" of a family they have treated while perusing these sections, and find they have gleaned information that is useful for furthering their understanding of those they have been treating and their particular kind of dynamic profile.

I found the chapter on immigrant stepfamilies particularly fascinating, since I often consult here and abroad about treating recently relocated families and the additional problems they confront that are often inherent in the immigration process and with being foreigners in a new land. Berger's treatment of this topic is sensitive, thoughtful, rich, and valuable, as are her portraits of black, gay, and lesbian remarriage families. She adds substantially to the literature of the field with her descriptions of the special factors that come to the forefront in these three groups of families.

In keeping with the rest of the book, the final section is succinct, timely, and well written. The multipronged emphasis on normalization of the stepfamily experience; utilizing psychoeducational approaches; promoting flexibility and creativity; and working in a collaborative paradigm in therapy are at once realistic and feasible. It fits well with recognizing that stepfamilies comprise a huge percentage of our population and that this is now a normal rather than an atypical family form.

I harken to and echo her call for a step-relationship language and have long challenged audiences I present to to come up with words and concepts that adequately depict relationships without being prejorative. How cumbersome to say "her first husband and her second husband" or the "fathers of children #1 and #2," and then "of children #3 and #4." How does one connote the relationship of the two men, each of whom has had the same wife, albeit sequentially? They may both be contributing to the same woman's financial support and/or to underwriting the costs of the same child's education, housing, and clothing. Do they become "husband-in-law" (my term)? If not, what term should we use, since frequently they will have a relationship to each other within the context of the stepfamily and the linked predecessor family? Suitable language would make conceptualization easier and more accurate, and would advance the field.

Berger has captured the complexity and variety of stepfamilies and helped us to glean their hopes and dreams by moving beyond stereotypes and overgeneralizations. I believe this book will constitute a valuable and important part in building a knowledge base about stepfamilies.

*Florence W. Kaslow, PhD*
*Director, Florida Couples*
*and Family Institute*

# PART I:
# THE NATURE AND HISTORY
# OF STEPFAMILIES

*Remarriage is the triumph of hope over experience.*

Samuel Johnson

# Chapter 1

# Introduction:
# The Changing Context of Stepfamilies

This book is about diverse types of nonclinical stepfamilies. It is geared toward learning about the lives of successful stepfamilies. Stepfamilies are different from non-stepfamilies in many ways. Often these differences have been viewed as problems, and efforts have been made to help stepfamilies become as similar as possible to first-time families. The more a stepfamily resembled an intact nuclear family, the more successful it was considered. We now know that this is not so. Stepfamilies are a different "creature" with unique characteristics. Knowledge about functional stepfamilies will help us to differentiate between what is typical of all stepfamilies (but not of non-stepfamilies) and what is dysfunctional. Consequently, we will know better how to guide remarried families.

As divorce rates continue to rise and most divorced adults continue to remarry, stepfamilies are becoming the fastest growing family structure. The nuclear family is no longer the typical American family (Whitsett and Land, 1992). Stepfamilies have become so common that they are predicted to be the predominant family structure in the United States by the year 2010 (Visher and Visher, 1996). Even though estimates of their numbers vary, it is clear that stepfamilies are a major type of family, and they are here to stay, to expand, and to become more and more visible.

Consequently, family therapists, psychologists, social workers, educators, pediatricians, family physicians, psychiatrists, and a wide variety of other professionals are servicing more and more stepfamilies in their practices.

To render stepfamilies services that promote their well-being and meet their needs, one has to recognize their normative structural features and dynamics. It is also important to understand how the members of stepfamilies perceive and cope with their situation. It is crucial to acknowledge that what is normal for a stepfamily differs from what is normal for a non-stepfamily. Conceptual systems designed for nuclear families are not always applicable to stepfamilies. A conceptual framework tailored to address the distinctive structure of stepfamilies will help us to distinguish issues related to remarriage from clinical syndromes. In a recent survey of 267 remarried couples regarding their experience in therapy, lack of therapists' familiarity with the unique issues and dynamics of stepfamilies emerged as the major retarding factor of the counseling process (Visher and Visher, 1996). Hence, better education about stepfamilies is necessary.

Yet, only in the 1980s did scientists and clinicians begin focusing their research on the study of stepfamilies. Until then, stepfamilies remained neglected, compared to the abundance of clinical, theoretical, and empirical knowledge about single-parent families, divorced families, and adoptive families. As such, stepfamilies remained a stepchild in family research. In a recent review of studies, Ganong and Coleman (1994a) concluded that:

> As recently as 1979, a review of the literature yielded only eleven empirical studies on stepfamilies, including unpublished doctoral dissertations. These studies had sampled a total of only 550 stepfamilies in the United States. (p. 11)

Clinical knowledge was no more abundant (Schulman, 1972; Messinger, 1976), and only a handful of popular books and articles was available (for example, Baer, 1972; Maddox, 1975; Roosevelt and Lofas, 1976; Green, 1978). The reluctance to study these families has been blamed on their complexity and the challenges they present to researchers (Pasley and Ihinger-Tallman, 1987) as well as a societal tendency to ignore their unique issues—If we do not deal with them, they do not exist as a social phenomenon (Robinson, 1991; Berger, 1993).

The 1980s witnessed an explosion of clinical, theoretical, and empirical interest in remarriage and stepfamilies. However, most works at the time unfavorably compared stepfamilies to first-marriage intact families. Inherent in this perspective is the idealization of intact families as the desired "normal" model, with other types of families viewed as inferior. This maintains the socially negative stereotype of remarriages as "second-grade" families. During these years, clinical knowledge about dysfunctional stepfamilies developed faster than empirical research on stepfamilies as a whole, which resulted in a distorted body of knowledge that dominated the field and reinforced the negative stereotypes. Consequently, most of the early as well as some of current books and articles pertinent to stepfamilies dealt mostly, though not exclusively, with troubled stepfamilies who experienced individual, marital, or family problems that motivated them to seek treatment.

Much of the literature focused on documenting problems, conflicts, and difficulties of stepfamilies, including the intense painful feelings involved in stepfamily living. Stepfamilies have been blamed for many social ills, such as delinquency and domestic violence and abuse, and associated with chaos, hurt, instability, and confusion. Studies and clinical discussions of stepfamilies often examined the effects of remarriage from a problem-oriented, pathologizing viewpoint. This yielded the "deficit-comparison paradigm" that implicitly assumes the inferiority of stepfamilies to nuclear families (Berger, 1993; Kaslow, 1993; Ganong and Coleman, 1994a). This attitude is reflected in, among other things, family terminology. Terms such as family disruption, dissolution, and instability, which bear negative connotations rather than neutral descriptive concepts, have been often used to refer to divorced and remarried families (see Spruijt, 1996).

As a result, stepfamily literature was heavily loaded with problem-oriented knowledge. For example, Melanie and Steve are married and are raising her two daughters and his three daughters from their previous marriages. When they were planning to marry, they researched stepfamily literature to collect information that would help them predict which issues they would face and guide them in what they should do. The dominant message they perceived was, "Do not do it. It is problematic and stressful."

My professional and personal experience and my research indicated that living in stepfamilies often involves painful feelings. However, such feelings do not necessarily exist as an inevitable experience in stepfamilies. For example, Mimi and Rick, who are raising her two girls and his two boys, state, "When we remarried, friends prepared us to expect tensions, complications, explosions, and a lot of sorrow and pain . . . now, seven years later, we are still waiting for any of this to occur." This raises a question: how do families that experience painful feelings differ from those that do not? The literature firmly established that the former are not pathological by definition. Are the latter bypassing early phases of the step-process? Are they living in denial? Did they come to the remarriage with more realistic expectations and therefore experience less of the pain of giving up fantasies about the perfect stepfamily?

The difficulty in letting go of the assumption that stepfamilies are "less good" is also evident in more subtle ways among professionals and laymen alike, such as efforts to portray "the perfect stepfamily" and pointing out successes "in spite of the fact that they are a stepfamily." To understand what does work for stepfamilies, we need to study nonclinical stepfamilies and identify their normative patterns and strengths rather than studying clinical families and generalizing from them to larger populations.

In addition to an overemphasized pathologizing focus, many of the early studies relied on an individualistic perspective, studying personal traits, attitudes, and adaptations of individual members of stepfamilies (Bowerman and Irish, 1962; Bohannan, 1975; Parish and Coopland, 1979). Data were typically collected from one family member. Information collected in this way naturally tends to be one-sided, forming a partial picture. Only a few studies included more than one family member as informants (see Berger, 1993; Quick, Newman, and McKenry, 1996). In the early 1980s, the systemic approach started to gain a central place in stepfamily literature. Although clinicians shifted to a systems conceptual framework, the individualistic perspective still dominates stepfamily research to a considerable degree, with a few exceptions of studies that collected data from more than one family member (see Berger, 1993; Quick, Newman, and McKenry, 1996).

The empirical and clinical knowledge on stepfamilies expanded markedly during the 1990s. Researchers and clinicians began to examine stepfamilies as a unique species, judging them by criteria relevant to their particular structural features rather than in comparison to non-stepfamilies (Visher and Visher, 1988). Scholars focused on understanding normative development, dynamics, issues, and strengths of stepfamilies within the broad context of their experience. This is not to say that stepfamilies cannot have problems; yet, a stepfamily is not necessarily problematic or dysfunctional. What is functional for stepfamilies is not always identical with what is functional for non-stepfamilies, since stepfamily structure yields different features, unique dynamics, and special needs. Current knowledge has begun to reflect this new understanding; different questions are being addressed, and nonclinical stepfamily populations are being studied.

However, current knowledge still approaches stepfamilies under one rubric, with limited differentiation of their diverse types. Although the uniqueness of stepfamilies has been well documented, the study of differences among types of stepfamilies has been neglected. Only very little research and clinical knowledge to date has focused on the diversity of stepfamilies; taxonomies are scarce, and only a handful of scholars and clinicians offer information about types of stepfamilies. Generally, the differences recognized among stepfamilies refer to structural characteristics: remarriage families following divorce compared with those following death; stepmothers and stepfathers; remarriage with and without residential children; or stepfamilies with and without children from the present union (Wald, 1981; Pasley and Ihinger-Tallman, 1982; Clingempeel, Brand, and Segal, 1987). Several researchers developed typologies of stepfamilies based on how children and adult family members perceived their family (Burgoyne and Clark, 1984; Gross, 1986). Studies pertaining to the diversity among stepfamilies and examining how issues are related to different types of stepfamilies are yet to be developed.

This book addresses these gaps in the literature. Its purpose is twofold: first, to shed light on different types of stepfamilies and, second, to discuss the implications of these typological differences for counseling. It describes the chief characteristics of diverse types of nonclinical stepfamilies and, based on these portrayals, builds an approach to assisting families throughout the step–life cycle.

# Chapter 2

# Stepfamilies: Who Are They?

•

## *WHAT IS A STEPFAMILY?*

Mr. and Mrs. Gould have been married for five years. Mr. Gould, forty-eight, is an engineer. He has three daughters by a previous marriage: Dona, twenty-two, works in an office in New York and lives with her boyfriend. Gail, nineteen, attends college in Rochester. Melissa is seventeen and lives with her natural mother, her mother's boyfriend, and his two daughters by his previous marriage—Arian, seventeen, and Georgia, sixteen. Arian's and Georgia's mother lives in California and they see her twice a year for short visits.

Mrs. Gould, a forty-four-year-old schoolteacher, has been married twice previously. John, her son from her first marriage, is eighteen and attending college in upstate New York. Her twelve-year-old daughter, Joan, by a short second marriage is a fragile child. She is often ill and requires a lot of attention from everybody. Mr. and Mrs. Gould themselves have a four-year-old daughter, Naomi. She feels very confused when describing to her classmates in kindergarten the different types of step-siblings, half-siblings, and full siblings in her family.

The Goulds are one of today's typical families. If we ourselves do not live in a family similar to theirs, we probably know somebody who does. In a recent presentation at a professional conference, I asked the audience how many were willing to identify themselves as members of stepfamilies. About one-third of the hands were raised. When I asked how many know intimately at least one stepfamily, almost no hand remained unraised. The picture is clear: stepfamilies are a substantial and permanent part of the current social landscape.

A stepfamily is created by a remarriage into which either one or both spouses bring at least one child from a previous marriage.

When only one spouse brings children from a previous marriage, while the other one has never been married or was in a childless marriage, the stepfamily is defined as a simple stepfamily. This concept is misleading; stepfamilies are never simple because of their complicated structure, intricate dynamics, and multifaceted issues. In compound stepfamilies, both the husband and the wife were married at least once before the current marriage and had a child or children in that previous marriage. Both spouses are divorced or widowed and have consequently remarried, bringing their children from the previous marriages into the new family. The children may be living in the remarriage family permanently, as is usually the case with children of the wife or with children of widowed husbands. In other families, parents may have joint custody, a situation in which children divide their time between living with their father and living with their mother. In many families, children live with one parent, visiting the new family of the other parent on a regular basis, mostly during weekends and vacations, as is often the case with children of divorced husbands.

As women are usually awarded custody of their children following divorce, the majority of stepfamilies are stepfather families. These families consist of a remarried couple, the wife's children from a previous marriage, and sometimes the husband's children from a previous marriage (Glick, 1989). It is estimated that the number of children in stepfather families is three times larger than the number of children who live in stepmother families (Robinson, 1991), and the proportion is even larger when counting only stepfamilies formed following divorce.

## HOW MANY STEPFAMILIES ARE THERE?

The number of stepfamilies is increasing, with more children affected now than ever before (Korittko, 1987; Ganong and Coleman, 1994a). Statisticians and sociologists debate the number of stepfamilies, and estimates vary greatly because in many countries there are no accurate census data on stepfamilies (Berger, 1993; Ganong and Coleman, 1994b). This may reflect social denial of the existence of stepfamilies as a special population, or it may be the result of the different definitions of what a stepfamily is. For example, some experts include among stepfamilies those households with visiting children (residents not permanent) from previous marriages and some do not. In a certain number of these families, the children from a previous marriage visit often, sometimes as frequently as two to three times a week, while in other families children from a previous marriage visit sporadically, seldom, or never.

However, available data enable us to develop good estimates of the numbers of stepfamilies and to realize that stepfamilies constitute a sizable segment of today's families. The rate of divorce is constantly rising. Even the most conservative estimates agree that at least every other marriage in the United States (some say 60 percent) in the 1990s will end in a divorce, and approximately 60 to 75 percent of these divorces will include children under nineteen (Martin and Bumpass, 1989; Robinson, 1991). Most divorced adults remarry; forty percent of all marriages each year are remarriages for one or both spouses, with the most frequent pattern being a previously married man marrying a previously married woman (Wilson and Clarke, 1992; Ganong and Coleman, 1994a). As the average age of remarriage is 34.5 for women and 38.6 for men, many of them are likely to bring children from a previous marriage, with half of these remarriages involving at least one minor child. One-fifth of American families with children (over 5 million families) are stepfamilies (Kaslow, 1993). Currently, one in three Americans is a member of a stepfamily (as a stepchild, stepparent, remarried parent, or stepgrandparent). This is expected to rise to nearly one in two by the turn of the century (Larson, 1992).

The United States has the highest remarriage rate in the world. The trend toward remarriage in the rest of the Western world is similar even though the numbers remain lower. For example, in England, one-third of all marriages in 1987 were a remarriage for one or both partners, as opposed to 9 percent in 1961 (Robinson, 1991). In Israel, stepfamilies are estimated to be about 5 percent of all families, but their numbers are rising rapidly (Berger, 1993). The same upward trend applies to the Netherlands, Australia, and other countries around the globe (Hartin, 1990; Schultz, Schultz, and Olson, 1991; Spruijt, 1996). The stepfamily continues to become more common worldwide.

## *A SHORT HISTORY OF STEPFAMILIES*

Stepfamilies are not a new phenomenon. Remarriage has existed as an acceptable solution to the loss of a spouse in all societies at all times and has long been an integral part of European and American social reality. The number of stepfamilies in Western Europe and in the United States in the seventeenth and eighteenth centuries is similar to current estimates (Chandler, 1991; Noy, 1991). For example, in the American cononies, 40 percent of married men and one-quarter of married women ages fifty and older were remarried; in Italy, France, and England, 30 to 50 percent of married people, during this same time, were also remarried (Beer, 1992). Around the turn of the twentieth century, about one-fourth of the children in Western society lived in stepfamilies. However, in the past, most stepfamilies were created following the death of a spouse. This reality is reflected by the term stepfamily since *steop* is an Old English word meaning bereaved or orphaned.

American presidents such as George Washington, Abraham Lincoln, Thomas Jefferson, James Madison, Ronald Reagan, Jimmy Carter, and Bill Clinton, many of the Kennedys, and most Hollywood stars were and are members of stepfamilies, as were famous artists such as Leonardo da Vinci and Constantin Brancusi. Proverbs regarding stepfamilies and specifically stepmothers are mentioned in Greek, Chinese, and English writings as early as 419 B.C. (for example, in Euripides' writings). Ancient Jewish laws refer to and restrict certain types of remarriage. For instance, people who belong to the Cohens, the descendants of the tribe that served in the Temple, are not allowed to marry a divorcée; a woman that has been widowed twice has limited rights to remarry, and women cannot be remarried within the first three months following their divorce to ensure that they are not pregnant by their previous husband. In Pennsylvania and in the Quaker community, similar restrictions existed, requiring the widowed to wait a year before remarrying (Pasley and Ihinger-Tallman, 1987).

Due to increased longevity and rising divorce rates, most of the remarriages since the 1960s have been established by divorced couples, making the original concept of stepfamilies misleading. A more accurate term to describe families created by remarriage following a divorce is yet to evolve, even though different concepts have been used, such as blended, reconstituted, combined, reorganized, REM, restructured, second, and merged families (Wald, 1981; Berger, 1993). The available concepts are inadequate and inaccurate; they carry negative connotations, and most stepfamilies resent using them and develop "acrobatic" ways of avoiding their use. Prosen and Farmer (1982) view the terms step-, reconstituted, and merged families as inappropriate because they may denigrate family members. Robinson (1992) saw the euphemisms used for stepfamilies as reflecting cultural negative stereotyping, and Ganong and Coleman (1994a) described stepfamilies as "the families with no name" (p. 1). In a recent study of stepfamilies, all the interviewees expressed dissatisfaction with existing terminology and pointed out that the time has come to develop a neutral, nonmoralistic, appropriate nomenclature for this type of family (Berger, 1993). One family in this study suggested the term refamily to convey the message that this is a real family, yet it carries with it the prefix "re" to indicate the sense of "again" or "in another manner."

Beer (1992) notes that political and economic conditions are the major forces shaping the family pattern that is typical for each era. The industrial revolution precipitated the transition from the cohesive, extended "tribal" family, within which most education, religious, and cultural life occurred, to a small, mobile nuclear family.

## WHAT DO WE KNOW ABOUT STEPFAMILIES? A CRITICAL REVIEW OF EMPIRICAL AND CLINICAL KNOWLEDGE

Empirical studies about stepfamilies focused on newly formed families and the initial phases of the remarriage, while little comparative knowledge was accumulated on long-lasting stepfamilies. Even though the difference between step- and non-stepfamilies has been acknowledged, sometimes it is implied that as the stepfamily settles down and reaches advanced phases it becomes more similar to first marriages. Often the question of what happens to stepfamilies down the road is not addressed at all. However, it is helpful for practitioners as well as for the families themselves to remember that stepfamilies remain forever different from first-marriage families.

Many studies of the remarried are of demographic nature. Data from these studies indicate that about three-quarters of divorced adults remarry. Men remarry more than women; whites remarry more often, at an older age, and sooner after divorce than blacks; young people, especially those who have no children or only one or two children, remarry more than others (Pasley and Ihinger-Tallman, 1987; Bumpass, Sweet, and Martin, 1990). On the average, the man's second wife is six years younger than himself (McGoldrick and Carter, 1989), but in some remarriages the women are older than the men (Berger, 1993).

Remarriage tends to occur soon after divorce. Wilson and Clarke (1992) drew a demographic profile of remarriage which indicated that the median interval between divorce and remarriage is slightly shorter for men than for women. On the average, men remarry within 1.3 to 7.1 years following the dissolution of the previous marriage, with an average of 3.6 years, as opposed to women who remarry on the average 3.9 years following the separation with a range of 1.5 to 11.2 years.

Although the exact figures vary, experts tend to agree that couples in stepfamilies divorce more often than couples in first-time marriages (Robinson, 1991; Cherlin, 1992). This is especially true regarding complex stepfamilies (Cherlin, 1978; Clingempeel and Brand, 1985; White and Booth, 1985; Benson von der Ohe, 1987). Martin and Martin (1992) refer to this phenomenon as the inherent potential for instability in stepfamilies.

Two models are generally used to explain this pattern: the institutional model and the processual model. Jacobson (1996) reviewed and assessed both models. According to the institutional model, lack of adequate social norms to regulate behaviors in stepfamilies leads to stress and uncertainty and eventually makes them particularly vulnerable to dissolution. This model has been criticized for being factually unwarranted and unnecessarily complicated. It has also been challenged by a recent study (MacDonald and DeMaris, 1995) which found that remarriage and stepfamilies are not necessarily associated with more frequent marital conflict. According to the processual model, it is more difficult to achieve a solid "family culture," which is essential for marital stability, in stepfamilies than in first-time families because of "baggage" carried from the past. Therefore, stepfamilies are at a greater risk of instability. However, both models define recursive divorces negatively, using terms such as instability and weakness. However, approached from a strength perspective, divorce and remarriage may be defined as an expanded repertoire of coping strategies. Having lived through one divorce, people realize that "it is not the end of the world" and consider divorce an additional option for change, since they are less afraid of a divorce than people who have never experienced one.

The higher rate of redivorce in complex families may also be related to the fact that complex stepfamilies experience higher stress and dissatisfaction in family relationships and lower marital quality than simple stepfamilies (Clingempeel and Brand, 1985; Schultz, Schultz, and Olson, 1991). Beer (1992) offered another perspective on this issue. He claims that if we exclude people who would avoid divorce at almost any cost, such as fundamentalist Christians and practicing Catholics, the rate of divorce among remarried families is a little lower than that of first-time marriages because people who remarry have learned from their mistakes. Clinical experience with people who attend therapy does not support this optimistic view. In counseling, it is common to see people in a second marriage who are repeating patterns that did not work for them in previous marriages (for example, much has been written about women who divorced one alcoholic only to remarry to another person with an addiction). On the other hand, interviews with nonclinical stepfamilies show that some people do learn their lesson from their first marriage and manage to establish a much more satisfying family the second time around.

Research efforts have sought to understand the effects of stepfamilies on their members. Remarriage of a former partner is often accompanied by reactivation of feelings of depression, helplessness, anger and anxiety, particularly for women, and by lessening of contacts between children and their noncustodial remarried parent (Hetherington, Cox, and Cox, 1981). Remarried couples often experience tension related to stepchildren living in the family. Coping with complicated issues of navigating among their natural children, stepchildren, and mutual children born in the remarriage, these couples often find it difficult to be satisfied in the marriage. Factors that affect the satisfaction, adjustment, and quality of a remarriage are the quality of stepchildren-stepparent relationships, the way in which families make decisions, and the birth of a common child (Hobart, 1989; Pasley, Dollahite, and Ihinger-Tallman, 1993).

The effects of growing up in a stepfamily are controversial. Although some studies did not find any significant psychological differences between children in stepfamilies and their counterparts from other family types, stepchildren were often reported as feeling more rejected and discriminated against than children in nuclear families, having more mental health and behavioral problems, having fewer social skills, having lower educational expectations, and being aggressively insecure (Langner and Michael, 1963; Rosenberg, 1965; Hetherington, 1993). The tendency to emphasize the negative effects of living in a stepfamily was significant in the past. In recent years, more and more studies and comprehensive reviews of the existing knowledge indicate no significant differences between children who grow up in stepfamilies and those who grow up in non-stepfamilies. It is important to remember that knowledge about what happens to children who live in stepfamilies when they become adults and build their own families is almost nonexistent. Efforts to investigate any such long-term effects yielded very few significant differences between adults who grew up in step- as compared to non-stepfamilies (Beer, 1992).

Some scholars indicated that the effects of living in a stepfamily vary and specified differential effects on children by age and gender (see Pasley and Ihinger-Tallman, 1987; Martin and Martin, 1992; Ganong and Coleman, 1994a). Numerous studies have shown that girls have more difficult relationships with stepparents than boys and that stepparents of either gender have more troubles with stepdaughters. Other factors that affect the adjustment of children are the relationship with the noncustodial natural parent, the personality of the stepparent, the composition of the sibling subsystem, and the attitude of the custodial natural parent (Beer, 1992).

Although the findings are inconsistent, many studies found stepfamilies to be less cohesive and more stressful than non-stepfamilies. Stepmother families and complex stepfamilies tend to display more stress than stepfather families (Martin and Martin, 1992).

Stepfamilies often have problems concerning poor communication, power issues, and conflict avoidance (Crosbie-Burnett and Giles-Sims, 1989; Pill, 1990).

Clinical knowledge of stepfamilies has generally reported that stepfamilies are beset by problems and difficulties and are more likely to be dysfunctional than their first-marriage counterparts (Pasley and Ihinger-Tallman, 1987). Children experience conflicts regarding split loyalties that are often followed by ambivalence toward various family members and guilt for parental divorce and for developing attachments to stepparents and stepsiblings. They feel angry toward the stepparent who took the place of the natural parent, toward the natural parent who "betrayed" the noncustodial natural parent, and toward the "deserting" natural parent (Sager et al., 1983; Visher and Visher, 1988; Pasley and Ihinger-Tallman, 1987). Children of stepfamilies were reported to experience intensive loss and pain, anxiety about belonging, and confusion about roles and rules.

Since families seek counseling when they experience difficulties, mostly in the initial phases of the step–life cycle and around pivotal transitions in their lives (for example, the birth of a new baby in the remarriage), these are the phases about which we know the most. A large part of the clinical literature focused on stepfamily formation during the first five to seven years of the step–life cycle, with the implied assumption that once integration has taken place, loyalties develop, and things become familiar and calmer, stepfamilies need less help.

Papernow (1993) studied the developmental process of stepfamilies from the viewpoint of family members. She described in detail the emotional stages experienced by stepfamily members as they move toward family identity and indicated that it takes four to seven years for a stepfamily to move through these stages. She identified seven stages to establishing a family identity:

1. fantasy—adults expect the new system to be established instantly;
2. immersion—characterized by constant conflicts and tension;
3. awareness—of difficulties and splits along biological lines;

4. mobilization—clashes between diverse needs of individuals and subsystems;
5. action—solidifying of the couple and responding to needs of children;
6. contact—stepparent-stepchild relationship develops and some stability has been achieved;
7. resolution—the family gains cooperation and stability.

Each of these phases presents different tasks for the stepfamily. A major concern in this process relates to unresolved issues from prior marriages. These issues concerning questions of money, custody, visitation, and the like, cause difficulties in the remarriage and may be either persistent or periodic problems (Kaslow, 1988).

## *SUMMARY*

Stepfamilies have existed throughout history, but they became the focus of social study toward the end of the twentieth century. Today we know much about their demography, structure, development, and dynamics.

Stepfamilies differ from each other. They vary according to spousal marital history (were both previously married and have children or only one of them), reason for the dissolution of previous marriages (divorce or death), number and ages of children and custodial arrangement, and existence or absence of mutual children in the current marriage (Ahrons and Rodgers, 1987; Pasley and Ihinger-Tallman, 1987; Berger, 1995). Despite this diversity, all types of stepfamilies share structural, dynamic, and developmental characteristics that are unique to this type of family configuration and that differentiate them from non-stepfamilies (Sager et al., 1983; Visher and Visher, 1988). These common stepfamily characteristics will be presented in the next chapter.

# Chapter 3

# Characteristic Features of Stepfamilies

## *STRUCTURAL CHARACTERISTICS OF STEPFAMILIES*

All stepfamilies have a complex structure, ambiguous and constantly changing boundaries, and unclear roles. The following material is a discussion that includes examples of these structural attributes of stepfamilies.

### *Complexity of Structure*

"In remarriage one marries a family or a tribe, not a wife," states Mr. Rand. He is a divorced father of two who through a second marriage, acquired three stepchildren and two new pairs of in-laws. His wife maintains warm relationships with her ex-husband's parents, and with many additional cousins, uncles, aunts, and other relatives.

Stepfamilies have a complex structure; they are composed of two previously separate units and include children who belong to two households, multiple parental figures, numerous relationships, and a collection of full-time and part-time subsystems. In all stepfamilies there is an underlying lifelong duality of the two original units. The split is especially clear when children from a previous marriage maintain an ongoing relationship and either live alternately with each parent (for instance, joint custody) or spend regular periods of time with a noncustodial parent (such as weekly or biweekly visits, alternative weekends, Thanksgiving, Labor Day, summer vacation, etc.). But even when the relationship with one parent is loose or nonexistent, the original parent is still a part of the "psychological reality" of the family. When a stepfamily has children in the remarriage, the split is more prominent because of age differences between the two (or more) sets of children from the previous and current marriages.

Visher and Visher (1988) refer to this complexity of stepfamilies as the remarried family's suprafamily system. Bohannan (1975) calculated eight possible dyadic relationships (such as husband-wife, father-son, mother-son, and so forth) in a nuclear family as opposed to twenty-two possible dyadic relationships in a remarried family with one remarriage. This number is further multiplied if a second divorce and remarriage occur.

Since there are different divorce and custody arrangements, stepfamilies may contain a variety of subsystems and relationships. Each stepfamily includes at least three, and often more, parental figures. At least one of them exists outside of the remarriage family, while a parent figure of the same gender exists within the family. The extrafamilial parent figure exists in the concrete reality, such as a divorced father who routinely spends time with his kids who are in the custody of their remarried mother, or psychologically, such as a dead parent or a parent who neglected the children or has limited contact with them.

A stepfamily may include a variety of subsystems: the remarried couple, parent-children, stepparent-stepchildren, and natural, half-, and stepsibling subsystems. In addition, stepfamilies always include at least three, often four, and sometimes five or more sets of in-laws, grandparents, uncles, and extended family both from previous and current marriages (Nelson and Nelson, 1982; Visher and Visher, 1988; Ganong and Coleman, 1994a). This raises questions regarding the relationships among in-laws from the previous and current family and other family members. Typical questions are: Do parents of current spouses see themselves as grandparents to children from previous marriages of the new spouse? How should in-laws from previous marriages be addressed and treated?

When a parent remarries, at least three sets of grandparents are affected: the parents of the remarrying parent, the parents of the noncustodial parent, and the parents of the new spouse.

## The Parents of the Remarrying Parent

The parents of the remarrying parent are often a source of help for their adult divorcing child and for their grandchildren as they go through divorce. They may provide financial help, temporary or permanent housing, child care services, and emotional support during and following the divorce. When their divorced adult child remarries, grandparents may feel displaced, as the couple builds a new life for themselves and the children. They may also feel concerned about whether the new partner treats their grandchildren properly. They want their children to be happy, but they are often concerned that the remarriage will cause their child to shift part of the energy and attention that was focused exclusively on the grandchildren to the new spouse. It is common to hear grandparents criticize their adult children for "being selfish" and "thinking about themselves" in their decision to remarry.

Anna is the only daughter of Jacob and Glenda. When Warren, her only son, was three, she divorced her husband of fifteen years. She moved to live near her parents who helped intensively with child care and baby-sitting tasks. When her son was seven, Anna started dating Gerald, whom she married three years later and then moved to another state. Anna's parents felt torn. They wanted their daughter to be happy, yet were worried about the relationship between her new husband and their only grandchild. Their first question when Anna announced her upcoming marriage was, "What does Warren think about it?" and this remained their primary concern. They began every telephone conversation by asking, "How does Warren get along with Gerald?"; "How does Gerald treat Warren?"; or "Who will take care of Warren when you are gone for a business trip?" Ultimately, they failed to accept Gerald as a real and reliable partner in raising their grandchild.

Some grandparents spoil the children from the previous marriage "to compensate" them for being "deprived," while others remain attached to the previous partner of their divorcing son or daughter and fail to allow space for the new partner.

## The Parents of the Noncustodial Parent

A divorce that involves children requires the ex-in-laws to shape their future relationships with grandchildren who remain in the custody of their previous daughter-/son-in-law. The way grandparents choose to handle this delicate issue depends on the nature of the relationship between the grandparents and their adult child's ex-spouse during the marriage and the divorce process. An ex-spouse who felt unwelcome and criticized during the marriage is not likely to foster a relationship between the child and the ex-in-laws after the divorce and especially not after a remarriage, if the new spouse has parents who welcome their new stepgrandchildren. In-laws who favored their divorcing child, blamed their daughter-/son-in-law and supported their child's interests during the financial negotiations of the divorce may find themselves "paying" by losing contact with their grandchildren. Children may distance themselves from the parents of the noncustodial parent because they identify with the pain and anger of their custodial parent. A custodial parent who encourages the children in this direction may cut them off from the extended family of the noncustodial parent.

The grandchildren-grandparents relationship will also be shaped by the existence of a new spouse in the life of the noncustodial parent and the grandparents' relationships with this new spouse. If their adult child remarries and the grandparents have a new daughter-/son-in-law, it may create additional loyalty conflicts regarding the relationship of the grandparents and their grandchildren from a previous marriage. Grandparents may choose to compromise their relationship with grandchildren from a previous marriage to prevent jealousy by the new spouse.

Anna was very careful to keep a relationship with her ex-in-laws after she divorced her husband of fifteen years. Being a child therapist, she believed in the importance of maintaining the relationship between Warren, her then three-year-old son, and his grandparents. However, Warren insisted that his mother also be invited when he went to his grandparents. When his father remarried, Warren was very resentful toward his paternal grandparents for praising his father's new wife and trying to talk him into accepting her. He accused his paternal grandmother of favoritism and "nagging," and gradually decreased his visits with her.

## The Parents of the New Spouse

When a parent remarries, the new in-laws have to take a stand regarding their relationship with the children of their adult child's new spouse. Their attitude will depend on whether they have other grandchildren from their other children, whether this is also a remarriage for their own adult child and they have grandchildren from his/her previous marriage, and whether the remarriage bears grandchildren. Some stepfamilies report that the parents of the second husband resented the idea that their son married a divorcée, especially when he has never been married before, and rejected her children. Grandparents whose son has divorced and remarried to a divorcée are often angry at the stepgrandchildren for "taking the place" of their natural grandchildren, who live with the grandparents' ex-daughter-in-law, while their father raises the stepgrandchildren "instead." Even though they are not always aware of this anger, it may affect how they accept the new spouse and his/her children from a previous marriage.

Some in-laws in a remarriage accept children from a previous marriage of their new daughter-/son-in-law as "equals among equals" with the rest of their grandchildren, buy them presents, and spend time with them. Colin, a former bachelor, married Richa, a divorced mother of two girls, and has a daughter with her. Colin's father (Colin's mother died prior to his marriage) states proudly, "I have three granddaughters," and takes all the girls for trips during the summer. In a similar way, Rosa's mother-in-law in the current marriage developed a very warm relationship with Rosa's daughter from a previous marriage. She states that Rosa's daughter will remain her granddaughter even if her son divorced her mother.

Other stepgrandparents discriminate stepgrandchildren from non-stepgrandchildren. This discrimination is sometimes open; they do not acknowledge birthdays and do not bring presents to stepgrandchildren, display only pictures of natural grandchildren, and do not count stepgrandchildren among their grandchildren. Some treat step- and natural grandchildren equally in everyday life but do not include stepgrandchildren in wills and do not open savings accounts for them as they do for other grandchildren. In other instances, the discrimination may be more subtle but still directed toward the new spouse and the stepgrandchildren.

## Stepfamilies Have Ambiguous and Ever-Changing Boundaries

Boss and Greenberg (1984) defined boundary ambiguity as "the family not knowing who is in and who is out of the system" (p. 55), and they identified the level of boundary ambiguity as a predictor of family stress. Ambiguity of boundaries is the bread-and-butter issue of stepfamilies. Because there is little agreement as to who is in the family, and because of constant changes that occur when children alternate between households, both external and internal boundaries in stepfamilies are unclear and permeable. This creates uncertainty regarding issues of affiliation, distance-proximity, and togetherness-separateness and becomes a fundamental source of stress (Visher and Visher, 1988). In addition, adolescents sometimes decide to live with the "other" parent as part of age-related struggles for independence. All adolescents wish to gain autonomy, but the situation of those from divorced families often provides them with an opportunity to fulfill this wish by choosing a parent with whom to live. Sometimes a desire to change custody arrangements in adolescence reflects a wish to build an intimate relationship with the noncustodial parent or to resolve a conflict with the custodial parent.

*External Boundaries*

In non-stepfamilies there is a "territorial" definition of who are family members, where they live, and to which family unit they belong, but in stepfamilies it is not clear where the family "starts" and "ends." Because there is at least one natural parent who lives outside the family, external boundaries are more permeable than in the intact family, creating ambiguity about who belongs (Furstenberg and Spanier, 1984; Ganong and Coleman, 1994a; Bradt and Bradt Moynihan, 1988). Examples of recurrent changes in the composition of stepfamilies occur when parents have joint physical custody and a child lives part of the time with each parent or when a child spends a month during the summer break with his father and his new family. One family defined the ambiguity: "A stepfamily is like an accordion; it shrinks and expands alternately." Mrs. M, a mother of two, whose second marriage is to a father of three with whom she now has two children, described the situation: "I never know for how many family members I have to do shopping, prepare dinner, and do the laundry. It is pretty exhausting to never be sure of the size of your family today."

In interviews with stepfamilies, it is important to ask each family member how many members are in the family and who they are

(Berger, 1993). It should not be assumed that all family members refer to the same people if they answer the question with the identical number. For example, both Mr. and Mrs. Rand reported that their family includes five members. A closer look revealed that he had counted his two children from his previous marriage and the child in the remarriage, while she had counted her children from her previous marriage and the child in the remarriage. Neither of them included the spouse's children from a previous marriage in the definition of their family. Although in this case all four children from previous marriages are young adults who do not live in the family, similar responses may come from stepfamilies in which children from previous marriages reside full- or part-time.

Frequently, there is disagreement among family members whether certain people do or do not belong to the family, depending on their feelings toward these people. Ron, a ten-year-old who lives with his remarried mother and stepfather, came home annoyed and sad from his visit with his father's new family, which included a never previously married wife with three children. Ron reported that his father's new wife (whom he refuses to refer to as his stepmother) forbade her children to address him as their half-brother, declaring that he "does not really belong in our family. It is as if he is your brother, but he is not your *real* brother."

Stepfamilies face a unique situation in which subsystems transcend the boundaries of the family created through remarriage. Thus, the original parents are still in a co-parental subsystem even though their marital subsystem has been terminated (Keshet, 1987). Children belong to two households and constantly alternate between them, changing roles and rules as they move to the "other" territory. An only child who lives with his mother and stepfather may be the oldest brother to younger half-siblings when he visits the new family of his remarried father. Eating manners, sleeping arrangements, acceptable interpersonal relationships, and religious patterns may be very different in the two households to which the child belongs, requiring him/her to constantly adjust to two different worlds (Visher and Visher, 1988; Giles-Sims, 1987).

Consequently, stepfamilies often depend on extrafamilial figures in making their decisions. For example, scheduling family vacations, family outings, and celebrations of holidays, birthdays, and family events requires cooperation of the noncustodial parent. This creates competition, limits the autonomy of the family, intrudes on privacy, and may lead to jealousy (for example, if a noncustodial parent takes a child on a ski trip, while the custodial parent is stuck at home). It also introduces uncertainty into the life of the stepfamily: Will the children from the first marriage be here tomorrow or not? Did the natural father pick up the child after school or is the child standing alone and waiting? Will the child-support money be in the bank to cover the payment for the child's private school?

*Internal Boundaries*

Remarriage requires reorganization and redefinition of internal boundaries. The most clear example is the building of a clear boundary around the new couple. In the process of constructing a marital world and establishing a sense of togetherness, the newly married tend to exclude others. Children from previous marriages often experience this as rejection and try to stop it.

The existence of a parental relationship that predates the marital bond leads to unclear intergenerational boundaries within the family, especially when there are two or three sets of siblings with considerable age differences between children from previous marriages and children from the current remarriage (Visher and Visher, 1988; Berger, 1995). Also, the blurred internal boundaries create questions regarding the hierarchy within the family and which rules apply to which relationships.

Unclear internal boundaries may lead to loosening of sexual boundaries. There is often an atmosphere of heightened sexuality because the remarriage couple is in the romantic phase of the relationship. At the same time, family members are not biologically related and did not grow up together, and there is no clear legal taboo against sexual relationships between stepsiblings (Sager et al., 1983). The situation is especially difficult for adolescents who live with stepsiblings of the opposite sex. On one hand, the situation encourages closeness and intimacy between young people who are not directly related and who are at an age when sexual attraction is a major interest. On the other hand, relationships between members of stepfamilies are not defined as rigidly as they are in nuclear families

(Phipps, 1986; Kaslow, 1993); sexual norms are not particularly clear regarding stepsiblings, at least those who do not live together.

Because the incest taboo either does not exist (for example, stepsiblings) or is not clear (stepparent-stepchild), it is not surprising that incestuous issues arise quite often in stepfamilies. Stepfathers sexually abuse their daughters more often and more seriously than biological fathers, increasing the risk factor for abuse by six or seven times (Finkelhor, 1984; Russel, 1984). Even when no actual incest occurs, sexual competition between a new spouse and children of the same gender from a previous marriage is common, especially when adolescent children are involved.

## Role Definitions in Stepfamilies Are Ambiguous

Roles in stepfamilies have no clear names, definitions, or expectations, and members of step-families have no opportunities to learn these roles through modeling.

### Step-Roles Lack Clear Names

Stepfamilies contain traditional roles and relationships such as father, mother, sister, and brother. They also contain additional relationships such as stepmother, stepfather, stepsibling, half-sibling, and some relationships related to the remarriage that do not yet have names or definitions. Garfinkel (1990), in his description of his ex-wife's wedding, indicated this lack and pointed out the need for "a glossary to help us identify who is what to whom in this era of the enlightened and expanded family. For instance, there is still no nomenclature defining my relations with my ex-wife's new husband. If he is my daughter's stepfather, does that make him my step-husband? Or half-husband? . . . And how about my relationship with my ex-wife's future children? . . . " (p. 56). How does one describe the relationship between in-laws from a previous marriage and the parents of the new spouse? What is the correct term for the relationship of a child who lives with his remarried mother to his father's new wife? And to her children? What should children born in the remarriage be called? Shared children? Common children? Mutual children? The answers to these questions require the development of satisfactory terminology.

This lack of adequate names for common stepfamily situations creates difficulties within stepfamilies and their environments. Situations such as social introductions and completion of medical, insurance, and other administrative forms becomes complicated, as the following example illustrates. Mrs. Rich, a fifty-year-old single mother who married a seventy-year-old divorcé, was hospitalized for surgery. When John, her husband's son from a previous marriage, who is a few months older than she, came to visit her in the hospital, she wanted to introduce him to her roommate. Should she introduce a person who is her senior as her stepson? Should she use the awkward language "my husband's son?"

These situations may also cause embarrassment and confusion. For example, Corinne and Neal have five children: her daughter and son, his daughter and son, and a mutual daughter. They recount a situation when the wife's son was playing with friends in the park when he noticed his stepfather passing by. The boy wanted to call to him to brag about how well he handles the ball, but felt uncomfortable calling his stepfather by his given name because he did not want to seem different from his friends. He therefore called "Dad," to which his stepfather did not respond because he did not realize that the boy had called for him.

### Step-Roles Lack Clear Norms

There are also no normative definitions of the social roles of step-kinship such as stepchildren, noncustodial parents, and stepparents. Western culture has not yet developed rules pertaining to stepfamily relationships that would regulate them (Bohannan, 1970; Cherlin, 1978; Fine, 1996). In a recent article, Fine (1996) summarized empirical studies pertaining to the stepparent role and concluded that social consensus on how stepparents should and would behave in given circumstances is lacking and that biological parents, stepparents, and children in stepfamilies experience ambiguity regarding the stepparent role.

For example, the role of a stepfather is unclear. Is he a substitute father, a nonfather, an additional father, a half-father, a second father, a friendly adult, the other father, or simply a father? James, a stepfather to the adolescent son of his wife, explains:

A stepparent experiences another kind of parenthood, full of contradictions . . . you want the impossible. On one hand, one wants to give, to invest in the child, to prove to one's wife that he is filling the gap in the parental domain as well as in the marital domain. On the other hand, one cannot be only giving all the time. The stepchild is an interference; he takes away your wife's attention, takes money, especially if there is no child support paid by the child's father, and one starts asking oneself about raising a child who is not yours. One wants the stepchild to be grateful and at the same time that he not be grateful and accept the step-relationship as natural; otherwise it is a failure. Yet, when the stepchild talks back, you experience rage that this is how he pays you back for everything you do for him. It's a catch—you send the stepchild double messages, "You are entitled; it's natural that I give to you—it's my duty," and at the same time, "I give you so much; you have to appreciate it; do not dare challenge me" . . . as a stepparent you are doomed if you do and doomed if you don't.

The stepfather's role may bring with it satisfaction as well as frustrations, as expressed by one stepfather:

You raise the child, you give him everything, you put food on the table, and you buy him the computer and the designer clothes that he wants, but he continues to idealize the father who does not pay child support. When you try to confront him for not working enough in school (for which you pay), he tells you not to tell him what to do because you are not his father.

To cope with this complicated role, the stepparent needs a lot of support from the natural parent, as well as a lot of patience and investment of time and effort on the part of the stepparent.

## Opportunities to Learn Step-Roles Are Limited

In addition to an absence of clear norms regarding step-roles, there are no socialization channels through which to learn them and no agreed-upon model with which to identify. We learn our roles as family members from direct experience within our own families and from families that we observe in our social environment. We internalize the models that we observe to develop our own version of a given role. Lack of acceptable norms regarding step-roles creates, at least for current generations, a shortage of appropriate role models. As the number of stepfamilies in society becomes more abundant, children who are raised in stepfamilies and who experience stepfamilies in their social environment will have a clearer perception of "how to do it." Role model examples are now appearing in some TV sitcoms, in movies, on popular talk shows, and in novels.

## What Affects the Degree of Role Ambiguity in Stepfamilies?

The degree of role ambiguity is related to a number of variables. The stepparent role is more ambiguous for stepmothers than for stepfathers, more for stepparents in families in which the noncustodial natural parent is highly involved in the child's life than when the original parent has a limited presence in the stepfamily's life, more in early phases of the step–life cycle, than later on, and more for families with young stepchildren than for families with adolescents (Fine, 1996).

This role ambiguity has been related by Cherlin (1978) to incomplete institutionalization. He assumed that when well-established norms regarding roles and relationships between family members exist, the need for families to make decisions is limited, diminishing the potential for conflicts. Since stepfamilies lack such cultural norms to guide them through the complexities of family relations, they need to develop their own solutions. This creates more room for choices and potentially for internal conflicts. For example, since the role of stepparents is not clear, the question arises regarding whether they should discipline stepchildren. However, this hypothesis has been challenged recently, as being unsupported by empirical evidence and lacking in analytic logic (MacDonald and DeMaris, 1995; Jacobson, 1996).

The role ambiguity of stepparent depends on the expectations of the natural parent and on the consistency of these expectations. Some natural parents expect stepparents to assume full parental responsibility; some do not expect them to be a parent to the child; others convey an ambivalent message of expecting the stepparent to fulfill parental roles, yet this expectation is qualified and conditioned. For example, some natural parents feel comfortable with the stepparents' functioning as parents as long as the stepparents follow the educational line of the natural parents.

## Consequences of the Ambiguity of Step-Roles

Role ambiguity produces confusion, stress, competition, role strain, and issues of loyalty, which will be further discussed later in this section. In one family, ambiguity was described as "the worst enemy of stepfamilies." It may also foster indirect and potentially ineffective communication among family members, with stepparents and stepchildren interacting indirectly through the natural parent (Whiteside, 1982). For example, stepparents often prefer to tell their spouses their ideas about disciplinary issues rather than deal with the stepchildren directly, and children often prefer to request help from their natural parent rather than from their stepparent.

In the absence of clear role expectations and social consensus pertaining to step-roles, each family has to develop its own standards and interpretations. This requires stepfamilies to be involved in elaborate negotiation processes to shape step-roles and has been known to lead to role strain, lowered family adjustment, and lower satisfaction of family members (Fine, 1996; Saint-Jacques, 1996). Two recent studies suggest that a growing number of stepfamilies successfully negotiate clear role expectations. Bray and colleagues (1994) and Ganong and Coleman (1994b) found that parents and stepparents tended to agree on appropriate child-raising practices and sharing of responsibility. This may be a beginning of the emergence of some consensus on the role of stepparents. Such consensus on norms will help to ameliorate the problems of role ambiguity and contribute to the quality of life in stepfamilies.

## DYNAMIC CHARACTERISTICS OF STEPFAMILIES

Typical issues in the dynamics of stepfamilies are the differences in developmental phases of all family members, the need to merge two cultures, the gap between their reality and the legal situation, split loyalties, social myths, and issues of power.

### *Stepfamilies Struggle with Diverse Phases*
### *of the Life Cycle Concurrently*

While non-stepfamilies go through predictable phases of the life cycle (Carter and McGoldrick, 1990), stepfamilies face different developmental phases simultaneously. In addition, the number and ages of children are not preplanned in stepfamilies. Therefore, they tend to include a larger number of offspring than non-stepfamilies, with a wider range of ages because children are from different marriages. This is especially true when stepfamilies opt to bear children in the remarriage in addition to the children one or both spouses bring from previous marriages. Stepfamilies must deal with competing and incongruent developmental needs of individuals, subsystems, and the family unit (Rosenberg and Hajal, 1985). This sometimes creates awkward situations. For example, when an older man marries a much younger woman (not an unusual situation), she and her stepchildren may be in similar personal phases in their lives, but their roles within the stepfamily will be much different.

As a result of this "crossing" of developmental phases, the needs of individual family members may be out of sync with others' needs, and the needs of the system may conflict with developmental needs of individual members, intensifying already existing tensions. Often, stepfamily members have to "jump" into a stage of life for which they have no experience and for which they are not yet ready in terms of their own personal development. A typical example is a never-married young woman who finds herself parenting the adolescent children of her husband while she is still inexperienced in parenthood. Also, when a mother of school-age children marries an older father with young adult children, the stepfamily must develop a new marital system that will meet the needs of both young children and postadolescents.

Since the needs of young children and adolescents are different, individual interests may conflict, amplifying the already present friction created by the effort to integrate two originally separate units. Age-appropriate needs of adolescent children for autonomy, privacy, and freedom are in conflict with the needs of the newly formed stepfamily system, which are to bring family members together and to promote cohesiveness and bonding. Conflicts between the needs of family members in different developmental stages and the needs of the stepfamily may pull the family in opposite directions.

Harold and Rose married four years ago. Harold is sixty-eight and Rose is fifty. Into the family, she brought Victor, her only son from a previous marriage, who was ten at the time of the remarriage. James, Harold's only son from a previous marriage, is thirty-two and is back in school after having dropped out of college and having worked in temporary jobs for nine years. He lives on his own and maintains a close relationship with his father's new family. This creates a four-generation system in which Harold is eighteen years older than Rose, who is eighteen years older than James, who is eighteen years older than Victor. Each of these individuals is at a different developmental phase in their lives. Harold is busy with questions of retirement, Rose is in the midst of an intensive academic career, James is building his future, and Victor is dealing with issues of identity typical for his age. This combination requires the family to cope simultaneously with a wide variety of issues while struggling to develop its identity as a unit.

### Stepfamilies Have to Merge Two Cultures

Every family develops its own "miniculture." This includes family rules about "our way to do things" for a wide range of life decisions, from table manners to disciplinary practices, from the nature of family vacations (or even whether the family takes vacations together) to financial strategies, from the typical family menu to priorities in spending money.

In stepfamilies, each subsystem brings to the family relationship a package of expectations, traditions, roles, and rules. The challenge that the family faces is to merge two "minicultures" into a "stepfamily culture" (Visher and Visher, 1990), a process viewed as a problematic challenge characterized by stress and resistance (Goldner, 1982).

### Stepfamilies Live with a Gap
### Between Legal Status and Reality

The legal status of step-relationships is unclear and confusing. Mahoney (1987) notes that stepfamilies and step-relationships lack adequate legal definition and many of the laws relevant to step-families lack clarity and cohesion. Remarriage creates a legal relationship between spouses, but in most countries and states, only minimal or no mutual legal obligations or rights exist between other family members, such as stepparent, stepchildren, and stepsiblings. In remarriage where the new kin-in-law are children who legally and practically depend on their remarrying parent, the stepfamily situation raises questions regarding mutual obligations and rights.

Traditionally under common law, stepchildren have no legal rights to claim financial support or inheritance from stepparents, and stepparents have no legal parental status, rights, or obligations regarding their stepchildren unless adoption takes place or the court grants a stepparent joint custody with the biological parent (Stacpoole, 1988). Consequently, stepparents are not allowed to take legal actions regarding stepchildren, such as medical consent, and have no right to claim custody if a divorce occurs. Although this situation is gradually being changed, as will be discussed at length in Chapter 13, we still live in a "twilight zone" regarding legal obligations in step-relationships, with ambiguity regarding eligibility and obligations of step-kin.

Incompatible with the absence of a clear legal definition of step-relationships is the reality of stepparents and stepchildren becoming intensively involved in one another's lives. They are often part of parent-child roles and maintain routine physical and emotional contacts. When a new spouse's children from a previous marriage live or visit with the remarriage couple on a regular basis, stepparents are often required to perform parental tasks and to make major decisions regarding their stepchildren's lives. They often participate in raising their stepchildren, educating them, and supporting them financially.

The gap between the situation of step-relationships de facto and de jure may cause stressful situations in the marital and parental subsystems. For example, a stepparent may feel left out and a natural parent may feel overburdened because of the asymmetric disciplinary situation. Stepchildren may rebel against the demand to obey a stepparent. "You are not my father and you have no right to tell me what to do" is a common statement heard from adolescent stepchildren. The following examples illustrate other typical situations.

Mrs. Ring had never before been married when she met and married a divorcée with custodial rights of his then three-year-old son, Ron. Ron's parents had divorced two years prior to the remarriage, following his mother's "coming out of the closet" and moving in with her girlfriend. Both women became involved with a cult and spent a lot of time in India, maintaining only sporadic contact with Ron. When Ron was six, his father traveled to the Far East on a business trip; his mother was on one of her spiritual journeys. Ron became seriously ill and when his stepmother rushed him to the hospital, she was informed that he needed to have surgery. However, Mrs. Ring was not allowed to sign consent, as she had no parental rights and the situation was not defined as life threatening (in such situations, consent is not always necessary).

Veronica, a thirty-four-year-old clinical psychologist, is married for the first time to Henry, a forty-seven-year-old psychiatrist. The couple has custody of Henry's eight-year-old son, mainly because of his natural mother's unstable lifestyle and cocaine abuse. After the child had lived with the couple for four years, his father, who was a recovering alcoholic, relapsed and was hospitalized. His natural mother, who lives about three hours away from the family, immediately sought and was able to gain custody, even though she had only seen her son once or twice a month during the past four years. This meant moving the boy to another school, away from the baseball team in which he excelled, and into an unfamiliar environment.

Sometimes, stepfamilies go through a second divorce. When this happens, stepparents often have no parental privileges such as custody or visitation rights. For instance, Mrs. Levine was eight months pregnant with her daughter, Dalia, when her husband left the family and emigrated from Israel to Argentina. He did not pay alimony or child support and eventually divorced Mrs. Levine. Except for rare telephone calls, Dalia had no contact with him and did not always know where he lived. While Dalia was still a toddler, Mrs. Levine married her second husband, Mr. Taylor, who became a loving and devoted stepfather. He could not have children of his own so Dalia became his "special child." He developed an intense and warm relationship with the girl, attended parents' school activities, and spent a lot of time with her. When Dalia was fifteen, her mother died of cancer. Her biological father, who learned about this from friends, made Dalia move to Argentina to live with him, despite her protests and pleas to remain with her stepfather, whom she had known and cherished most of her life. Although Dalia's reluctance to move was supported by her paternal grandparents, who had come to love and respect Mr. Taylor for raising their only granddaughter, Dalia had to move to Argentina to live with her natural father.

### *Split Loyalties in Stepfamilies*

Loyalty conflicts have been identified as a major issue in step-families, especially, though not exclusively, for children. Remarried parents experience conflicts between their loyalty to their children and to their new partners; parents, between their loyalty to their step- and to their natural children; and children, between their loyalty to their step- and to their natural parents and between their loyalties to each of their divorced natural parents.

Stepchildren do not know how they are expected to feel toward each of the adults involved in their lives. Will their mother be angry if they like their stepmother? Will their father feel betrayed if they become attached to their stepfather? Is a warm relationship with both their father and stepfather mutually exclusive? If they do not develop a good relationship with a stepparent, will their natural parent married to the stepparent be disappointed?

Preadolescent and adolescent children frequently have intense loyalty conflicts, especially if one parent is not remarried or is not in a new relationship. Such conflicts often lead to children boycotting a remarried parent, refusing to visit or accept presents from him/her. In extreme cases, adolescent and young adult children may refuse to talk with a divorced parent who has remarried or refuse to invite the "betraying" parent to weddings, birthdays, etc.

Ella, thirteen, lives with her older sister, her remarried mother, and her stepfather. Her natural father lives on his own and leads a "happy bachelor's life." Ella avoids developing a close relationship with her stepfather, believing that, "This is not fair. We have a family while poor Daddy does not have anybody. He is very lonely. I wish he remarried and would have somebody to care for him." These feelings may remain with children when they grow up. Brad, twenty-eight, was an adolescent when his parents divorced. His father, Richard, remarried and had Gerri with his second wife. When Brad got married, he invited his father but refused to allow him to bring Gerri to the wedding. When confronted by his father, Brad argued that the presence of Richard's child by another woman might upset his mother on what is supposed to be a happy day for her.

Adults share a similar confusion between loyalties to their children and stepchildren, their spouse and children, and their current spouse and previous spouse. Regarding natural and stepchildren, stepparents may feel guilty because they have "left" the former to live with the latter, and they may maintain lack of involvement to protect themselves from this guilt as well as from distress and rejection by a stepchild. Sometimes this is given as a reason for "keeping my distance" from the stepchildren, "to avoid the feeling that I give her children what I deprived my own children of," as Mr. Everest described.

Stepparents also feel torn between their current spouse and children from a previous marriage. Mrs. Neil divorced her first husband when she was pregnant with her now eighteen-year-old daughter. Two years later, she married her current husband, who is ten years younger than her. The couple had two sons together. "A difficult situation occurs when I find myself between my husband and my daughter. I feel torn and I get confused. She sees me as the adult responsible for her. When my husband intervenes in issues of her education and she does not like it, I feel torn . . . betraying one of them. The same conflict occurs regarding the spending of money. How much should be spent on each child . . . my daughter wants things that I would have bought her, but my husband opposes this, he considers it unnecessary, exaggerated, and again I feel torn between the two."

Adults may feel disloyal to the previous spouse or a previous relationship. This happens more often following the death of a previous spouse. Remarried widows and widowers often have difficulty sharing activities, rituals, and experiences they used to enjoy with their deceased spouse as well as information about him/her with a current partner since they feel this is disloyal. However, divorced adults also may experience feelings of disloyalty on either a conscious or unconscious level. Ruth, who was married to her high school sweetheart for twenty years and who remarried ten years after their divorce, becomes defensive whenever her current husband criticized her previous husband for late payment of child support, refusal to participate in medical and dental expenses for his children, and not keeping in contact with them. "I feel as if his criticism is directed at me for being stupid to live with such a person . . . after all, we shared a life and two kids."

### Stepfamilies Live in the Shadow of Widespread Myths

In the absence of norms for step-roles, myths develop. Several myths cast their shadow over stepfamilies. One is the myth of the inferiority of stepfamilies. "American culture presently considers any form of family life that does not conform to the traditional politically correct nuclear family as problematic" (Atwood and Zebersky, 1996). This trend has become even more manifest with the recent refocus on family values. Both the media and folklore portray stepfamilies negatively as deficient, inadequate, and deviant, or they foster the myth that a stepfamily can become yet another ordinary (that is, "nuclear-like") family and measure its success by the degree that it does so (Fast and Cain, 1966; Perkins and Kahan, 1979; Ganong and Coleman, 1987; Robinson, 1991).

Negative stereotypes of stepfamilies are not new phenomena. They appear in many cultures. For example, the Babylonian Talmud warned 1,500 years ago against marrying a divorced woman while her husband is alive. An old Chinese proverb advises, "Good women will not drink the tea of two families"; the Germans say, "A good stepmother is as rare as a white raven"; and the English version is, "Be a stepmother kindly as she will, there is in her love some hint of winter's chill" (Stevenson, 1976).

Negative images of stepmothers and stepsisters as wicked and cruel are persistent in the folklore and fairy tales of all cultures (for example, Cinderella, David Copperfield, Snow White, Hansel and Gretel). Interestingly, stepfathers were less subject to negative myths, probably because prior to the women's emancipation era they were often perceived as saviors who rescued the single mother and her children from poverty and misery. The negative stereotypes also include the use of the phrase "being a stepchild" to mean being deprived, second-rate, neglected.

The negative images of step-relationships have ramifications for the stepfamily and its members because they affect individuals who live in stepfamilies, their personal environment, including social organizations such as schools, and the general public. Stepfamily members may develop unrealistic (negative or positive) expectations of themselves and of their new family as a result of the culturally unfavorable definitions of stepfamilies to which they have been exposed. A woman who grew up believing that a stepmother is inevitably bad may try to become a "super stepmom" when she remarries. She may be frustrated if her adolescent stepchildren rebel, or she may give up from the beginning because "No matter what I do I will remain the terrible stepmother." By the same token, a child who grew up with the same idea may approach his/her stepmother with negative expectations and not allow a positive relationship to develop. Thus, a self-perpetuating cycle is often set in motion, maintaining negative perceptions: Children will expect their stepmother to be cruel, nasty, and demanding and will relate to her as such without checking the reality. Their unpleasant behavior may cause the stepmother to be unaccepting of them, thus validating the false original negative expectation (Kaslow, 1988). Studies have found stigmatized perceptions of step-relationships incorporated in the self-concepts of stepparents and stepchildren (Amato, 1987; Kupisch, 1987).

Stepfamily members are also exposed to the effects of the negative myths on their environment. Stepmothers especially feel that they constantly live under a social magnifying glass; they feel that neighbors, relatives, teachers, and others inspect their performance, judge them, and compare them with the original wife in the "real" marriage (Schulman, 1972; Fine, 1996; Hughes, 1991). This creates stress within stepfamilies and may eventually affect their functioning. (Who can perform effectively when every step is being observed to catch a mistake?)

This experience has been described by my student, Tammy, who presented her family of origin genogram in a class on advanced practice with families. Tammy was raised in a stepfamily. Her widowed father married a divorcée who had two daughters from her previous marriage. When Tammy presented her genogram, she started by saying, "I was raised by my father and my stepmother, who is a wonderful person unlike what you may expect." When challenged, Tammy explained that her defensive statement follows from numerous societal experiences with negative expectations pertaining to the woman who raised her, whom she loves, and to whom she is deeply attached.

Professionals are not immune to the effects of these myths. Ganong and Coleman (1987) studied stereotypes of stepchildren held by teachers, social workers, lawyers, students, and others. With the exception of experienced therapists, most respondents shared negative preconceptions regarding stepfamilies. Stepfamilies report experiencing anti-stepfamily biases in their contacts with educators, social agencies, medical staff, and other professionals. Emma, a remarried divorcée, reported that when she discussed her son with his teacher and described the family configuration, the teacher responded, "I did not know David is from a broken family."

Rita, the remarried mother of nine-year-old Monica, went to meet her daughter's new teacher. She reports, "In the beginning the teacher asked about my daughter's strengths and abilities, what she likes to do, and so forth. When I shared with her our being a stepfamily, she started asking about problems, tensions, and difficulties. Rather than asking about possible effects of the family situation in a neutral way, she immediately assumed problems." Reports of similar encounters were very common in research interviews with remarriage families (Berger, 1993) as well as in counseling with stepfamilies.

Such stereotyping is often used, or perhaps abused, to "explain" problems. Stepfamilies often express their concern that these stereotypes are conveyed to their children and to the other students, thereby creating negative preconceptions.

### Issues of Power

The complexity of structure, ambiguity of roles and boundaries, and split loyalties create unique issues of power within stepfamilies. First, the role of a sole custodial parent carries with it considerable overt power as well as emotional, legal, and social obligations. At the same time, children from a previous marriage have considerable control regarding this parent—a power that is often covert. It derives from the existence of an additional parent external to the stepfamily. The child perceives this parent as a source of support against the custodial parent. An additional source of the child's power is the guilt felt by the custodial parent ("I caused my poor child to live in a stepfamily therefore it is my obligation to compensate him/her.").

This power may take the form of overdependency, an overdemanding attitude, and efforts to create a cross-generational coalition with the natural parent against the stepparent. Bob, whose mother remarried to Bill when her son was seven, uses every opportunity to complain to his mother about his stepfather: "When you were not here he ate these cookies that you saved for the guests." "He said he would be here with me at five and he came late." In the Fisher family, both partners have been married previously. Each brought a daughter from the previous marriages into the stepfamily. Each of the girls turns first to her natural parent for support and advice. Each also tries in subtle ways to manipulate her own parent to side with her against the stepparent or stepsister.

The lack of symmetry in parental power may strengthen the position of the natural parent in the spousal relationship but, in extreme cases, marginalize the stepparent. Jane, twenty-seven, is married to Andrew, thirty-eight. Her eight-year-old daughter from her previous marriage lives with them. His twelve-year-old daughter lives with her mother and visits regularly with the stepfamily. Jane states, "My girl is the most important person in my life. I invest everything in her. She comes first." Her husband agrees, saying, "She raises her daughter alone. They gang up on me. I often find myself against a solid coalition."

Visher and Visher (1996) suggested that a hierarchy of power exists among adults in stepfamilies so that the natural custodial parent has the most power and the stepparent married to the noncustodial parent has the least power regarding his/her spouse's children. The noncustodial parent has more power than his/her spouse and, at least in the beginning, also more power than the stepparent married to the custodial parent. Some of this power relies on the parent-child relationship prior to the divorce, and some of it may be based on the child's feelings of guilt. Tom, nine, lives with his affluent mother and stepfather, while his father, who spent time in jail because of white-collar crimes, lives alone in poor conditions. Tom's father persuaded Tom to maintain a relationship with him by playing on Tom's guilt—"father is alone, miserable, and has no money." Tom's natural father uses his situation to make Tom call him and spend time with him.

When the stepfamily is first formed, the stepparent who resides with the stepchildren has little legal power but often substantial actual power delegated by his/her spouse. Gradually, the stepparent gains more and more direct power through the relationship with the stepchildren. This is especially true when the stepparent fulfills parental roles for the stepchildren. Therefore, stepmothers often have more power than stepfathers because stepmothers typically get involved earlier and more intensively in fulfilling roles such as cooking and attending parent-teacher conferences. Beer (1992) noted that when the stepparent also becomes a parent through the birth of a mutual child in the remarriage, his/her role in the family becomes more central and he/she gains more parental power. The custodial parent has the most legal and actual power regarding his/her children, even when adoption by a stepparent takes place, since the parent and children have a lifelong shared history, intensive common memories, and experiences together during various critical phases (first family, divorce, single parenthood, and remarriage).

Rivalry among step-, half-, and natural siblings is also associated with issues of power. Invisible coalitions among siblings from the various marriages may create power struggles within the family—"Your children and my children hit our children." Children who live permanently in the stepfamily may feel more powerful because they are always there; they are a consistent part of the family system. They also may feel less powerful because they are often expected to perform more chores than their younger half-siblings or visiting stepsiblings.

Children who only stay with the family part-time may feel more powerful because of their status as "guests." Noncustodial stepfamilies are often a "Disneyland family," with more fun and fewer demands because of reluctance "to waste" the visits on routine chores. At the same time, these children may feel relatively powerless because they witness references to events of which they are not part, they may not understand certain family jokes, and they always remain outsiders to some degree.

Children of the remarriage also experience a mixture of feelings regarding power. On one hand, they gain power by having both parents in the household. On the other hand, they are the youngest, and unlike the children from previous marriages, they do not have potential sources of support outside the family. Edna, a mutual child of a remarriage that included children from previous marriages, reports:

> When I was young, I felt jealous of my brother and sister who went to their parents and returned with gifts and stories about the wonderful time they had. I used to feel deprived being the only child in our family with just one Daddy and one Mommy and demanded to join my siblings in their visits to their noncustodial parents.

Sibling rivalry among the different sets of children may affect the well-being of the whole stepfamily system. Out of the differences in power, animosity, jealousy, and anger may be born. Disagreements regarding disciplinary and child-rearing issues have been consistently found to be major sources of conflict in remarriages (Visher and Visher, 1996). A complaint by one child about a step- or half-sibling often falls on "open ears" if a parent already feels guilty for having caused the child to live through divorce and remarriage. This parent frequently intervenes on behalf of his/her child. Consequently, the stepparent will support his/her own child. The tension between the two camps can easily ignite a marital conflict.

Difference in economic situation is another source of power struggles. Research has shown long-term financial decline for most women and children following divorce, while the standard of living for men generally improves (Bogolub, 1995). Consequently, men enter remarriage financially stronger than women. This gap in economic strength may affect the relative power of the partners in the marriage.

Power issues exist between the noncustodial natural parent (ex–spouse) and the stepparent (the current spouse). The conflicts often pertain to children and to the remarried parent and are often exacerbated if the noncustodial parent is not remarried. For example, the natural father may feel displaced by the current partner of his ex-wife and make efforts to demonstrate that he is more powerful than the stepfather. This is done by a variety of ways, such as contradicting the stepfather's ideas, challenging his statements, expressing opposite opinions, and criticizing and making fun of him. An ex-wife may demonstrate her control by constantly summoning her ex-husband to help with emergencies and calling him when her children visit their father and his new wife. Mildred, a childless divorcée, married Tom, a father of three boys. She says that her husband's ex-wife used to interrupt each visit by her husband's children with some urgent message: "The children's hamster is sick"; "My parents came for a visit and the children need to come back earlier"; "My car is broken and you will have to drive them home" (when she knew that they had tickets for the opera).

There also exists a power issue between the custodial and non-custodial natural parents, in which the remarried parent may try to control the household of the noncustodial parent. The parents of seven-year-old Joan divorced when she was a baby. When Joan spends the night with her father, her remarried mother gives her an ironed shirt ("her father will not make sure that she is neatly dressed") and calls to tell her ex-husband what lunch to give Joan for school in the morning.

## DEVELOPMENTAL CHARACTERISTICS OF STEPFAMILIES

The common developmental characteristics of stepfamilies include experiencing many changes, dealing with multiple losses, and having a complex history.

### Stepfamilies Experience Many Changes

Stepfamilies go through many transitions—from an intact family to a divorcing family to a one-parent family to remarriage. Each of these changes creates a period of uncertainty, disorganization, and disruption of the balance that had been achieved in the previous phase. Following a divorce or a death, a new balance has to be reached. Tasks previously fulfilled by the absent parent are taken care of by the members of the single-parent family, by a relative, or by an external figure such as a paid child care worker. When a parent remarries, the newly achieved balance is disrupted again. Therefore, even though remarriage is often thought of as a "repair" of the undesirable situation of divorce or widowhood, it is a change that disrupts the previous balance and may lead to a crisis.

Furthermore, the transition from pre-remarriage to stepfamily is a total and rapid change that is often initiated by the decision of two adults, who wish to join their separate lives together, and children are brought along as a "package deal." Remarriage requires everybody to adjust quickly to a new situation in which some of the participants did not choose to be (Kurdek, 1989; Visher and Visher, 1988). Edgar, a remarried divorcée who raises his wife's daughter from her first marriage, says, "In stepfamilies, one marries the wife and her children."

Although all marriages require partners to go through a process of constructing a marital world out of their different individual perceptions of the world, building a common worldview in a remarriage is more complicated. In a second (third, fourth, etc.) marriage, the couple must simultaneously develop their construction of reality as a marital unit, while they disassemble the "realities" constructed in their previous marriages and between marriages (Jacobson, 1996).

Also, in stepfamilies, spouses do not enjoy the luxury of an adjustment period that allows for a gradual change; they must "jump" immediately into multiple roles. This does not allow time for the new couple to gradually work through issues typical to a new marriage such as power structure, decision-making processes, coping with extended family, and making time for intimacy. Remarriage couples often do not have a private honeymoon, either because children accompany them on the honeymoon or because limited child care resources do not allow them to take more than a very short trip.

In a remarriage that involves children, family members may have to assume multiple new roles at once. A mother of two young children may become instantly a wife, a mother of four adult children, an aunt, and even a grandmother. An only child may become the middle child of five, and the youngest child may become an older brother.

These recurrent upsets cause confusion and bewilderment, especially for children because they feel they have no control over what is happening in their lives. They often blame the stepparent for the situation, since they are afraid to risk an additional experience of abandonment by blaming their custodial parent.

### Stepfamilies Deal with Multiple Losses

Stepfamilies live with a "built in" experience of loss. Visher and Visher (1988) contend that stepfamilies are born of loss. People who go through the cycle of divorce, to single-parent family, to remarriage, lose exclusivity of relationships, autonomy, social status, fantasies, roles, assets, and economic security throughout the "journey" across their diverse family configurations. In the process, the remaining parent and children often develop exclusive and close relationships. Divorced adults frequently become more independent and self-sufficient and may have a hard time resuming relationships that require sharing and compromises. Children often become autonomous and sometimes parentified, filling the role of the absent parent. This is especially true for an oldest child who becomes "Mommy's helper" in taking care of younger siblings. These children often resent losing their special role, being "pushed back" into a child's role, and sharing their parent with "a stranger."

The transitions that accompany divorce and remarriage often involve relocation, which means losing the familiar house, neighborhood, and school. When remarriage means the sharing of rooms, pets, books, and toys, it involves losing privacy and often leads to rivalry.

In addition to creating these fresh losses, the transition to stepfamily life reactivates the loss of the original parent through divorce and emphasizes its finality. Very often children in stepfamilies do not accept the loss that was caused by the termination of their parents' marriage and continue to carry the fantasy of reunion. When a parent remarries, this dream is challenged by the new reality. Still, some children continue to hope that the remarriage couple will not be united, or even be separated, thus enabling their parents to get together again. The dream of reunion may survive for many years. Joan, a therapist in her thirties, told me that her parents divorced when she was twelve and her mother quickly remarried to a family friend. Her father also remarried but redivorced after a short time. Joan maintained a warm relationship with her biological parents and her stepfather. When Joan was thirty, her stepfather died of a heart attack at the age of sixty-three. Her first thought when she learned about his death was, "Now Mom and Dad can remarry."

Some writers insist that family members must resolve losses associated with the dissolution of the previous family prior to constructing a successful stepfamily (Sager et al., 1983; Visher and Visher, 1988; Meyers, 1992; Atwood and Zebersky, 1996). However, this is easier said than done because past events can hardly be worked through "once and for all." Even though resolving issues from a previous marriage can be done to a certain degree, various events in the life cycle of the stepfamily may revive the feelings of loss associated with the previous marriage. Such events are the birth of a new child, the remarriage of the previous spouse, and weddings, confirmations, and bar/bat mitzvahs of children from a previous marriage. Consequently, stepfamilies must learn to live with loss as an inevitable component of their existence.

## Stepfamilies Have a Complex History

All families have a past. However, in stepfamilies, this past is more complex for three reasons. One reason is that the stepfamily's past includes, in addition to personal history, "baggage" from the families of origin of each spouse and "ghosts" from previous marriages and divorces. These "ghosts" are people, relationships, assets, and financial obligations as well as unresolved issues, disillusions, disappointments, and expectations that are connected to the previous marriage. Such "past agents" are ex-spouses and their extended family, a house from a previous marriage, children in residence or visiting, photo albums, rituals and habits, friends and colleagues of the previous couple, and child support and alimony payments. Less concrete examples include feelings, perceptions, unresolved issues, emotional wounds, memories, patterns, and sensitivities. For instance, Mrs. Campbell's first husband was an alcoholic. Although her second husband does not have a personal or family history of drinking problems, whenever he drinks at a party she overreacts. Both spouses are aware of the roots of this reaction and of its inappropriateness to the present. Yet, it is very much an active part of their current marital relationship. Mrs. Blow behaves in a similar fashion. Her first husband had a long affair with his secretary. He frequently came home late and often was not available when she called. When confronted, he offered various excuses. Mrs. Blow remarried five years ago. She calls her husband several times each day and gets easily upset if she cannot reach him or if he is delayed in coming home.

The second reason past issues in stepfamilies are complicated is because family histories of all subsystems and dyads are different. Only some stepfamily members share a common history. Each subsystem carries diverse remnants of the previous marriage(s) in the form of roles, values, lifestyles, and loyalties. For example, Mr. and Mrs. Prince married three years ago. Maria, thirteen, Mrs. Prince's only daughter from her previous marriage, lives with the couple. Mr. Prince shares with his ex-wife custody of their fourteen-year-old son, John, who is with the family three nights a week, every other weekend, and most holidays. Maria and her mother have been used to a strict division of household chores and a set curfew time, while John's parents have been flexible in demands regarding schedule and duties. Consequently, the family contains two units with very different standards. In non-stepfamilies, expectations and customs are gradually developed throughout the life cycle of the family, whereas the units in remarriage families "import" with them preconceived agendas.

The last reason a stepfamily's past is complicated is because it includes at least one and often more parent-child relationships that predate the current marriage. This deprives the couple of an opportunity to establish an intimate relationship without children around. It also creates a potential infrastructure for triangulation and cross-generational coalitions. This works in different ways regarding children in residence versus visiting children. Children who reside in the stepfamily have usually lived with their natural parent through a divorce and a single-parent phase. The experience they shared with their parent creates an intimate and close relationship; the stepparent remains an outsider. The parent of children who visit the family may use the past to intensify the relationship with their children to compensate for the guilt they feel for leaving their children and establishing another family. In an effort to "win" the children, the parents of visiting children may side with their children, even at the cost of excluding the new spouse and limiting their functioning as stepparents.

## *SUMMARY*

This chapter described and discussed structural, dynamic, and developmental characteristics of stepfamilies. Typical characteristics are: a complex structure, ambiguity of boundaries and roles, differences in developmental phases of all family members, the need to merge two cultures, a gap between reality and the legal situation, split loyalties, social myths, issues of power, multiple changes and losses, and a complex history. These characteristics lead to common key issues that all step-families must resolve. All stepfamilies need to decide how to handle people, assets, memories, and patterns that are related to the past; they have to define themselves vis-à-vis non-stepfamilies, and they need to develop a way to manage the diverse subsystems. These issues will be discussed in the next chapter.

# Chapter 4

# Key Issues of Stepfamilies

In spite of their diversity, all stepfamilies share unique issues derived from special remarriage characteristics. Three such major issues refer to the stepfamilies' attitudes toward the past, their perception of themselves vis-à-vis other types of families, and the subsystems that are dominant in the families. To assess stepfamilies and develop strategies for preventive and curative interventions, it is necessary to understand how these issues shape the course of families, what is normative, and what becomes dysfunctional and requires clinical help.

## PAST ORIENTATION: THE ATTITUDE OF THE STEPFAMILY TOWARD THE PAST

Past orientation describes how the family perceives, conceptualizes, and handles pre-remarriage history. The concept of past orientation was developed in theoretical and clinical literature about families. The family's orientation toward the past significantly affects its present functioning and its ability to plan toward the future (Sluzki, 1983; Rosenfeld, 1989). Different schools of thought in family therapy point out how current family patterns relate to patterns carried over from the families of origin of the spouses. This relationship can be played out in two ways. First, patterns from the families of origin may be repeated in the present family. For example, a woman who grew up with parents who were abusive to each other develops abusive relationships with her husband because this is the pattern of marital relationship that she knows. Second, the current family may be used to "correct" the past by doing now something totally different than what was done in the past. For example, a husband who grew up with a demanding and strict father becomes a soft, receptive father to his own children.

In stepfamilies, past orientation has special prominence (Wolpert-Lur and Bross, 1982; Sager et al., 1983; Hodder, 1985; Kaslow, 1988; Bradt and Bradt Moynihan, 1988). Although all families must make decisions regarding the presence and effects of the past in their current lives, in stepfamilies the past is complicated and loaded with sensitive and painful issues from previous marriages that almost always spill over into the new family (Kaslow, 1993). How much space is the pre-remarriage past, and especially the past related to previous marriages, allowed in the present family? What is the relative focus on past versus present? How are past-related patterns, relationships, memories, and objects incorporated into current family life? How much of the "heritage" from previous marriages penetrates the present? Who is allowed to refer to the past, under what circumstances, and in what manner? To what extent are expectations from the remarriage colored by experiences in previous marriages? How is the past played out in the present? All these questions need to be dealt with, and family mechanisms to regulate the presence of the past need to be developed.

Families with a high past orientation are those in which the past has a considerable presence. People and events from the pre-remarriage are often referred to, and ways of doing things in the past have considerable impact on the present. Mr. Neil, a previously single man now married to a divorcée, expresses this experience in the following words:

> My wife's first marriage is always in the air . . . it is part of our collective memory as a family, a part of our recollections and experiences. It is not her first marriage but our first marriage . . . it serves as a reference point in our life. In a way I live as if I was married to him. We refer to the past sometimes jokingly like claiming that the son that my wife and I have in our marriage inherited his artistic talents from my wife's first husband . . . Sometimes references to the past are done in a more serious tone . . . but the past is a consistent part of our life now.

Mrs. Fridman, a remarried mother of three (one in a previous marriage and two in the remarriage), says, "You cannot totally disconnect from the past; you need to respect it, to let it penetrate your current life, not to cancel it."

Mr. Henry, a remarried, previously childless stepfather of a ten-year-old, explains the presence of the past in his current family:

> The natural father did not disappear and he is very much a part of our daily life. We have to take his opinions into consideration. For example, if we wished to send my stepson to a left-wing youth movement, according to our political tendency, his biological father would have resisted. We can't fully exercise our educational preferences with the son, since his father is in the picture. We would like to move to another state for several years, but the divorce agreement limits us. The past dictates much of what we can and can't do in the present.

Perry Garfinkel (1990) described his experience of the intense presence of an ex-wife in the reality of the husband's new family in the following words: " . . . there is no forgetting of the ex . . . there she is, forever a part of your past and often enough, your present. She has become a permanent fixture . . . a reference point for gleaning new insights from old patterns" (p. 24).

In some stepfamilies with high past orientation, the past is colored mostly as negative. For example, Clifford, a remarried father of three young adults, two of which refuse to talk to him, and a stepfather of three girls, says, "In families like us members carry a warehouse of pains. The pains of hatred, revenge, and anger. These pains serve as a point of reference to every move in the remarriage either by penetrating into the new family or as a guide to what should not be done." His wife adds, "My first marriage is the model of what we should keep away from in every possible way."

In families with low past orientation, the focus is on what *is* rather than on what *was*. The past is ignored and its place in current life is trivial. They seldom compare the present to the past; they focus on the current situation and minimize, to the point of extinction, references to the past. They cut off all relationships rooted in the past, including the extended family of the previous spouse and friends from the first marriage. When asked about their attitude toward the past, typical statements are: "We erased the past; it does not exist." "What was was; it's dead . . . this is the real family." "We think about the previous marriage as nonexisting . . . One should not allow the past to enter the present." "It is important to ignore the first marriage as if it never was." "We disconnected any relationship with friends from the past . . . we want to have nothing to do with people who knew the previous marriage."

Past orientation is reflected in the decisions stepfamilies make regarding financial issues, living arrangements, terms of address and of reference, and parenting style. Families with low past orientation base their decisions on the current situation. Families with high past orientation base their solutions to current issues on previous experiences.

Some stepfamilies with high past orientation consciously or unconsciously repeat, continue, and preserve the past in the new family. They often use the remarriage as an "improved version" of previous marriages in which families try to amend failures and correct mistakes made previously. Other stepfamilies with high past orientation go in the opposite direction and refuse to allow in their present life any similarity to the past. These families wish to negate the past so intensely that sometimes they make decisions not based on the matter at hand, but by choosing the extreme opposite of decisions made in the past.

While families with low past orientation seldom compare the present to the past, families with high past orientation use the past as a criterion for judging the present: "it helps you sketch sensitivities and boundaries." Comparisons to the past are either explicit (e.g., "in my previous marriage I was used to having coffee prepared for me") or more subtle. Adults may use comparisons to the past to cement the current spousal relationship (e.g., "we agree on most things, unlike the previous marriage"). By contrasting the current "we" with the past, they solidify the marriage as a unit. Children often make comparisons with the past to preserve their loyalty to their parent of the same gender as the stepparent (e.g., "my mother prepares better pasta dishes than my stepmother").

Most stepfamilies have to deal with assets, expenses, and income from previous marriages, such as child-support payments from a previous spouse. Families with high past orientation tend to lead a "two-pot economy" (Fishman, 1983). Ownership of assets is determined according to their source. Spouses often have a pre-remarriage financial contract and keep separate bank accounts. Each is responsible for the needs of the children, and an agreement is negotiated regarding daily expenses. Mrs. Zeis describes the situation in her stepfamily, which includes her son and her husband's daughter from previous marriages: "In families like ours, balances are kept strictly in a mine-yours format and money is spent based on who brought what and who is entitled to what from whom." In contrast, families with low past orientation tend to adopt a "common good" economy, merging all income and expenses irrespective of sources. Spouses have shared bank accounts, and money is spent on the basis of need and availability rather than according to its source.

Patterns of spending money may become an issue especially when considerable gaps exist between the pre-remarriage financial situation, and obligations of spouses and in times of financial stress. It may cause distrust, intimidation, and tension and emphasize the difference between the two units of which the stepfamily is composed (Kaslow, 1993).

The Prides are a complex stepfamily with Mrs. Pride's son and daughter and Mr. Pride's two sons from previous marriages. The family experienced difficulties in cash flow when they bought their new house. Mr. Pride suggested borrowing money from the savings account of his wife's children to offset the family's temporary financial stress. His wife decisively vetoed the request because "this money belongs to my children and not to our current family."

The decision of where to live also reflects how much emphasis families place on past versus present. Families with high past orientation may continue to live in a house of one of the spouses, maintaining the same room allocation and keeping articles and furniture from the past. This provides stability for family members who lived there, but newcomers are viewed by children as invaders who rob their parents' and their own territory (for example, if rooms need to be changed to provide place for the new spouse's children) and try to assume the role of the parent who moved out. The spouse and children who move in feel like strangers on somebody else's turf. Families with low past orientation insist on moving not only to a new house without memories, but also to a new neighborhood, a new town, or another state. They create a new household and allow only a few, if any pictures, art works, and items from previous marriages in the residence of the remarriage family.

Choice of concepts for mutual reference also reflects the past orientation of the family. Without proper terminology to accurately describe the step-relationship, family members have to develop ways to introduce one another to people outside the family and to refer to one another inside the family. In families who rely heavily on the past, members tend to prefer "my spouse's children," "my Mom's husband," and similar concepts in which preservation of the past is embedded. Members of present-focused families opt for "my children," "our children," "my stepdad" to underscore the current role relationship.

Parenting style is another aspect of family life that differentiates families by their past orientation. In families with high past orientation, parental commitments are divided along biological lines. Adults remain the primary, and in extreme cases the exclusive, disciplinary and nurturing figures for their children from previous marriages, often serving as a buffer between the stepparent and the stepchildren. The Dayan family illustrates this pattern. Mrs. Dayan's six-year-old daughter from a previous marriage is completely her responsibility: "She is 100 percent Mommy's. A natural parent has to be responsible and a stepparent should maintain distance." Some biological parents perceive this situation as undesirable, yet have difficulty changing their patterns. Mrs. Gold says, "When my husband scolds my son, whom he has been raising since babyhood, I know this should be this way but I cannot stand it . . . sometimes I bite my lips not to intervene but I can't, it's stronger than me . . . he is *my* son." In families with low past orientation, however, spouses fully share parental responsibilities for all children. In the Hart family, "all children are ours. If we ever divorce we will fight over custody for all of them." Stepparents attend parent-teacher meetings, discipline the children, and function as full parents.

Clinicians and researchers debate about the optimal level of past orientation in stepfamilies. Experts in the field of treating remarriage families stated that stepfamilies need to balance past and present to be functional (see Bowen, 1978; Sager et al., 1983; Visher and Visher, 1988; Kaslow, 1993), and families who do not make space for their past in their present lives are bound to have problems. For example, it is recommended that whenever feasible, stepfamilies should live in a new place "clean" of memories or at least rearrange their home so everybody will feel "at home." Research findings on the issue are inconclusive. Some studies indicated that stepfamilies tend to preserve the past (Kalmuss and Seltzer, 1986; Groll-Barnes, Tompson, and Burchard, 1989) while other research found that stepfamilies are located anywhere on a continuum from families who focus on the present and minimize the past on one end, to families who are geared heavily toward the past on the other (Berger, 1995). However, both clinicians and researchers agree that past orientation must be understood and considered when assessing and working with stepfamilies.

The past orientation of all family members is not necessarily the same. Children may want to preserve the past, while adults wish to erase it to fulfill fantasies of extinguishing previous marriages. In other families, children want to blur their past as a means to resemble their peers (this is changing with the rise in the prevalence of remarriage families) or to distance themselves from painful memories, while adults wish to preserve it because they believe it to be right, they feel obliged, or they want to limit present commitment. Also, one adult may be inclined to foster a higher past orientation, especially if there are children from the previous marriage who reside with their other parent, while the other adult, usually childless or with children who live in the stepfamily, tends toward a low past orientation. However, despite personal differences, the family as a whole has to negotiate a family system perspective regarding orientation toward the pre-remarriage past. This perspective is often a compromise between the wishes and interests of individual members and subsystems.

The past orientation, as with any family feature, is dynamic and may change throughout the family life cycle and under varying circumstances (e.g., the birth of a child in the remarriage—the "glue" child). Yet, these changes are limited, and many stepfamilies do have stable differences and may be assessed about their overall attitude toward the past, regardless of temporary changes.

### *ACCEPTANCE/REJECTION OF DIFFERENCE: THE SELF-PERCEPTION OF THE FAMILY VIS-À-VIS OTHER TYPES OF FAMILIES*

Acceptance/rejection of difference describes the self-perception of the family relative to other families. How similar to or different from non-stepfamilies do members of stepfamilies see their own families? Specifically, how do stepfamilies see themselves vis-à-vis nuclear families, who are still considered the "normative," "correct" type of family? If a stepfamily perceives itself as different, how is it different?

The concept of acceptance/rejection of difference was first coined by Kirk (1964, 1981) in relation to adoptive families. Even when stepfamilies appear structurally the same as nuclear families because the household includes two married adults and children, they are different in several important ways, and life in a stepfamily is clearly not the same as life in a non-stepfamily (Martin and Martin, 1992; Ganong and Coleman, 1994a). Acceptance/rejection of difference reflects the attitude of the stepfamily toward these differences.

Stepfamilies can be located anywhere on the continuum of acceptance/rejection of difference. At one extreme, families deny any difference and foster the myth of identity between stepfamilies and non-stepfamilies. They cling to the myths of instant love and of "we are one big happy family, à la the Brady Bunch." The Decker family illustrates this position: "We are just like any other family. The fact that one of our children was born to another father is not really relevant. There is nothing special about being in a second marriage. It's only in the papers, but in real life it's all the same as in any other family . . . relationships, feelings, behavior." Some families deny any difference from non-stepfamilies, especially outwardly, in the way they present themselves to neighbors, friends, colleagues, and society at large: "We are not handicapped and do not need any special attention . . . if we present ourselves as different it may cause problems."

At the other end of the continuum, families perceive stepfamilies as inherently different from non-stepfamilies. This difference is sometimes defined in pathologizing terms: "Something is not natural even in the best stepfamily . . . more sensitive and fragile . . . It does not matter what the stepmother will do for the children . . . she will always remain the wicked stepmother . . . Every month it improves, but it always remains not just like a real family. A stepfamily is like a glass that has been broken and repaired. It is good, but it is never like new again." Some stepfamilies define themselves as "a wound," "a deficient model," "a compromise."

Other stepfamilies describe their difference from non-stepfamilies in more neutral terms: "We are special for good and for bad. Our family is more complex . . . stepfamilies are another species . . . it is not like all other families . . . friction is a normal part of everyday life . . . we struggle with our being different but we also use the special opportunities it offers."

A few stepfamilies see themselves not only as different but even as preferred to non-stepfamilies: "Families like ours are happier because they can apply lessons learned from the past to make the second family better . . . stepfamilies are an improved model. Members invest more and gain more." "My wife had to be married to her first husband, so she could learn and prepare to be married to me properly."

Burgoyne and Clark (1984), who studied forty stepfamilies in Sheffield, England, found that 40 percent of them wished to think of themselves as ordinary families, and Berger (1993), who studied sixty-three stepfamilies in Israel, found that 20.7 percent of the families wished to deny any difference from non-stepfamilies, 22.2 percent acknowledged differences, and 57.1 percent presented a mixture of denial and recognition of differences.

The question arises regarding which level of acceptance/rejection of difference is functional. Experts generally agree that to be functional the family needs to accept and come to terms with these differences (Kaslow, 1993; Carter and McGoldrick, 1990; Hartin, 1990). Berger (1993) found no difference in satisfaction or adjustment between families who acknowledge their difference from non-stepfamilies and families who deny it. More clinical and empirical work remains to be done to determine which levels of acceptance/rejection of difference are functional for which types of stepfamilies and for the diverse phases of their development.

## *THE DOMINANT SUBSTRUCTURE OF THE FAMILY:*
## *THE FOCAL SUBSYSTEM*

The focal subsystem describes which subsystem (marital as distinguished from parental) is dominant and has priority in situations of conflicting interests.

A warm and stable relationship between the adults in the remarriage is desirable in all families. However, in some families adults unite through their position as parents, while in other families they build their closure through the marital bond. Families of the first kind are parental-focused and the latter are couple-focused stepfamilies.

Competition (hidden or explicit) between parental and marital subsystems occurs in all families. It becomes obvious in situations that require prioritizing between subsystems. For example, the wife-mother needs to attend at the same date and time an important event at her child's school and a significant event at her husband's workplace.

In stepfamilies, these situations carry unique complications and are more emotionally loaded than in non-stepfamilies (Goetting, 1983). Stepfamilies include parental figures both within (biological parent and stepparent with whom the child lives) and outside the family (noncustodial parent with or without his/her new family). Consequently, stepfamilies have a "parental coalition" that transcends the stepfamily boundaries and includes three or more adults who fulfill some parental role toward children from previous marriages (Visher and Visher, 1988). The internal co-parental subsystem is part of this "parental coalition," which includes the parent and stepparent with whom the child lives (for example, the mother and her current husband). Each stepfamily needs to develop principles for prioritizing subsystems if a situation arises that requires making such a choice.

The marital versus parental subsystem issue results from two of the aforementioned characteristics of stepfamilies. First, since remarriage establishes a new relationship and fosters intimacy among adults, but not necessarily between stepparents and stepchildren, the new spouse is perceived by children from previous marriages as an intruder with whom they are forced to share their previously exclusive relationship with their natural parent. At the same time, the new spouses struggle to maintain the priority of their relationship with each other as newlywed partners, and each often perceives their partner's children as overdemanding and as trying to sabotage the remarriage to keep their parent's attention for themselves. This can lead to a full-blown crisis between the stepparent and the stepchild, with the natural parent caught in the middle. To avoid such conflict, the family needs to establish rules regarding prioritizing parental and marital subsystems.

Furthermore, stepparents who are not fully confident in their marital relationship may be concerned (sometimes with good reason) that their spouse's children are trying to provoke their parent and undermine the remarriage. The natural parent of the same gender as the stepparent occasionally encourages, overtly or implicitly, such efforts, especially if he or she is not remarried.

Second, while in a non-stepfamily the relationships and commitment of parents and children are symmetric because the children are offspring of both parents, in stepfamilies the relationship is unbalanced. Natural parents have longer and more intensive relationships with their own children than do stepparents; they have more commitment to and responsibility in the parental subsystem than the stepparent, whose major vested interest is in the marriage rather than in step-parenthood. This unbalanced investment of the spouses in the marital and parental roles intensifies issues regarding the focal subsystem. The Wexlers illustrate the difficulty of balancing commitment to one's own children and commitment to one's new spouse in an asymmetrical situation. Mr. Wexler gained custody of his four preadolescent and adolescent children when his first wife came out of the closet as a lesbian, divorced him, and moved with her girlfriend to another state. He remarried to a never-married young woman. The new Mrs. Wexler felt that her husband put his children before their marriage and that he was often too busy with activities with and on behalf of his children from which she was excluded.

When timing of an event that is important for the child and an event that is important for the husband conflict, the decision about which event to attend may often be interpreted as a preference of one relationship over the other: "Your son [whereas in a non-stepfamily it is our] is more important to you than our marriage" or "You love your husband [in a non-stepfamily it is Dad] more than me."

In more extreme cases, the situation may reach an ultimatum of "him/her or me" by either the child from the first marriage or the current spouse. This tends to happen especially when a child from the first marriage reaches adolescence and experiences problems in school, uses drugs, acts out, and so forth. The stepparent in some families takes the position of "this is not my problem, who needs it?," refuses to put up with the difficult situation, and demands that the biological parent choose between loyalty to the child and loyalty to the marriage. By the same token, an adolescent who does not get along with the stepparent may confront the biological parent with an ultimatum of "either me or your spouse." At this stage, adolescents sometimes request to move in with their other biological parent's household, go to a boarding school, go to live with a relative (a grandparent, an aunt), or threaten to run away.

In families with a marital focal subsystem, spouses have remarried exclusively for the couple relationship and put the spousal relationship in the center: "We married because we want to be together. Children are a 'package deal' and they will have to accommodate . . . In a remarried family the most important question is what happens to the couple . . . husband-wife relationship is the heart." For these families, the remarriage is the glue that holds the family as a unit: "If one of us died the family would not hold." In these families, people often enter the remarriage with a strong commitment to do anything they can to make the marriage work. Berger (1993), in the study described previously, found a marital focal subsystem in 38.1 percent of the nonclinical stepfamilies she interviewed. Visher and Visher (1996) report that 25 percent of remarriage families in therapy identified that making a commitment to the spousal relationship was the single most important factor and that this helped stabilize their family.

Families with a parental focal subsystem focus on building a family together. Adults perceive the remarriage as a commitment to a parental role as much as to a marital role. Joseph, a ten-year-old whose mother remarried to a never-married man, expressed the spirit of his family, "Mom and I married David." These families ascribe to the parental relationship a central place in the family: "Stepparent-stepchild relationships are the core. Everything depends on how well this works. . . . The nature of the bond between me and my wife's children from her previous marriage determines if our marriage is possible." "Acceptance of the second husband by children from the previous marriage is crucial to the success of the remarriage . . . if this does not exist the remarriage will disintegrate." At the extreme, some families focus so intently on parenthood that they become a family with a one-dimensional focus on children (Martin and Martin, 1992).

The focus on the parental subsystem is expressed in prioritizing stepchildren as well as children born in the remarriage. It often takes the form of extreme permissiveness and dedication to children's needs to the point of denying spousal needs. For instance, visiting children may not be requested to fulfill household chores, and family rules regarding bedtime, table manners, and relationships are "bent" for them. Children in residence may be protected by the parent in confrontations with the stepparent and be excused from rules because "it is enough that they have to live with a stepparent." For example, Ann, an eight-year-old, describes her mother's remarriage as, "When Mom and I married John. . . ." Ann also accompanied the couple on their four-day honeymoon.

The choice of a focal subsystem reflects different approaches to coping with a history of a dissolved marriage. Stepfamilies with a marital focal subsystem struggle to prevent another failure because they carry with them the previous experiences of dysfunctional and unsatisfactory spousal relationships. Having realized how fragile a marital subsystem may be, they regard protecting it as a priority in their subsequent marriage. This approach is reflected in the following quotation: "We both work hard for this marriage. We invest, cherish, and protect it. We compromise for what we would have never compromised for in the past. We know what may happen. We are determined to prevent it from happening and we make our marriage come before anything else."

Stepfamilies with a parental focal subsystem often focus on children as a precaution against a total commitment to the marriage, which is vulnerable while parenthood is consistent, as expressed by Mrs. Blau: "Children are the center because they always remain, whatever may happen to the marriage . . . we already learned what may occur to a wedlock. Children are the most consistent in one's life." The new couple's focus on a parental subsystem may also be related to guilty feelings from "imposing" on children to live in a stepfamily because of their own "selfish" interests. As one couple stated, "The children did not chose to live with Mark or with Rita. We did. Since we chose to remarry it is our obligation to make sure that this decision does not deprive them. We give them our very best."

## *SUMMARY*

This chapter discussed three major issues of stepfamilies: orientation toward their past, self-perception vis-à-vis non-stepfamilies, and the focal subsystem. Stepfamilies view these issues and deal with them in different ways. These differences create different types of stepfamilies. The next part of the book presents a typology of stepfamilies and discusses the different types.

# PART II:
# TYPES OF STEPFAMILIES—
# AN INNOVATIVE CLASSIFICATION

Stepfamilies are not made from one mold. Although in the past functional stepfamilies have been described as families that balance past and present, choose the marital subsystem as their focus, and accept their differences from other types of families (Goetting, 1983), adopting a singular dominant model of a functional stepfamily seems to be incompatible with the realities of the 1990s. There is no universal model of a successful stepfamily. Stepfamilies differ from one another in demographic, structural, and dynamic characteristics. Contrary to Tolstoy's observation in *Anna Karenina* that all happy families are alike, stepfamilies are happy in different ways.

Scholars and clinicians suggested diverse methods for classifying stepfamilies. Most of these typologies are based on demographic and structural features, such as the reason for the dissolution of previous marriages (death versus divorce), presence or absence of children from previous marriages, existence or absence of children from the remarriage, complexity of the remarriage family, or custody arrangements (Ahrons and Rodgers, 1987; Robinson, 1991; Ganong and Coleman, 1994a).

Taxonomies of stepfamilies based on dynamic variables are scarce. Gross (1986) suggested such a classification based on the perception of the stepfamily by adolescent children who live in it. She identified four patterns of family perceptions by adolescents: augmentation, reduction, alternation, and retention. Augmentation describes an adolescent perception of the family as including both the divorced natural parents and the stepparent. Reduction is a pattern of including only the remarried natural parent and excluding both the noncustodial natural parent and the stepparent. In alternative families, the adolescent's perception includes the remarried natural parent and the stepparent but not the noncustodial natural parent. In retention, the adolescent's family perception maintains the original situation by including the natural parents and excluding the stepparent.

Burgoyne and Clark (1984), in their study of stepfamilies, distinguished five types of stepfamilies based on the self-perception of the families. The "not really a stepfamily" type are families formed through remarriage while the children were very young, and they perceive their stepfamily as an ordinary family. The "looking forward to the departure of children" stepfamilies were formed through remarriage when the children were adolescents or young adults and no plans are made to have children in the remarriage; the couple waits for the children to leave so that they can focus on the marital relationship. The "progressive" type are families who emphasize the advantages of their current situation. The "concious pursuit of an ordinary family life together" type imitates a non-stepfamily, with new children and with the stepparent accepting a full parental role. The "conscious pursuit of ordinary family life frustrated" type finds its efforts to be similar to a non-stepfamily undermined by continuing problems from the first marriage.

The case for an ongoing professional dialogue toward developing classifications of family relational systems has been made in the most compelling manner by Kaslow (1996). A special schema is required to address the unique situation of stepfamilies. Such a schema has been developed in a recent study that identified three distinctive types of stepfamilies: integrated stepfamilies, invented stepfamilies, and imported stepfamilies (Berger, 1993, 1995).

The study was based on the interpretive tradition of qualitative research. This tradition is built on the assumption that families (as well as individuals) interpret their experience in a unique way and act upon their interpretation. Therefore, to understand families, it is important to understand their interpretation of their physical, social, and emotional situation, their environment, and their relationships.

The three types of stepfamilies that were identified in the study differ in the way they perceive and handle the issues of past orientation, acceptance/rejection of difference from non-stepfamilies, and the focal subsystem, which were discussed in Chapter 4. The following three chapters will describe and illustrate these types of stepfamilies.

A word of warning is in place here. The types that will be discussed are ideal types in the sense that they represent abstract generalized categories rather than describing any actual family (Gould and Kolb, 1964). In reality, most families tend to differ from the "pure" types presented in the next three chapters. However, since these types were shaped on the basis of examining actual stepfamilies rather than on preconceived theoretical categories, they proved to be helpful in thinking about and working with stepfamilies in clinical and psychoeducational practice. Although families demonstrate a mixture of traits, they still tend to be predominantly similar to a given type.

All types of stepfamilies do not differ in every characteristic. For example, invented and imported families deny being different from non-stepfamilies; integrated families and imported families have in common a marital focal subsystem. However, it is the combination of the features that creates different gestalts, gives each type of family its unique character, and makes it a distinctive type.

The general profile of each type of stepfamily will be described. Their past orientation, attitude toward their unique family configuration, and focal subsystem as well as typical issues generated by these features will be discussed and illustrated. Different family portraits will be presented to illustrate each type.

# Chapter 5

# Integrated Stepfamilies:
# Combining Then and Now
# Around the Couple

## *PROFILE OF INTEGRATED STEPFAMILIES*

These stepfamilies are integrated in the sense that they combine the past and present realities and live concurrently in the old world and the new world, allowing their pre-remarriage past to play a considerable role in their present life. They acknowledge the inherent split between the original units of which the stepfamily is built and develop modes to incorporate these units.

In integrated families, spouses enter the remarriage for the sake of the marital relationship, which is their primary interest and the central axis around which all other relationships are organized. The marital subsystem is the focus, while children, relatives, and friends are expected to adjust to the new reality. Typically, integrated stepfamilies are formed through remarriage in a relatively late phase of the spouses' lives, bringing into the new family children as well as considerable assets, memories, relationships, and family patterns as remnants from previous marriages.

## *COMBINING PAST AND PRESENT*

In integrated families, past experience is very much alive, and these families tend to continue or revive patterns from the past for use in the present. Even though all integrated families maintain a large space for the past in their current lives, the degree of their reliance on the past may vary. Mr. Hull was a bachelor when he married a mother of two. He describes the situation:

> Somehow, the past always penetrates the present . . . you do not start from a blank page . . . my wife's previous marriage is always in the air . . . not longings but wondering, curiosity . . . what would it have been like if she did not divorce him? We do not think or talk about it nonstop but it's there; it's present.

The past has been reported by some integrated families to be a source of tension. Mr. Hull continues, "When marrying a previously married individual one faces many existing patterns which are difficult to change. Insisting on changes leads to inevitable conflicts."

For children, fostering the past in the present may create confusion. Ron was almost six when his mother remarried. Six months after the remarriage, as he was having dinner with his mother and stepfather, he stated suddenly, "Now there is no more Ron Goldberg" (his natural father's surname). "There is only Ron Meyer" (his stepfather's surname). About a year later, he requested to go back to his original name, and when he turned sixteen, he requested officially to have a family name combined of both his fathers' names, indicating in a symbolic way that he had resolved the confusion and had come to terms with having past and present combined in his life.

The past serves as a guide for the present and as a criterion against which to judge the present. As a guide, the past is used to set both a positive and a negative model for life in the current family. As a positive guide, the past is used as a source of rituals, patterns, and relationships from the first marriage that are preserved in the remarriage to establish a sense of continuity. As a negative guide, the past reminds families of mistakes they wish to avoid.

Sometimes the tendency to avoid repetition of past patterns and the failure of marriage associated with them leads families to insist on adopting the opposite of what they did in the past. Arnold, a childless divorcée, remarried to Jane, a mother of two, explains:

> In my first marriage, there were many secrets. Now I decided on a no-secrets policy; my wife used to reject any help from her first husband but she is willing to get a lot of help from me.

One tries not to do again what did not work, while maintaining some connection to what was.

Adam, a previous bachelor who married a divorcée, agrees: "I believe that my wife learned how to avoid mistakes she did in her first marriage. If she had not been married before, things would have been different here." This observation is supported by many remarriage families. Integrated stepfamilies often say, "If we had worked on our first marriage the same way we do now, we probably would not have divorced."

The past is also used as a measure against which the present is judged, either overtly or in more subtle ways. Even though comparison to the past exists considerably more in the first phases of the remarriage, the high awareness in integrated families of the past as a part of the present preserves its function as a yardstick. Joan remarried to Bob. Each has a child from a previous marriage, and they have two kids together. They describe how the past affects their life together:

> We often compare the the present to the past because then we realize how much better our current life is. Financially, both of us had a more comfortable life in our first marriages and occasionally when we experience economic stress we think about how much easier it was then, but the next minute we think about the price that we paid and we are happy we are not there . . . the past helps us put things into a correct perspective.

The combination of past and present is represented in names, living arrangements, and orchestration of finances. Martha was divorced when she married David. Her ex-husband remarried at the same time. Martha has one son, Simon, from her previous marriage and David has never been married before. The couple has a five-year-old daughter and a three-year-old son in the remarriage. Martha and Simon have two last names. Simon lives with Martha and David and sees his father at least twice a week but only for a couple of hours; he chooses not to sleep over or spend weekends or vacations with him. There is no fixed schedule for the meetings, and they are arranged according to Simon's and his father's availability. Simon refers to his stepfather by his given name; the younger children imitate him and do the same. The family lives in the apartment where

Martha lived with her first husband, "to prevent unnecessary changes for the son such as school and friends," but they renovated it, completely changing the inner structure to create a room for each child and a new bedroom for the couple. Simon's father pays child support on a regular basis. The money is used partly for special expenses for Simon, such as a bar mitzvah trip abroad, and partly for routine expenses of the family. Simon's father, mother, and stepfather have a relaxed relationship and they cooperate well regarding Simon's needs. For example, his stepfather may drive him to a soccer practice and his father drive him home from the practice. The three adults and the children attend extended family weddings and celebrations with little stress. Both paternal figures encourage Simon to develop a positive relationship with the other.

## ACKNOWLEDGING DIFFERENCES

Integrated stepfamilies perceive themselves as different from non-stepfamilies, sometimes to the point of emphasizing their uniqueness and negating any similarity to intact first-remarriage families. They live constantly with a built-in split between the two units of which the family has been assembled. Mrs. Silner divorced her first husband when she was pregnant with her currently thirteen-year-old daughter and remarried three years later, a never-married man with whom she now has a ten-year-old boy. The Silners view stepfamilies as "more complicated, with all kinds of advantages and traps that do not exist in first-marriage families. Some of it is more problematic. Some of it better . . . you learn from the experience . . . some is just different, neither better, nor worse . . . just another kind of family."

The difference from non-stepfamilies is conceptualized by integrated families as psychological, emotional, logistic, legal, and/or economic. Some families see differences in all those areas while other families emphasize differences in several of them but not in others.

Martha and David, previously described, see stepfamilies as "different to a certain degree both emotionally and technically. There are many arrangements regarding visits of nonresiding children, managing money, etc. . . . at the same time there is more friction."

The main differences are related to the children from previous marriages, the existence of a parental figure outside the family, and the existence of two types of children within the same system. Even stepparents who take a relatively active part in parenting their stepchildren comment that "it is like in other families, yet it's different . . . it's as if similar but not really similar."

Because of these differences, integrated families often express the need for specialized services for stepfamilies. Some families indicate the need for pre-remarriage counseling for couples and for guidance to help parents know how to deal with unique issues related to their family configuration. Other families believe that society as a whole should acknowledge the existence of stepfamilies as a unique group and better accomodate their needs, such as changes in taxes, Social Security, and attitudes and regulations of the school system and of community organizations. They believe schools should be more sensitive to the existence of this type of family in planning celebrations, graduations, mailing report cards, and preparing holiday cards. Several families identify the need to run support groups for stepchildren in the school. Other families suggest the need to grant authority to social workers or social agencies (such as Child Protective Services) to intervene regarding the treatment of children by their noncustodial parents and stepparents, since the stepfamily where the child lives cannot control what happens in the other household.

## *MARITAL FOCAL SUBSYSTEM*

In integrated families, the focal subsystem is the remarriage. Consequently, most power lies in the couple's relationship. Martha and David describe their marriage as the core of the current family:

> Our relationship is the center, the axis, the raison d'être of the family. This is the basis . . . the begining and the end. Children grow up quickly and before you know it they are out of the house to establish their independent lives while we are here . . . we stay together. As heartless as it sounds, if we were to choose between the relationship with the children and our relationship, our bond is the most important and the children have to fit in.

## CHARACTERISTICS OF THE INTEGRATED
## NATURE OF THE FAMILY

The integrated nature of the family is reflected in its general approach and in specific aspects of family life such as housing, managing family finances, and parenthood.

### Living Arrangements

Living in the house that belonged to one spouse prior to the remarriage is not uncommon. These families often deny any unpleasant aspects of living in what was the house of a current spouse, while in a previous marriage. Furniture, artwork, and household objects from the previous marriage are used along with new purchases made by the stepfamily.

### Finances

Assets and money are divided and used according to their origin, often in separate bank accounts. The family handles daily expenses as a unit, but special expenditures for children from previous marriages (e.g., college tuition, a car, a trip abroad) are paid by the natural parent. In many integrated families, the natural father pays child support. In some families, these payments are saved for special purposes for the children from the first marriage and are not part of the family's income. The use of prenuptial and postnuptial agreements (Dreyfus, 1990; Du Cato, 1991; Kaslow, 1991) occurs mostly in integrated families because spouses in these families are anxious to protect assets accumulated prior to the remarriage and to guarantee channeling them to their own families rather to the other spouse's family.

### Parenthood

Since they are most often interested in creating a new couple rather than a new family, integrated families tend not to bear children in the remarriage. In most integrated families, both husbands and wives have been married before and already have children.

Their children are grown up, and both partners feel that they are beyond the child-raising phase of their lives. The wives' children tend to be adolescents and the husbands' children are young adults. These children either live independently or are preparing to leave the family and establish their own lives.

Spouses observe "parenthood territory," with each excusively or primarily responsible for his/her own children: "My children are my taboo turf." Parental resposibilities are often coordinated and shared with the noncustodial natural parent. In some integrated families, natural parents are exclusively in charge of their children's discipline, and when the stepparent wants to make a comment, it is usually done via the natural parent. In other families, the natural parents are responsible for the discipline of their children in general but the stepparents discipline regarding issues that directly concern them.

In some families, following biological lines in the allocation of parental roles may be taken to a the extreme. Jane, a divorcée remarried to a divorcé, declares:

> My daughter is my sole responsibility. It is my turf. No one touches me and my "cub." She is first of all mine. My daughter is my business, it is "not his business," they are like tenants in the same household but do not have much to do with each other. One way to prevent troubles in stepfamilies is to negotiate prior to the remarriage the level and quality of involvement the stepparent will have with the stepchild. Natural parents should not expect stepparents to be "as-if parents" and need to take full responsibility for their own children. This creates a clear arrangement based on reality and not on an illusion.

Stepparents feel somewhat as "strangers" to the stepchildren because they have not raised them from birth. They often report that they are more careful with stepchildren than with non-stepchildren regarding disciplinary measures as well as emotional and concrete investments. Edward had been single prior to his marriage to Suzi, who brought to their family her daughter by her previous husband. He recalls situations in which he would have slapped his own child, but avoided doing so to his wife's daughter. Amos, who also was a bachelor prior to marrying Miriam, who had a daughter with her first husband, says:

> I always have been careful not to hit her even in situations that I would have done so if she was my biological child . . . I made a point of giving her more as the firstborn so that she will not feel deprived because she is not mine like our other children.

Similarly, Mr. Hull states:

> I restrict my involvement with issues concerning my wife's children. For example, if she had decided that the child-support payment will go to the children's account, I would not protest even if the money was very necessary.

Developmental models of stepfamilies suggest that in the beginning of the remarraige a stepparent should not start disciplining and only gradually assume a growing degree of parental status when the relationship with stepchildren is established and the stepparent gains more credibility. However, the speakers in the previous excerpts have been remarried for eight to fifteen years, supporting the differential model that suggests the existence of consistent differences among stepfamilies. According to this model, a stepfamily maintains its basic nature despite variations and accommodations along its step–life cycle.

Maintaining the parenting-according-to-biological-lines model can serve as a buffer against commitment toward stepchildren. If stepparents restrain themselves from becoming full parents for their stepchildren, they may have two secondary gains. First, they do not risk being rejected by stepchildren (for example, the "You are not my father and cannot tell me what to do" reaction, especially from adolescents); second, by limiting their commitment toward stepchildren they defend themselves against guilty feelings for "neglecting" biological children for the sake of parenting other children.

### Names and Reference Terms

In integrated families, adults typically refer to previous spouses as "my/my spouse's first/previous spouse" or use concepts that pertain to parental role such as "my child's parent," indicating that there was another relationship prior to the current family.

Children from previous marriages often have either their natural father's last name or the names of both their natural father and their stepfather. They call their stepfather by his given name and refer to him as "my stepdad," "my mother's husband," or alternate between these references and "Dad" (especially when they resent appearing exceptional in social circumstances). Sam, a six-year-old, calls his stepfather "Dad" and his natural father "Daddy" while his eight-year-old sister calls her stepfather "Dad Joseph" and her natural faher "Dad Jonah." Stepparents in integrated families refer to stepchildren as "my spouse's children."

Sometimes children's questions drive families to define themselves. When Gail was three, her mother remarried to Adam, who was a bachelor. Gail's father left her mother when she was pregnant with Gail, joined a spiritual group, and severed contacts with his ex-wife and daughter. The couple has month-old twins in the remarriage. Gail started asking if Adam was her father. She was very upset with the response that he is her mother's husband and like a father to her, but she has a biological father who lives elsewhere. Gail was angry with her stepfather because she perceived this as a rejection: "You do not love me if you say that you are not my father." She also pressured him on different occasions: "Are you already my father?" "You are my father." The couple insisted that even though Adam loves her and performs parental roles, Gail still has a biological father. They felt this was important because they believe that their pre-remarriage history is and always will be a part of who they are as a family.

### Sibling Relationships

"I am not afraid of your father." "You will run to your father to squeal and complain." The speaker is Lora, a thirteen-year-old girl who lives with her remarried mother, stepfather, a stepsister her age, and two half-brothers, ages seven and three.

The structure of sibling relationships in integrated families reflects the blended nature of this type of stepfamily. Although children born in the remarriage form with their parents a nuclear unit, children born in previous marriages represent past relationships.

The integrated nature of the stepfamily is reflected in the structural relationships between these different subsystems of siblings: they are related to other family members in a variety of ways (blood kin, quasi-kin, nuptial-kin), their emotional proximity and feeling of mutual reponsibility varies, and their daily lives are a mixture of shared experiences and unshared experiences, such as visits and vacations by children from a prior marriage with the noncustodial parent.

## TYPICAL ISSUES

Integrated families point out that a major issue is the lack of opportunities for focusing on the marital relationship. Even though this reality is common to all stepfamilies, it emerges mostly in integrated families because they have a marital focal subsystem and are especially sensitive to any factor that interferes with it. This issue has been widely addressed in stepfamily literature, possibly because many families seen by professionals are integrated stepfamilies. Since they experience difficulties as a result of their family complexity and they recognize their difference from non-stepfamilies, integrated stepfamilies are usually receptive to the idea of therapy.

Suzi, a remarried mother of sixteen-year-old Ronnie from a previous marriage and ten- and six-year-old Sharon and Tom from her current marriage, describes this situation: "The couple in a remarriage family does not have time to be together. We could not go naked, make love in the living room, etc. We always had to remember that there is a girl in the picture. We did not have the chance to build our relationship without the presence of children." Mrs. Hull, a divorced mother of two, who remarried to a bachelor, expresses a similar experience: "We never had an opportunity for 'couplehood' . . . it has always been marriage 'in the shadow' of parenthood."

The issue of limited control over events that affect family life is also mentioned by most integrated stepfamilies. Since integrated stepfamilies recognize the existence of relationships from the past, their freedom to plan family trips, vacations, and holidays is limited, and the logistics involved in such planning is complicated by the need to take into consideration the schedules of the noncustodial parent and the extended family from his/her side. Amir and Ruth have been married for three years. Amir has a fourteen-year-old son from his first marriage and Ruth has a twelve-year-old daughter from her first marriage to Nathan, who remarried and has two stepchildren in his current marriage. Amir and Ruth have together a one-year-old, Rachel. Amir describes how the family makes plans to go to a resort for a weekend:

> On one Friday we can't go because my son comes to visit and he refuses to join us since there are no computers in the resort and he will be bored. However, we cannot change his weekend with us since his mother and her husband are busy on this weekend with some event of her new husband's twin girls. The next week is not feasible because my stepdaugther is not around and we want her to be part of the trip. The following week it is my wife's ex-husband's birthday and we give him a party at our place . . . maybe if we start planning in February we get to go for the three days sometime in August . . . that is if nobody in any part of our family has an exam or a broken leg.

An additional issue of control refers to the experiences to which children from the previous marriage are exposed in their visits with their noncustodial parent. Jack reports that:

> Roy, my eight-year-old stepson, wishes to meet his father often and while we do not want to limit this relationship, we are not always happy with the things he picks up there and with the places his father takes him to. Whenever Roy comes back from a weekend with his father, where he has no chores, no bedtime, no organized schedule, it takes a while to reorient him to the rules in our family. We tried to talk to my wife's ex-husband, but to no avail. After all, we cannot control from here what happens there.

Sonya sounds helpless when she describes her situation: "My ex-husband is a wild driver. When he takes our son I am constantly nervous. He sits him in the front seat in spite of his young age. He does not always belt him. When the child was a toddler, his father refused to install a safty seat, even though I bought one for him. I confront him on this but. . . ."

Although some integrated families see the need to cooperate and coordinate with additional people in a matter-of-fact manner, others accuse the noncustodial natural parent or his/her kin of abusing flexiblity of visitation arrangements. David, a thirty-nine-year-old childless divorcée, is married to Eileen, thirty-five, and is stepfather to Andy, her nine-year-old son by her first husband, Abe. The couple decided that allowing Andy unlimited access to his natural father is desirable for his development. However, they claim that Abe abuses the open-ended access they have allowed him by being intrusive in their current life and by trying to control Eileen as he did during their marriage.

Integrated stepfamilies report facing numerous questions and reactions from teachers, neighbors, and institutions. Since they incorporate a considerable orientation to the past in their lives and see themselves as different from non-stepfamilies, integrated families are easily visible. Consequently, they face a wide range of reactions from their social environment regarding their family configuration.

Lack of symmetry has been noted as an issue in integrated families. Most integrated stepfamilies include a remarried wife and her children and a remarried or never-married husband who does not have children or whose children live elsewhere. This creates a "maternal majority" and leaves the husband-stepfather as a minority. Such a structure may affect the allocation of power in the family. Many husbands feel overpowered and imposed upon when expected to share their wives with their stepchildren. Mr. Hull describes the situation as follows: "I am only one and I encounter my wife's camp that includes herself plus her two children. Therefore, very often I suggest rather than decide."

## CASE ILLUSTRATION: THE EVEREST FAMILY

Nili, a thirty-nine-year-old accountant of Middle Eastern origin, and Josh, a forty-six-year-old Israeli-born pilot of European origin, have been married for four years. Nili is an attractive, rational, and calm woman, who measures her words carefully and presents herself as assertive and composed. Josh is a heavy, reserved, and quiet man, who says as little as possible. Both spouses have been married before. Nili divorced her husband of fifteen years six months prior to meeting Josh, who is divorced from his wife of eighteen years. Nili has two sons from her first marriage: Yair, who is fourteen, and Jonathan, who is eleven. The children live in the stepfamily. Josh has two daugthers: twenty-year-old Tamara and eighteen-year-old Ruth. Tamara lives on her own because she does not get along with her natural mother. Ruth lives with her mother. The following genogram presents the structure of the family.

The Everest Family: An Integrated Stepfamily

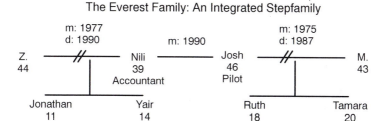

The family lives in a luxurious three-bedroom apartment in a middle-class suburb. Nili lived in the same apartment with her first husband. When she met Josh, he moved in with her. The furniture in the living room is a combination of pieces brought by the spouses and items they purchased together, creating a mixture of styles and colors. Nili's children have on display in their bedrooms pictures of themselves with their natural father and family pictures with the current stepfamily.

Jonathan and Yair visit their father every week. When he comes to pick them up, he often enjoys a cup of coffee with Nili and Josh. The couple's relationship with the boys' father is friendly and relaxed. They collaborate in decision making regarding educational and medical issues of the children and celebrate the children's birthdays together.

Josh's daughters visit their father's new family routinely and have indirectly expressed their wish to come to live with the Everests, which Nili declined, claiming there is no available space. Josh's relationship with his ex-wife is limited and tense.

The marital relationship is clearly the focus of this family: "Our bond comes first. This is the basis of this family. Everything starts and ends there. The rest is peripheral. We invest the most in our marriage and this is the secret of our success. This is the only way to make it as a stepfamily."

The pre-remarriage past is very much alive in the Everest family, and they allow it to play a considerable role in their current life. The following interaction illustrates their approach regarding the past:

> **Interviewer** [to both partners]: What place does your previous marriage have in your current family?
>
> **Josh:** I am in a way married to Dan [Nili's first husband]. He is part of our family. You cannot ignore the past. It is very much alive.
>
> **Nili:** We both came with "a full load" . . . from another life with other habits . . . we try to merge it all together.
>
> **Josh:** When you remarry the wife brings to the remarriage her previous husband and the husband brings his previous wife and we try to live all four of us . . . to find a way between all the dyads and tryads without creating too many knots.
>
> **Nili:** A second marriage is not a first marriage . . . you carry the past with you . . . you cannot come "clean," you bring with you "leftovers" and they color the present.
>
> **Interviewer:** In what way?
>
> **Josh:** We try to learn from mistakes in the first marriage, not to repeat them. I find myself overly cautious at times when it is not relevant because Nili is a different person than my ex-wife; but I guess one may say that sometimes I react to my ex-wife in my reactions to Nili.

Family members often talk about the first marriages of both spouses and compare life in the current family with their previous experience. Nili expresses the presence of the first marriage: "The comparison between what was and what is, is always there. One does not compare in a planned way, but a word, a gesture, an incident immediately brings to mind how my first husband would have reacted in a similar situation, how I would have felt in my previous marriage." Josh adds: "In a stepfamily one constantly lives with the past . . . sometimes overreacting to something that happens today because of connotations it carries from the previous life . . . the past very much affects the present. For example, I have a hard time giving a hug or a good-night kiss to Nili's children . . . it feels as if I betray my own girls."

Formally, the previous marriage is recognized by the fact that Yair and Jonathan bear their natural father's name and their mother uses a double last name Everest-Brick. Everest is Josh's name and Brick is her first husband's name. They opted to do so to link the children's name with their mother's and because Nili feels it has been a part of her identity for so many years: "You cannot take off your name like a nightgown just because the legal status has been changed. I feel Brick; I am Brick. It would be like erasing a part of me. Being a Brick is part of my past and one does not get rid of the past because one divorces and remarries." The family joke is that Josh should also carry both names since Nili's ex-husband is part of his life too "and anyhow half of Jonathan's and Yair's teachers call me Mr. Brick."

Though presumably trivial, the names cause confusion and difficulties in dealing with the school system, health insurance companies, and social agencies. For example, the local country club insisted on registering all family members by Josh's last name, to which his stepsons reacted with resentment. Also, since Josh pays for his stepsons' education the school refused to issue them student passes with their own last name.

All four children call their stepparents by their given names and introduce them as "Mom's husband" and "Dad's wife." Both spouses introduce the children from a previous marriage as "My husband's (wife's) children." This use of language shows that the Everests are constantly aware of having been two separate units in the past; this situation is carried into the new family and maintained there.

The relationship with Nili's ex-husband is friendly and all three adults cooperate in parenting Yair and Jonathan. They go together to parent-teacher meetings and discuss major decisions regarding the boys, such as choice of appropriate schools and planning of bar mitzvah parties.

Even though both Josh and Nili function as parents, each of them is the main parental figure for his/her natural children. The following exerpt illustrates the issue of parenthood in the Everest family:

**Interviewer:** Who is generally in charge of discipline of the children?

**Josh:** My feeling is that their mother makes the decisions regarding her children.

**Nili:** This is a mistake.

**Josh:** Both of us do the technical part of "take this," "go there," "do this," but she has an overall responsibility . . . they are her children. I may suggest but I leave her to make the final decision.

**Nili:** I am more easygoing in this respect. I may tell his daughters more than he will tell my sons.

**Josh:** For example, yesterday I drove Yair to a piano lesson and he wanted to go somewhere. I discussed with him possibilities but referred him to Nili to get a final decision. After all, she raised them, she knows them better, and she should decide. I can't decide for the children of my spouse without consulting with her.

The Everests perceive themselves and other stepfamilies as completely different from intact first-marriage families because of the major crises they have experienced. The existence of previous spouses, guilt of the husband for having left his daughters, the consistent effort to balance giving to children from the different marriages, relationships with extended family members from the previous marriages, additional financial burdens—they see all these unique issues as creating in stepfamilies more complexities, sensitivities, and higher levels of tension, even when ex-spouses co-parent as well. Both Josh and Nili perceive stepfamilies as having more problems than first-time families, and they recommend that teachers should be informed about the family situation. They indicate that emotional relationships in a stepfamily are different: "You love carefully."

## SUMMARY

Integrated stepfamilies share a strong commitment to the marital relationship as the core of the family, maker considerable room for the past in their current lives, and perceive themselves as different from non-stepfamilies. These families vary in the degree and the ways in which they "translate" these features into their daily lives. Attention to these characteristics can help therapists as well as stepfamily members and the general public to better understand individual stepfamilies and to help them meet their needs effectively.

# Chapter 6

# Invented Stepfamilies:
# The Time Is Now
# and the Family Is the Focus

We know a lot less about invented stepfamilies than about Integrated families because their striving to pass for a non-stepfamily makes them less visible as a unique type of family, and their motto "We are a typical family and everything about us is normal" often prevents them from seeking counseling regarding their situation.

## *PROFILE OF INVENTED STEPFAMILIES*

Invented families try to recreate the intact nuclear family. They deny the duality that results from the fact that stepfamilies are constructed from two separate partial families and treat this duality as if it is nonexistent. These families are invented in the sense that a new unit is originated as if nothing existed prior to it. This unit is present-oriented and geared toward "forgetting the past." The past is absorbed into the new family.

Invented stepfamilies tend to deny being a different type of family and usually adopt an attitude of "nothing is unique about families like ours." The focal subsystem of invented stepfamilies is parental; they are committed to raising children together.

The spouses in invented families often have remarried in a relatively early phase of their lives. Typically, the husband has never been married before or was in a short, childless first marriage. The wife usually is in the early stages of child raising, she often has one young child from a previous marriage. Some invented stepfamilies do include two or three children from the wife's previous marriage and one or more children from the husband's previous marriage. These children are "absorbed" into the new unit, and the spouses are expected to fulfill parental roles toward each other's kids.

Invented families were abundant until the first half of the century because the death of a spouse was the most common precursor of remarriage, and the typical response of the remarried was to re-create the nuclear family (Ganong and Coleman, 1994a).

## DISCARDING THE PAST: THE TIME IS NOW

Invented stepfamilies create a unit that is focused on the present and that allows a very limited, if any, space for the past in its current life. The family is originated anew and is perceived by family members as "the real family," while the past is ignored: "The previous family has been closed. A new family has been opened. The previous chapter in our life is dead. We are in a new chapter, a new life. We are not interested in and do not remember what once was. We totally crossed it out."

The context of relationships, events, and memories that are re-lated to the past is erased. Wherever possible the family relates to events from the first marriage as if they occurred in the current family. When this is impossible, the origin of "things from the past" is blurred or disguised to minimize the presence of the past in the current life. For example, when Marie, the fourteen-year-old stepdaughter of Brad, answers a call for her stepfather when he is not at home and is asked who is speaking, she replies, "the daugh-ter," rather than presenting herself as his stepdaughter or using her given name.

Rejecting the past is nurtured and driven by an effort to distance family members from what is perceived as a failure—the first mar-riage. Since invented stepfamilies tend to include fewer and youn-ger children from previous marriages than integrated stepfamilies, the past is more amenable to obliteration and re-creation, as opposed to families with adolescents who have a solid history with and memories of the pre-remarriage life and the noncustodial parent.

Angela and Jerome got married five years ago when Angela's son and Jerome's daughter were eleven. Together they have two boys, a three- and a one-year-old. Jerome has joint custody of his daughter, who spends with the family three nights a week, every other weekend, and half of her vacations and holidays. Angela has sole custody of her son, who keeps very loose relationships with his father who lives abroad. They describe their prescription for a healthy and happy stepfamily: "It is important not to allow ex-spouses to affect life in the current family. To be successful, families need to opt for the present, kill spirits from the past."

In invented families, the members rarely compare present life to the past, and when they do, it is mostly on an anecdotal level. They tend to make decisions without considering their effect on the non-residing parent and his/her new family. Sometimes this practice stems from a wish to "erase" the past and sometimes because of circumstances. Ruth, a forty-five-year-old Israeli, had been divorced for four years when she met Henry, an American eighteen years her senior, who spent a sabbatical in Israel. Ruth's son, then seven, saw his father one to three times a month. Ruth maintained a regular relationship with her ex-in-laws, whom she and her son saw weekly. When Henry returned to the states at the end of his sabbatical, the couple maintained the relationship by frequently visiting each other during the next year. Then they decided to live together. Because of professional and economic constraints, it was not feasible for Henry to move to Israel, so Ruth and her son had to move to the United States. Consequently, the relationship between the child and his biological father decreased significantly. They do not write to each other, hardly speak on the phone, and meet only a handful of times during summer vacations taken by Ruth and her son in Israel.

## DENIAL OF DIFFERENCES: WE ARE A REGULAR FAMILY

Because invented stepfamilies see the current union as *the* family, they deny differences from non-stepfamilies and try to disguise their family configuration. They describe themselves as "a regular family. There is nothing special about the fact that we married twice. We are not exceptional and not different, just a normal family with normal issues"; "We never think about ourselves as a combined family, a reconstituted family, or a stepfamily. We are absolutely a normal family. Nothing unusual"; "The question of which concept should be used to describe a family like us is irrelevant, as there is no need for a special concept because this is not a special family."

Some invented families see the denial of difference from non-stepfamilies as a condition for the success of the remarriage: "One ought to treat this marriage as if it is the only marriage. Not to think about being different, not to talk about it. Just ignore it, if the current family is to exist and succeed." Other families emphasize that acknowledgment of differences may work against the family: "It is not wise to call attention to us being a remarried family because this may trigger negative reactions that are born out of biases . . . we do not want to give people the opportunity to say, 'well, no wonder you have such issues, since you are a stepfamily' . . . sharing such information may be a boomerang. If you perceive the situation as not problematic, it is not problematic."

Those invented families that recognize any differences tend to minimize their significance. As George, a remarried father and stepfather says, "You do not have to illuminate differences with strong flashlights." When differences are recognized, they are defined mostly in organizational/technical rather than essential terms. Differences from non-stepfamilies are related to the need to drive children for visitation, to coordinate with ex-spouses concerning allocation of chores, such as taking children to dental appointments and ballet classes, and to inform a larger number of people about events regarding the children.

Marie and Brad are parents to seven- and ten-year-old daughters from Brad's first marriage, a five-year-old daughter from Marie's first marriage, and a nine-month-old baby born in the remarriage. When asked how living in a stepfamily differs from a non-stepfamily, they state:

> It is actually not different. We are a regular family. We have fun together, we fight together . . . like every normal family. We do have somewhat more complicated logistics because children go to their previous parents, but that is all . . . many families have complicated logistics. For example, families with many children, families of children who are heavily into

sports and need to be taken to practice all the time. There is nothing special about us.

Stepfamily issues that are too obvious to be denied are often claimed to be related to other characteristics of the family rather than its configuration. For example, the Bond stepfamily includes the remarried couple, their two toddlers, and the wife's son from a previous marriage. The adolescent daughter of the husband lives with her mother but visits with the family often. The family is experiencing typical issues of stepfamilies with adolescents. The boy rejects his stepfather, wishes to change his residential arrangements, withdraws from a previously warm relationship with his stepsister, and often criticizes his mother for the way she dresses and for expressing affection to her husband in front of the children. However, they strongly resist any definition of the issues as related to their family structure: "The son's adolescence is a difficult period in our family, but it has nothing to do with the family status. Adolescence is a difficult developmental stage in all families." Although this statement is true for many families, the Bonds clearly prefer to reframe step-related issues as nonstep issues.

Invented families often convey the message of "we are just another regular family" explicitly or implicitly to children. For example, the Grano children know that they are expected to prepare for Mother's Day a present for their stepmother as well as for their mother. In the first year of his remarriage, Mr. Grano took his daughters, who live with their mother and often visit with their father's new family, to buy Mother's Day presents. After the girls chose their gift to their mother, he asked them, "And what would you like to get for Justine [the current Mrs. Grano]?" Since the girls liked their father's new wife and had quickly developed a good relationship with her, they easily went along with their father's message and also got their stepmom a present. This started a tradition that has been kept ever since. When the relationship with the stepparent is not so positive the message from the adult to treat his/her current spouse as a parent figure may meet opposition and resentment.

The message of "we are like all other families" dominates the social relationships of invented stepfamilies. They convey to relatives, neighbors, and friends a demand to treat them as a nuclear first-time family. The Bond family, described previously, states:

> As for us everything is natural and we "broadcast" this to the world, the world treats us as a not unusual family . . . some of our friends even comment that it looks like we are the norm and they are the exception . . . When one sincerely believes that the situation is normal, it is normal . . . we would have reacted negatively to anybody who would treat us as a different type of family. Actually, we broke off our relationship with one family because we felt that their attitude toward us was affected by our being in a second marriage.

The Roberts family expresses a similar view:

> We tell everybody that our family now has three children and this is how we are being perceived. The environment "buys" you according to the way you "sell" yourself. We sold ourselves as a typical family and this is the attitude we get.

Since they do not want to be singled out as different, invented stepfamilies object to the idea that society needs to do anything for stepfamilies. Invented stepfamilies resent any implication that their family configuration requires special attention: "Remarriage is not a disease; unlike widowhood, we do not deserve a special label or special attention." George, a remarried father of his two daughters from a previous marriage and stepfather of one son, says, "Remarriage is not a disease. It is a private affair and nobody from outside should intervene or even know about the fact that once there was another family. Everything is just the same as in all other families except in formal documents."

## A PARENTAL FOCAL SUBSYSTEM

Since the partners in invented families get together to build a new family and raise children, the parental subsystem is dominant in this type of stepfamilies. This is reflected both in the centrality of parenting in their life and in the absence of biological lines in allocation of parental roles.

### The Centrality of Parenthood

Parenting is a central axis in the life of invented families. They are highly invested in raising the children from previous and current marriages, fostering close relationships among natural, half-, and stepsiblings, and making child rearing a priority in their functioning as a family. They often indicate that the quality of family life is reflected in and depends upon the stepparent-stepchild relationship: "The relationships with each other's children and among the children are the barometer of the family's quality of life . . . the family will rise and fall on the stepparent-stepchild relationship. If this does not work, the family is bound to fail; nothing will work." "The relationships with each other's children are the mirror of life in the family."

Some families even see the stepparent-stepchild relationship as the key to a successful marriage: "If this relationship is good, the marriage will be good, but if this relationship does not work, the marriage is bound to fall apart." This perspective puts a heavy burden on the stepparent-stepchild relationship.

Some families go so far as to say that they remarried and established the stepfamily for the sake of children, to raise them in what the partners perceive as the best setting. A stepparent is often defined as "the new parent" or "the current parent," indicating that the stepparent is *the* parent in the present. Mabel, a remarried mother of two, declares, "If my children did not like my husband, I would not have married him. After all, he was going to be their new father and this would not have worked if they could not stand him."

In integrated families, the focus is on the marital union and children come along as "a package deal." As Stephanie describes, the situation is different for invented stepfamilies: "Everybody is an equal part of the deal. There are no 'appendices.' Everybody belongs."

In a joint interview, Angela and Jerome, who were described earlier in this chapter, emphasized that their life revolves around the children: "We devote a lot to the children and make a point of fostering their relationships. . . . We remarried since this seemed the healthiest way to raise him [Angela's son] . . . that this will be the way to minimize his suffering from the situation."

Most invented stepfamilies have at least one child in the current marriage, even if both partners had children in a previous marriage. This creates two distinctive "sets" of children with a wide age difference between them: a cluster of older children from the previous marriages and young children from the remarriage. These children are related to everybody in the new family and are often referred to as the "glue" because they symbolize the stepfamily's hopes for rebirth and renewal. Angela and Jerome point out that, "It is important to bear children in the remarriage. They unite everybody and abolish any "camps" that may have existed unconsciously. These children become the focal point of the family because they are the only family members that we can all love free of guilt or fear of stepping on eggshells. These are the children that everybody can give to without having to be cautious."

Other invented families tend to think differently. The DiCaprios, a religious family that raises three children of each spouse from a previous marriage, explain that they refrained from having a seventh child together "because this child would have had something more than the rest of the siblings and we did not care to create such a gap."

### The Allocation of Parental Roles

In invented stepfamilies, parenting roles regarding all children are shared. Both spouses count and treat all children as their own, irrespective of which marriage they were born into. Division of parental roles is similar, as far as natural and stepchildren are concerned: "This is a family of the two of us."

Mrs. Rosenberg, a remarried mother of one and a stepmother of two adolescent girls, explains: "When the girls are here I raise them, feed them, wash their clothes, help with homework, and give them money; therefore, when they are here, they are my daughters and I discipline them just like I do with my son. This makes them feel that they are an integral part of this family and not guests."

In their effort to emphasize the unity of their family, many invented stepfamilies tend to adopt an equal division of parental roles. Both parents discipline all children from all marriages, attend parent-teacher conferences, and function as full parents.

Rachel, a twenty-eight-year-old remarried mother of six-year-old Jasmin, explains: "My current husband is Jasmin's father in every sense. He washes her, feeds her, helps her with her homework, and punishes her when necessary. If he would not have been her father, he could not have been my husband . . . we could not have been a family." Fred, her husband, adds: "Each of us does, regarding the children, what we do best. I am better in making rules and observing that they are followed, therefore this is my job; Rachel is better in problem solving and coping with emergencies, so that is her share of the parenting cake."

Unlike integrated families that clearly distinguish between patterns of parenting and stepparenting, invented stepfamilies foster equality of parenting and stepparenting. Dina and Michael have been married for ten years and are raising Dina's daughter from her first marriage and the son they have together. Michael's son, who lives with his mother in the same neighborhood, spends most afterschool hours with the family, often sleeping over and eating with them because his mother's career in journalism requires her to work long hours and travel frequently. Michael is an electrician and is the main breadwinner, while Dina works in a part-time clerical job and spends most of her time at home with the children. She is the main parental figure for all three children. In the Rivera family, the husband is the main parental figure for the two sons of his wife, his son who lives in the stepfamily, his son and daughter who live with their natural mother, and the mutual daughter born in the remarriage. When any child is in trouble and needs help, they come to him. He is the soft-hearted, giving parent while his wife is more demanding. If one of the children from any marriage needed to get somewhere, the wife would tell them to go by public transportation; the husband would give them a ride.

Parental roles are divided not along biological lines, but according to tasks or timing. For example, in the Hart family, the husband has the disciplinarian role while the wife maintains contact with the school and attends parent-teacher conferences for all children.

**Wife:** We share parental responsibilities, but when we want to establish order, my husband [stepfather] is called to duty.

**Husband:** I am more strict and I care more about discipline, therefore, I am the "sergeant major" of the family.

The Carrino family presents a similar picture. Mrs. Carrino is a housewife, mother of two boys, ages fifteen and thirteen, from her first marriage and of a baby boy from her current marriage, and a stepmother of two boys, ages eight and nine. She describes role allocation in the family: "I am softer than my husband. All the kids take advantage of this and get from me much more than what they get from my husband." Her husband adds: "I am the policeman of all the children. They know that with me they cannot play games like they do with my wife." In the Fast family, the wife performs most parental roles during the day, while in the evening the couple "shares equally all parental tasks regarding all children alike." In the Bross family, the mother and the stepfather discipline different behaviors. The mother deals with school-related issues and household chores and the stepfather deals with social manners.

In invented families that tilt toward a more traditional model, the wife has more child-rearing responsibilities, or the husband maintains instrumental parenting roles while the mother focuses on addressing emotional needs.

When the wife is a major parental figure, she parents biological and stepchildren in a similar way. The Pattersons have been married for four years. Each brought a ten-year-old daughter from a previous marriage. The girls grow up in the stepfamily because both previous spouses live abroad. Mrs. Patterson is exclusively responsible for the parental role in the family, a pattern that both spouses brought from their families of origin. Mrs. Patterson has sole responsibility regarding the health and educational needs of the girls, and when in need of help in child care, she cannot rely on her husband. She says, "This is my thing and it's up to me to find a solution." And her husband adds, "I put the bread on the table and she has to raise the kids. This is how I grew up and this is how I wish my girls [referring to his natural and stepdaughter] to grow up."

In many invented families, the wife is in the early stages of childrearing. This makes the stepfather becoming a major paternal figure relatively easy, as compared to stepfamilies that include adolescent children from a previous marriage. In the latter, the biological parent has had a long history with children from a previous marriage, and often the noncustodial parent also has maintained a continuous relationship with the children. Consequently, both biological parents have a strong position as disciplinarians, and the stepparent may have difficulties assuming such a position.

## MAIN ISSUES:
## INVENTED FAMILIES—WHOSE INVENTION?

What happens to children who live in a family invented by parents? This, in fact, happens to all children in all types of families. Adults create a family based on their wishes, expectations, and belief system, and children live in these families and gradually contribute to shaping them. Thus, adults may construct a religious family, a liberal family, or an adoptive family, and it is their decision that determines for children in which kind of family they are born and raised. Stepfamilies are unique in that the "invention" of a new family occurs after the children have lived in another family. In many invented families, children accept the adults' picture of the family. Eileen, thirteen, comments, "I have the nature of a redhead, just like Daddy. It runs in the genes [referring to her stepfather]." This acceptance may be guided by a wish to please, fear of losing affection, or a desire to belong.

Experts in the field point to the damaging effects on children of a decision by adults to foster an invented family profile. For example, Visher and Visher (1996) comment that, "Attempting to create a nuclear family negates the children's original family and robs them of their tie to the past" (p. 21). Kaslow (1993) warns that the attempt of a family to act as if the nonresidential parents never existed is detrimental to children. Boszormenyi-Nagy and Spark (1973) and Ahrons and Rodgers (1987) emphasize the importance of acknowledging the past and maintaining contacts with nonresiding parents and their extended families for the well-being of children and point out long-term detrimental effects of efforts to erase the past. However, in a recent study, invented stepfamilies scored equal to other types of stepfamilies in satisfaction and functioning (Berger, 1995). Albeit, in this study, since the information came from the adults who decided to foster an invented profile for their family, it raises questions regarding the absoluteness of the afore-mentioned generalizations regarding invented families. The effects of growing up in an invented family on children remain to be studied.

A typical issue in these families is that of competition between parent and stepparent over natural, step-, and remarriage children. This issue arises from the focus on the parental subsystem. Since the parental role is so central and important in these families, it is a source of power and potential cause of disagreement. The person who holds this role and exercises parental rights has power. This role and the associated rights become commodities/assets over which members compete.

Because invented families emphasize the parental subsystem and cohesion of the family as a unit, they often plan family outings to include all the children. Sometimes this involves complicated logis-tic strategies to ensure that the nonresiding children of the husband visit the family on the same day that the children of the wife are home and not visiting their biological father. Some invented fami-lies make extreme efforts to ensure that "everybody is included, no matter what"; they will not plan or will cancel family events if only some of the children can participate. This attitude often stems from parents' feeling guilty for "betraying" their biological children by having fun with their stepchildren.

## CASE ILLUSTRATION: THE FOX FAMILY

Ruth is a forty-one-year-old travel agent who runs her own busi-ness. She was married to Benjamin, her first husband, for six years and had one daughter with him, Sharon, who is currently seventeen and a senior in a prestigious and highly competitive high school. Shortly after Sharon was born, Ruth left her first husband and got a divorce three years later, following a nasty battle and considerable financial compromises. Five months after her divorce, Ruth met and started dating Gabriel, who was a popular bachelor. Gabriel is an engineer and works for the government. The couple married two years later and has been married for nine years. They have two girls together: ten-year-old Lea and five-year-old Liz. The following genogram presents the family configuration.

The Fox Family: An Invented Stepfamily

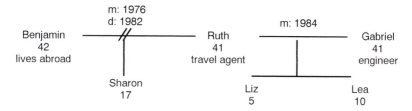

The family lives downtown in a modest townhouse. The two young girls share a bedroom and all three girls share a bathroom and a closet. They moved into the house after the remarriage. Both spouses came to the remarriage practically penniless. Gabriel had to use a considerable portion of his salary to support his sick and elderly parents and his mentally challenged older brother. His parents passed away during the following years and the brother lives in a supportive-living residence. Ruth had limited financial resources because of the numerous compromises and expenses that her divorce demanded. Despite the financial stress, the couple insisted on buying a new house "to have a fresh start in a neutral place that is *ours* and will not carry ghosts from the past."

The stepfather's last name serves exclusively as the surname of the family, including Sharon. When Sharon started to attend grammar school shortly after her mother remarried to Gabriel, Ruth worked as a teacher's aide in the same school. She registered the girl in school by the stepfather's name "to prevent Sharon from feeling uncomfortable and not to leave an opening for questions." Now Sharon follows through and presents herself by her stepfather's last name. The high school administration demanded that Sharon be registered by her official name, which is her biological father's last name. Although the family complied with the demand and all official documents go by Sharon's legal name, the girl uses her stepfather's last name on notebooks, etc. Her mother and stepfather strongly support this strategy.

Sharon calls Gabriel Dad at home and introduces him to others as her father. Gabriel refers to Sharon as "my oldest daughter." He

attended parent-teacher meetings at her school and often accompanied her class on field trips and was active in her school when she
was younger. He states that he perceives her as his own daughter as
much as he does his biological younger daughters:

> **Ruth:** The fact that she was such a beautiful girl helped.
>
> **Gabriel:** She is beautiful today too.
>
> **Ruth:** Today she is impressive . . . not beautiful . . . she has
> presence.
>
> **Gabriel:** She is more than impressive . . . [turning to inter-
> viewer] she always has had her special status with me . . .
> she was an only daughter.
>
> **Ruth:** She was a mature, successful, delicate, special girl;
> therefore, we were always very proud of her.

Family members state that all children are treated equally, having
the same rights and chores. Sharon does claim occasionally that she
is discriminated against and is required to do more and it is not fair.
However, the couple relates this to her age and personality rather
than to the family configuration.

While Sharon's relationships with her stepfather are warm and
close, her contacts with her biological father are minimal. When she
was eleven, he moved to Germany, where he practices medicine.
They talk over the phone two or three times a year, exchange holiday cards and birthday presents, and have seen each other only
twice since he emigrated, when her father came to visit his elderly
mother. Sharon also visited him once in Germany but she minimizes her relationship with him: "Actually Gabriel raised me. He
does for me things that fathers do for their children." Ruth and
Gabriel support her argument: "She is not really attached to him
[her father]."

However, Sharon maintains a warm relationship with her paternal grandmother and visits her routinely. The two young girls, Sharon's half-siblings, often join her on these visits and refer to the
elderly woman as "Grandma." In the family, these visits are referred to as "the girls go to visit Grandma Rebecca."

The family never discusses past-related issues and denies any
comparison to the past. Most of their friends, neighbors, and col-

leagues do not know the wife is in a second marriage. Their attitude toward the past is reflected in the following excerpt:

> **Interviewer:** How do you relate to the past prior to your marriage?
>
> **Ruth:** What is there to relate? The past is "passe." It is not part of our life and we do not look backward. We look at our life now and forward. Never backward.
>
> **Gabriel:** What was is dead, as if it never existed.
>
> **Ruth:** Right from the start we knew that we left the past behind and we do not want to go back to deal with things from the past . . .
>
> **Gabriel:** We never deal with the past, talk about it, or relate to it.
>
> **Ruth** [decisively]: It was disconnected and this is it!
>
> **Interviewer:** Do any of you compare life now to life before?
>
> **Gabriel:** No, never. Even in the beginning of our marriage neither Ruth nor Sharon ever compared the two families. I do not even think Sharon remembers how it was . . .
>
> **Ruth:** I think that it is not a question of memory . . . there is no reason to compare . . . now it's another life.

Both spouses deny any difference between stepfamilies and intact first-marriage families. Their philosophy is that adopting an all-is-normal position helps both step- and mutual children and is the healthiest perspective for stepfamilies.

> **Interviewer:** Is life in a family like yours different than life in first-marriage families? And if so, how are they different?
>
> **Gabriel:** It is not different at all, except in formal documents. When a man marries a mother, he must accept the child as his own. Any other kind of attitude disrupts the remarriage.
>
> **Ruth:** There is nothing different about a remarriage family. We do not inform new people we meet that I have been married before. There is no reason for anybody to know. It's irrelevant and meaningless.
>
> **Gabriel:** One has to act natural, not make a big deal of being in a remarriage, accept the child as your own. If one cannot do it, it is better not to get married because any other situation may not be comfortable to all involved.

**Ruth:** Only when all family members accept the situation as normal can the family function well.

**Interviewer:** Does your being a remarriage family have any effect on your social relationships?

**Ruth:** We do not share the information with new colleagues and friends, and those who knew it forgot about it because we are a normal family; we carry on with our life and deal with normal issues like all other families.

**Gabriel:** Most of the time we ourselves do not remember that this is not Ruth's first marriage. It feels like a first marriage, we behave like a first marriage . . . to us it is a first marriage.

**Sharon** [who was watching T.V. in the family room adjacent to the living room where the interview took place and obviously was listening to the conversation]: I do not remember living with Mom and Benjamin. I feel as if all my life I lived with Mom and Dad [referring to Gabriel]. I know that you psychologists and counselors have all these theories that I should feel different because Dad is not my biological father, but the fact is that to me he is my dad and that is it. End of story. That's why it goes well.

**Interviewer:** Let's assume for a moment, just for the sake of argument, that one or some of you would not have felt that the picture is so clear-cut . . . that there are differences between step- and non-stepfamilies. How would you guys have dealt with it?

**Sharon:** The whole question is irrelevant . . . it shows that you do not understand the atmosphere of our family . . . we all feel free to say whatever we want, in family talks and so on . . . it is that there is no need for that . . . we feel that this *is* the family. . . . I have a great family.

**Interviewer:** What is your secret? How did you make it work so well?

**Ruth:** We went naturally with the flow; both extended families were supportive from the beginning . . . it just went well. Our environment was open. Everyone and everything just flows smoothly.

## *SUMMARY*

This chapter introduced the invented stepfamily. Even though these families come in various sizes and formats, they all share certain characteristics: minimizing the place of the pre-remarriage past in their current lives, denying differences from non-stepfamilies, and focusing considerably on parenthood. They live as if they reinvented the family in the current unit. Working with these families requires special attention to determine the effect on children of choosing to detach from and minimize the past and ignore differences.

# Chapter 7

# Imported Stepfamilies:
# Living the "There and Then"
# in the "Here and Now"

Imported families are more complicated to define and illustrate than either integrated or invented families, because theirs is a less "pure" profile that shares more characteristics with the other two types than the latter two share with each other.

## *PROFILE OF IMPORTED STEPFAMILIES*

Imported families restore the previous family in the new unit as if it were the original family. Unlike integrated families that maintain the "old" or invented families that create the "new," imported families revive the "old" in the "new." They bring components from the past into the present and treat them as if they are part of the present and not part of the past at all. They do not make room for the past like integrated families or minimize the past by focusing on the present like invented families. Some imported families even spell out this process. Danny, a remarried, childless widower who remarried a divorced mother explains: "Our family imported from our previous marriages ways of doing things and beliefs, and from my wife's marriage, we imported her daughter, Maya." In another stepfamily, members state: "Everything remained as it was. What was, is what will be." To effectively re-create the original family in the stepfamily, imported families tend to focus on the past as the present and deny any difference from non-stepfamilies.

Imported families tend to be structurally simple stepfamilies, that is, families into which only one spouse brings a child from a previous marriage. As in invented families, this parent is typically the wife, who brought into the remarriage one young child from a previous marriage. The husband has frequently never been married before or was in a childless previous marriage. Even though they are less typical, imported families with more than one child and with children of both spouses do exist.

Unlike invented but similar to integrated families, the focal subsystem in imported families is the couple. These families tend not to bear children in the remarriage, and the children of the wife are treated as if they are "children of the family." Consequently, imported families are often smaller than other types of stepfamilies and the range of children's ages is more limited.

## *RELIVING THE PAST IN THE PRESENT*

While integrated families live in a combination of the past and the present and invented families live the present and eliminate the past, imported families live the past *in* the present. They do not view the current family as a new unit or a separate unit; instead, they relate to it as an extension of the original family or as its "substitute." Maya, Alex, his three daughters, and her son stated in a recent family interview, "In our family the previous families and the current family dissolved into each other to the point that sometimes we cannot remember in which context something happened and we start arguing if a certain event occurred with father Alex or with father Mike [Maya's first husband]." This situation is reflected in the terminology imported families use to describe themselves, such as "instant family," "ready-made family," and "prefabricated family."

Heather is a remarried mother of an eleven-year-old boy from her previous marriage and a three-year-old boy from her remarriage to Billy, a divorced father of a ten-year-old girl. She describes the experience of her stepfamily: "It's like a jigsaw puzzle. You take out one piece, the first husband, and you put in another, the second husband."

Unlike invented families that ignore the past, imported families "mask" it. They allow space for elements from the past in their current life, but they do not relate to these elements in their original context. Instead, they "absorb" these elements, assimilate them into their current life, and make them an integral part of the present.

These elements include relationships, rules, roles, patterns, and so forth. Alex, an adolescent stepson, expressed this experience: "When the second family is good and pleasant, we project all the good things on it and forget the good things in the first family. We feel as if all the positive things are in this family and remember the other family mostly with the unpleasant things even though we know that it probably had also good things."

Fourteen-year-old Barbara, who lives with her remarried mother and stepfather, comments that, "He [her stepfather] always says 'in my family things are done in such and such way' and you always wonder which family does he mean? His previous family? Us? All his families? It is as if he has one family which he started with his first wife and continues with my Mom."

Figuratively, imported families can be described as using a rehabilitation model. Rehabilitation works to bring a person (or unit) back to the precrisis level of functioning. Similarly, imported families operate to bring the new family to its predivorce-remarriage situation. In fact, some stepfamilies speak about themselves in rehab terms. Jeff, a father and stepfather, responds to the question "To what extent do things from the original family interfere with life in the current family?":

> Similar to all rehabilitation, living in a family like ours requires efforts from the rehabilitator and the rehabilitated, except for us it is not clear who is what . . . we all are rehabilitating and being rehabilitated at the same time. Stepfamilies are like one big rehabilitation center . . . when there is a child involved one has to be extra careful and devote a lot . . . yet when one succeeds one feels good, it is a big challenge.

Sometimes they describe the current family as an improved version of the "previous round." Often, imported families express their belief that they would not have divorced the first time if they had then the experience with which they entered the second marriage. Consequently, they see the stepfamily as an opportunity to do what could have been done in the first family. The Bonito family includes the couple, Mrs. Bonito's eleven-year-old son, and two mutual toddlers. Mr. Bonito shares with his ex-wife custody of their eleven-year-old daughter, who spends with her father's new family half the week, every other weekend, and half her vacations. The Bonito's describe life in the family as "the previous families amended."

These families are similar to a production in which actors have been "recast" but the show, the plot, and the roles remain the same. The divorce that dissolved the original marriage left roles unstaffed, and the new spouse steps forward to occupy a vacant role.

Miriam and Amos Baruch describe how this "change of guards" happened in their family. They have been married for four years. Mrs. Baruch's fourteen-year-old daughter lives with the couple, while Mr. Baruch's three daughters, ages nineteen, fourteen, and twelve, live with their mother half an hour away from the stepfamily. Prior to the remarriage, Mrs. Baruch's first husband maintained routine contact with his daughter. As soon as the couple married, the natural father "stepped out," and Mr. Baruch "stepped in" to fill the fathering role. Currently, Mrs. Baruch's ex-husband keeps very sporadic contact with his daughter while her current husband has assumed the father's role.

Children describe a similar picture. Seventeen-year-old Michelle, who lives with her remarried mother and stepfather, explains:

> My father was the soft-hearted and giving parent . . . With my stepfather I continue the same pattern of relationships . . . when I cannot get something from my mother I go to my stepdad. I know that often he will side with me and convince my mother . . . this is the kind of father I am used to.

In the Enrico family, the two stepsisters, ages twelve and sixteen, each from one of the spouses' previous marriages, express their perception of the current family as a continuation of the original family: "All of us together are one large family, including all the parents [that is biological and stepparents] and all the children [from each spouse's first marriage and the mutual daughter in the remarriage]."

Imported stepfamily members not only step into a role in general such as "a father" or "the oldest daughter," they often also inherit a specific mode for performing that role; they completely replace the previous family member in that role and follow the footsteps of their predecessor in fulfilling the role. The original role player developed and shaped a certain way of performing a given role, and family members are used to this and expect the new player to maintain this tradition. Those expectations are conveyed either directly and openly or implied indirectly. Members in the new unit find themselves facing these expectations and often complying with them.

Mrs. Hutchison is a divorcée remarried to a widower. The couple raises her three adolescent sons and his four adolescent boys. Mrs. Hutchison, who is in charge of discipline of all seven teenagers, stated:

> My husband and my stepchildren were used to a mother who was the disciplinarian. When we remarried it seemed that the easiest way was adapt to the ready-made "job description" rather than to struggle to change everything for everybody. This worked best since my children were used to me as the parent in charge because I raised them alone; my stepchildren were used to a mother as the disciplinarian, so in a way it was all figured out for me.

In some imported families the taking over of roles by a stepparent is supported by the noncustodial natural parent. This approval of "passing the torch" to the new spouse further fosters the experience of the new family as a continuation of the previous family. In the Patti family, Steve, the wife's son from a previous marriage, and the mutual daughter from the remarriage live in the stepfamily. The wife's daughter, who lives on her own, and the husband's daughters, who live with their mother, visit often. Mrs. Patti's first husband, George, remarried and went to live close to his family of origin in Argentina, his native country. The Pattis maintain a friendly relationship with George and his family. On visits to the United States, George stays with the new family of his ex-wife. He openly expresses support of his wife's second husband assuming the parental role toward Steve:

> It is true that I am his father but you raise him. If it is necessary to punish him, or even to spank him, I give you my permission and encouragement to do so.

Together with importing into the current family relationships, rules, roles, and patterns from the previous family, imported families allow issues that were experienced in the first family to reoccur in spite of the changes in performers. For example, Dennis, the middle of three sons of a divorced family, whose custodial parent subsequently remarried, used to feel deprived and discriminated against in his family of origin. He was sure most of the time that his older brother enjoyed many privileges because of his seniority and his young brother was spoiled and overprotected because of being the "baby" of the family. Now Dennis has an additional older stepsister and a baby half-sister. He is still sure that each of the other children gets more than he, and he is constantly jealous and embittered. By the same token, Olga describes in her first and second marriage a similar pattern of sweeping frustrations "under the carpet" and avoiding open discussion of problems: "I changed my husband, but I brought with me the same pattern of marital communication or, more accurately, lack of communication."

Many imported families continue to live in the residence of one of the spouses, often without total renovations. Furniture, kitchenware, and decorations from the original family are brought into the stepfamily, and the family continues relationships with the same social circle, creating a strong sense of continuity. This sometimes invites reactions toward the stepfamily as a continuation of the first family. Edward moved into his wife's apartment when they married. He reports that one of the neighbors met him in the elevator and mentioned that he had lost a lot of weight. Edward, who was slim all his life and had never met this neighbor before, was surprised that the neighbor had confused him with his wife's first husband.

Imported stepfamilies tend to preserve a sense of continuity for children, who often stay in the same school and play with the same friends. While this provides children with comfort because of familiarity and helps them to deal with the changes in the family following the remarriage, it may also introduce some confusion. Eight-year-old Samantha explains:

> In the beginning this was my home with my mother and my old father, and then my mother divorced my father and now this is the home of me, my mother and brother, and my new father. I have girlfriends that do not understand this, and one of them even said that this is not possible because children have

one father, but I had first one father and now another father, but my first father is also still my father. Sometimes I wish that we could all live here together.

In the DeHan family, the first family was imported almost literally into the stepfamily. The first Mrs. DeHan is remarried, parents a child born in her remarriage, and shares with Mr. DeHan custody of Cara, their mutual daughter. Mr. Dehan and the current Mrs. De-Han's first husband are business partners, while the first Mrs. De-Han and the second Mrs. DeHan maintain a close relationship with each other. The previous Mrs. DeHan shares with her successor recipes for Mr. DeHan's and Cara's favorite dishes and advises her on how various aspects of family life have been addressed, which the current Mrs. DeHan often adopts and follows. Similar situations are not uncommon in imported families.

Bonnie and Thomas married seven years ago. Each of them brought into the remarriage a boy and a girl of similar ages from the previous marriages. Bonnie's ex-husband had custody of the children until three years ago, when they moved in with Bonnie and Thomas. Several months later a mutual daughter was born. Bonnie and Thomas and their children knew one another in their previous families. Currently, Bonnie's ex-husband lives in another state, and the children get to see him once a year. They also keep sporadic telephone contact with him.

When Thomas divorced his first wife, he stayed in their home and his ex-wife, with her new family, moved into another house on the same block of identical houses in a small town about half an hour from a major city. Thomas' children stay with their father's new family twice a week and on all weekends. They also drop in occasionally during the rest of the week; they practically use both their mother's and father's homes together as their house. When they need money, are hungry, or wish to make a telephone call, they would drop into one of the houses. When all children are in the stepfamily, the boys share one bedroom, as do the older girls. The baby has a tiny room of her own. Although Bonnie's children are more reserved about going with their stepsiblings to their mother's house, this happens occasionally. In the beginning, Thomas's ex-wife would also come into the stepfamily's house (which was previously hers) to take a photo or another item, since she and her ex-husband never really finished dividing their possessions. Eventually, Bonnie demanded that her husband establish a clearer boundary and stop these "invasions"; however, there is very much a feeling that the previous family "spills" into the current family.

Sometimes stepfamily members extend their positions held by a previous spouse into extrafamilial arenas. Mr. Zeldin is a remarried father of two boys and stepfather of two girls, all in their teens. When discussing the effect of living in a stepfamily on social life and relationships with friends, he comments, "I lost most of the friends I had in my first marriage, but I inherited many of my wife's friends, often at the expense of her first husband. I replaced him in existing social networks. He walked out and I walked in. In a way I was marrying into a preexisting position."

## *DENYING DIFFERENCES FROM NON-STEPFAMILIES*

Marie, Jack, and Marie's daughter, Janice, are an imported stepfamily. The following excerpt is from a recent interview with them:

**Interviewer:** Can you tell me what is special about life in your family?

**Jack** [previously married without children]**:** There is really not much to tell. We continue our life as it was before . . . there is really not much change . . . we live in the same house. When I divorced, my wife moved in with her young boyfriend while I remained in the apartment. Marie and Janice [her daughter] lived in the same building, so the only change was moving three flights higher . . .

**Marie:** We have the same neighbors; Janice has the same friends and attends the same school; we have the same social circle. The new family is very much like the old family . . .

**Janice:** I have another father and I see him whenever he has time and I do not have tests or rehearsals [Janice is active in a theater group in her school] but otherwise, all is pretty much the same like in all the families of my friends.

**Jack:** You may almost ask if it is so much the same why we bothered to make the change.

**Interviewer:** Why indeed did you make the change if it's more of the same?
**Marie:** I cook better.
[Everybody laughs.]

To be able to carry on their agenda of rejuvenating the original family in the current one, imported families need to disregard any difference from non-stepfamilies. Similar to invented families, they tend to disguise their being a non-first-marriage family and to pass for a non-stepfamily.

Mr. Nichols, a remarried father of one child in each of his marriages and a stepfather of one, says:

> Living in a stepfamily is neither a disease nor an accomplishment . . . it is nothing special either for the good or bad and therefore need not to be recognized. Sure we have problems, all families have problems . . . we do not relate to them on the basis of stepfamily/non-stepfamily; we relate to them on a specific basis and address issues as they come up, not in relation to family configuration.

When asked to identify criteria for "good" stepfamilies, imported families state, "They are the same criteria that you would use for the first marriage. We are just as if it was a family created by a first marriage and should be judged the same way." Although this may be mostly the "slogan" of the remarried couple, children in imported stepfamilies also do not want to be exceptional among their peers and often adopt the same attitude.

As different last names for family members are a statement of difference from non-stepfamilies, in imported families, often all family members go by the current name or develop all kinds of strategies to avoid having to make a decision about which name to use. Mr. McMurty explains:

> We do not want to use two names because we are one unit. We are a regular family . . . we feel like in a normal family, the children know that we are a regular family, the neighbors accept us as a regular family . . . the only difference is that now I am the head of the family instead of Ross [Mrs. McMurty's first husband].

Children in stepfather imported families often choose to abide by the family's unwritten rule and adopt their stepfather's last name. Fourteen-year-old Peter resides with his mother, stepfather, stepsister, and three half-siblings. He is formally registered at school by his natural father's last name. However, he prefers to sign his drawings by his stepfather's last name.

When asked why he should not carry his original name, Peter explains that he feels that his family has changed: "We were Good, now we are Long; now I am a part of the Long family and prefer to carry this name." Peter pleaded with his mother and stepfather to have his name changed legally. As this effort was met with difficulties (his natural father would not approve: "You are my son and I want you to carry my name"), Peter intends to wait for the time when he can independently request to change his name. It is possible that Peter pushes toward this change in response to overt or implied pressure from his mother and stepfather. Sometimes children act in certain ways to gain approval, to feel accepted, or to fulfill parental expectations. However, an interview with Peter revealed no such signs. It seems that Peter genuinely feels that the current family is his family now and he wishes to acquire the name that symbolizes this situation as well as maintain his relationship with his natural father and his new family.

Imported families transform the split between the two original units of which the stepfamily is built. They know that the split is there (as with integrated families) yet try to function as if it is not there (as in invented families). For example, imported families tend not to sign pre- or antenuptial agreements because such contracts undermine the continuance of the previous family in the current union and imply the existence of separate pre-remarriage assets and/or income. These families emphasize their unity: "We think together about it, we discuss it, and we are in one mind what to do."

Mrs. Compton, a remarried mother of one son from her first marriage and one son from her current marriage, says: "It's all the same as if I stayed in my first marriage . . . I have two sons, each with a different name, none of them with my name since I kept my maiden name, which is the name under which I am known in my professional field." Her husband who also has a son from his previous marriage adds: "The only difference between us and other families is that each of us [the spouses] has two children and together we have three children, but this is really the only difference . . . all the rest is just the same."

To reject difference from non-stepfamilies, imported families often make a point of not parenting children along biological lines and of bridging cross-parental lines: "I gave his children what I wanted my son to receive." Spouses intentionally discipline, set limits, and parent each other's children to establish the lack of difference from non-stepfamilies. Families often foster rituals to establish this message such as the giving of an allowance by a stepparent. To cement the built-in division spouses support each other in performing parental roles. Rita, a remarried mother of two, says:

> If my husband acts toward my children in a manner that is not acceptable to me, I will not confront him in front of the children and not jump to defend them. I will wait until we are alone to explain my opinion because I do not want them to feel that he is a lesser parent; I want them to feel that he is just like a father in any other family.

If they acknowledge differences at all, imported families tend to restrict them to the existence of children and to describe them as limited, existing mainly in the beginning and gradually fading: "The only difference between us and other families is the fact that some of our children grow up with one parent who does not raise them from birth, but with time this difference also disappears gradually. As far as the rest of our life, it is just a normal regular life like all families."

Some imported families reject the difference because they are concerned about negative effects that recognition of difference may have on their lives: "If you let the environment see you as something exceptional, it is like a snowball; it rolls and rolls and you can never know when it will turn as a boomerang against you. Therefore, it is best to behave like all other families and to convey the message to children and to the world that you are now the family instead of the original family."

Imported stepfamilies emphasize that they make a point of presenting themselves as one unit. Variations of the message, "We behave naturally to be accepted naturally," are typical of imported families. The following statement by Mr. Myers, a remarried father and stepfather, is representative of many imported families:

> We convey to people that we are a cohesive family; we do not let anybody notice anything special about us because we do not want them to treat our children as exceptions . . . we want them to be treated like all their friends are treated.

### *MARITAL FOCAL SUBSYSTEM*

Imported families, similar to integrated families, emphasize the marital relationship. However, this focus has a somewhat different quality. First, unlike integrated families in which the spouses often create "a new perfect marriage," in imported families, they "slide" into familiar spousal positions and roles. Mrs. Green reports that both her marriages have been characterized by tension concerning the husbands' tendency to spend beyond their ability and to write checks that bounce: "It seems that I choose my husbands to be irresponsible financially."

Also, although the couple is the dominant subsystem and is seen as "the nucleus of the new unit," there is a strong focus on children in imported families. The importance of the couple is emphasized not only for the sake of the adults, but also for the children. Saul, a remarried father of three, one from a previous marriage and two from the remarriage, and a stepfather of one girl, explains:

> The marital relationship is the cornerstone of the family. This relationship is of utmost importance not only for my wife and I, but also for all of our children. If things are good for the couple, there is a high probability that all the rest will be good. A good spousal relationship in the remarriage has positive implications for children . . . I am willing to do a lot of things for the children of my wife for her sake. I love her, therefore I am willing to do for her children.

Other imported families mention the effect of the spousal relationship on children: "When we are happy it's good for the children . . . good couple relationship in the remarriage is crucial for the well-being of the children."

Children of the wife in imported families are typically younger at the time of the remarriage than children in integrated families. Therefore they become "children of the family," and raising them becomes a significant task in the family's life. Consequently, couples in many imported families talk about their struggle to protect and foster the spousal relationship, as compared to couples in integrated families who often present the priority of their relationship as a fait accompli and who expect their often adolescent and young adult children to adjust to the new situation.

The Suntrock family describes a typical process in imported families:

> When we remarried we had one daughter from Elena's first marriage. When our son was born, he was a first to the husband and a second to the wife . . . so we were both first-time and experienced parents at the same time . . . when the second son was born three years later, it was clear that he is a third child for all of us.

## CASE ILLUSTRATION: THE DUNCAN FAMILY

Jeremy and Lois Duncan have been married for five years. She is a skinny, petite, and girlish woman who wears heavy makeup, and he is a macho type of muscular, athletic build. Jeremy comments early in the interview, "She likes us [men] stoutly built." They are raising together eight-year-old Ted, Lois' son from her previous marriage to Zachary. That marriage was shaky from its beginning. Zachary is described by Lois as infantile and irresponsible. He often made risky, miscalculated financial decisions that led to losses. He changed many jobs, often got fired or left after a short time, and was unemployed for long periods. Lois was the primary breadwinner. The marriage finally dissolved following three years of ups and downs when Ted was two years old. At that time, Zachary was found guilty of fraud and started serving a three-year sentence in a state jail. A couple of months later, Lois met Jeremy on a blind date arranged by mutual friends. Within a few weeks, she and Ted moved in with him and the couple decided to get married, which they did three months later. Zachary is living in another town with his current wife, Renne.

The couple has no children, and they rarely see Ted. The following genogram presents the Duncan family.

The Duncan Family: An Imported Stepfamily

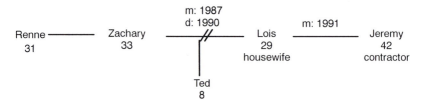

The family lives in a carefully tended two-bedroom apartment in a modern complex in a university town. Jeremy was the contractor of the complex and has lived in it since it was built.

Jeremy was never married before and relates to Ted as his own son: "Her child is now my child. He is our only son. I am an anxious father. I guess it is normal to be overprotective when you raise an only child." Ted sees his natural father frequently but there is no organized visitation schedule, as Zachary failed in the past to keep any agreed-upon plan. However, Zachary functions more like an uncle, while Jeremy carries all paternal responsibilities regarding Ted. Lois and Jeremy see themselves as equal partners in raising Ted. They attend together parent-teacher meetings and school events and share disciplining Ted. At the same time, Jeremy says, "I am more careful with him than I would have been with my natural child."

All family members, including Ted, use only the current last name everywhere, since "this is easier, makes things less complicated, and prevents unnecessary questions." The only exception is that Ted is registered in school by his natural father's last name, "because they would not allow us by law" to use another name. The child introduces himself by both last names and refers to Jeremy as his stepfather, calling him by his given name at home but "Daddy" in public.

The family tends to minimize the past in their current life: "The history has been erased. The only things that remained are Ted and the lesson learned." Ted, a highly intelligent eight-year-old, explains: "We are an instant family . . . Jeremy accepted a ready-made child and now he is my dad."

The marital relationship is presented as the center of this family: "First is our marriage." Jeremy indicates that part of the paternal roles he fulfills is for the sake of his relationship with Lois: "He is the child of my wife. I love her and want her to be happy; therefore I do things for Ted because he is her son."

> **Interviewer:** Please tell me about the relationships between the adults in your family.
> **Lois:** Just like in any other marriage. Mostly happy. Sometimes we argue but the frequency of arguments diminishes as we live together longer and learn each other's sensitivities.
> **Jeremy:** And this is directly reflected in the relationship with Ted. In the beginning, he had a hard time to accept me as his father and we had many power struggles. Gradually the good relationship between my wife and I radiated on the relationship with Ted . . . now we have fun together, he respects my demands and comments . . . we are like all fathers and sons.

Overtly, Jeremy is presented as the dominant figure, but at the same time he declares, "My wife always had a husband that was the sergeant major at home. I had no choice. I came into a pretailored role." The couple relationship is based on the model the wife "imported" from her previous marriage, and the same basic roles are preserved despite the changes in casting.

> **Interviewer:** How similar is life in your family now compared to life in the previous family?
> **Ted:** Now is fun and I can do many things that I could not do before.
> **Interviewer:** Such as . . .
> **Ted:** I don't know, I cannot think about anything. Something I could not do because I was little . . . maybe it is the same, I cannot remember.
> **Lois:** This is how I feel; it is as if this is my first marriage; I am the same, life is more stable financially, but many things are similar . . . I was always a pedant in matters of cleanliness and order. First I had to train Zachary; now I have to train

Jeremy. Ted is very much like me. Very particular about order in his things.

**Jeremy** [with a big smile]: You like to turn your husbands into being as obsessive as you are.

## SUMMARY

This chapter introduced imported stepfamilies. The most dominant characteristic of these families is that they seek to establish the current unit as a continuation of the previous family. Similar to invented families, imported families belittle the place of the pre-remarriage past in their current lives and emphasize their being not different from non-stepfamilies. Similar to integrated families, they have a marital focal sub-system, even though they underscore the importance of the couple for the sake of children as well as for the sake of the adults.

### A Comparative Analysis of Three Types of Stepfamilies

Table 7.1 and Figure 7.1 summarize the types of stepfamilies that were discussed in Part II of the book.

Table 7.1. Similarities and Differences Between Integrated, Invented, and Imported Stepfamilies

|  | Integrated stepfamilies | Invented stepfamilies | Imported stepfamilies |
|---|---|---|---|
| Past orientation | High | Low | Low |
| Acceptance/rejection of difference | Acceptance | Rejection | Rejection |
| Focal subsystem | Marital | Parental | Marital |
| Husband had children from previous marriage? | Yes | No | No |
| Number and age of wife's children from first marriage | 2+ adolescent | 1 young | 1 young/preadolescent |
| Children in remarriage? | No | Yes | No |
| Range of children's age | Large (between children of husband and wife) | Large (between children of first and second marriage) | Small |

FIGURE 7.1. A Comparison of Profiles of Stepfamilies

**Integrated Families**

| PO | A/C D | FSS | HC | WC | CN | RA |
|----|-------|-----|-----|-----|-----|-----|
| High* | Accept* | Marital* | Yes* | 1 | Yes | Large* |
| Low | Reject | Parental | No | 2+* | No* | Small |

**Invented Families**

| PO | A/C D | FSS | HC | WC | CN | RA |
|----|-------|-----|-----|-----|-----|-----|
| High | Accept | Marital | Yes | 1* | Yes* | Large* |
| Low* | Reject* | Parental* | No* | 2+ | No | Small |

**Imported Families**

| PO | A/C D | FSS | HC | WC | CN | RA |
|----|-------|-----|-----|-----|-----|-----|
| High | Accept | Marital* | Yes | 1* | Yes | Large |
| Low* | Reject* | Parental | No* | 2+ | No* | Small* |

| | |
|-----|-----|
| PO | Past Orientation |
| A/C D | Acceptance/Rejection of Difference |
| FSS | Focal Subsystem |
| HC | Does the husband have children from a previous marriage? |
| WC | Number of wife's children from previous marriage |
| CN | Does the stepfamily have mutual children in the remarriage? |
| RA | Range of differences between ages of children from all marriages |

# PART III:
# STEPFAMILIES AND CULTURE

When I started writing this book, my plan was to include a section on cultural aspects of stepfamilies and culture-sensitive practice. I did not consider developing special chapters about step-relationships in specific cultures. However, while writing this book, I became so involved with the topic that nobody around me could escape a discussion of stepfamilies. On one occasion I mentioned to my undergraduate students that I was working on the book and a young black woman suggested that I interview her since she is living in a stepfamily and would like to discuss the uniqueness of the experience of black stepfamilies. When I assigned a paper to graduate social work students that required them to interview a stepfamily and discuss systemic issues, one of them confronted me regarding the heterosexual-exclusive language that I used and suggested interviewing a gay stepfamily. At the same time, I was lucky to receive an institutional grant from my university to study immigrant stepfamilies. All these experiences were very exciting and before I realized, I was deeply involved in and fascinated by researching, interviewing, and counseling stepfamilies of different cultures and gaining a tremendous amount of knowledge from them. In the following three chapters, I share some of this knowledge.

Culture plays a central role in the lives of all families, and cultural factors play a major role in how families go through various life cycles (Carter and McGoldrick, 1990; McGoldrick, Giordano, and Pearce, 1996). Stepfamilies are no exception. Sociocultural context of the stepfamily affects how stepfamilies are perceived and how they perceive themselves. Western society is undergoing a gradual but consistent cultural change that makes stepfamilies more acceptable as an alternative family configuration. The status of stepfamilies in other cultures varies. However, cultural aspects of step-relationships have hardly been discussed or studied (Berger, 1997).

Integrated, invented, and imported stepfamilies exist in various cultures. However, each culture shapes its own unique version of these types. Thus, an integrated stepfamily from Hawaii is both similar to and different from an integrated stepfamily from New York City.

Different cultures also tend to favor specific types of stepfamilies more than others, and therefore, we will find diverse frequencies of these types in different cultures. For example, people who have been raised under the Soviet regime have a significant inclination toward developing the invented type of stepfamily. As discussed in Chapter 6, these families have a strong present orientation, deny being different from non-stepfamilies, and have a parental focal subsystem. This combination is compatible with the cultural heritage of families from the former Soviet Union. Having lived under oppressive conditions, they tend to repress experiences and feelings and adopt a present orientation. Adhering to the "party line" was a survival necessity and fostered denial of difference from others. Also, in the typical Soviet family, the parental subsystem is much stronger than the marital one (Mirsky and Prawer, 1992).

In studying stepfamilies within a cultural context, one has to explore the legitimacy and prevalence of stepfamilies in different cultures as well as intercultural, interracial, and interreligious remarriages. For example, what are unique issues of stepfamilies created by a remarriage with a black and a white spouse? Such a family may include white, black, and mulatto siblings. What is life like for stepfamilies with one Jewish and one Christian spouse? What happens with stepfamilies in Africa, Asia, the Moslem world, and so forth?

A full discussion of the diverse cultural perspectives of stepfamily life requires a book of its own and is beyond the scope of this book. However, the following chapters will allow the reader a glimpse at stepfamilies in three specific cultures: immigrant, black, and gay and lesbian.

# Chapter 8

# Immigrant Stepfamilies

Moving into a stepfamily has been compared to emigrating from one culture to another, causing culture shock with its associated stress (Burt and Burt, 1996; Visher and Visher, 1996). Immigration and remarriage are similar in that both are major transitions in the life cycle of a family that involve multiple losses and discrepancies between expectations and reality. Both follow a given developmental process and require flexibility in adjusting to a new situation and integration of two cultures within one unit. This chapter focuses on families that experience immigration and stepfamily life simultaneously.

## *THE EXPERIENCE OF MULTIPLE LOSSES*

Both stepfamily life and immigration involve multiple losses. The losses associated with stepfamilies have been discussed earlier in this book (Chapter 3). By emigrating from their country of origin to a new society, immigrants experience physical, social, cultural, and emotional losses.

Physically, they move from a familiar environment to an environment with unfamiliar weather and landscape and into a new house and neighborhood. Sights, smells, directions—everything is different, new, and confusing. As an example of what this involves let me share a personal experience. I immigrated to the United States from Israel, where I grew up and lived in Tel Aviv. Tel Aviv is a city that lies on the coast of the Mediterranean and the sea serves as a compass. To define directions, one refers to the sea in the west as a point of reference. When I first immigrated to New York and people gave me instructions to go north, east, and so forth, I could never understand how anyone knew where each direction was without the sea in the west.

Socially, immigrants lose significant relationships with relatives, neighbors, friends, and colleagues. Children lose classmates, familiar teachers, friends, and often grandparents, cousins, uncles, and aunts. Sometimes pets that have been with a family for years cannot come along and must be left behind. Immigration means to experience a shift from being "somebody," that is, a person with an identity, achievements, and recognition, to being "nobody." Often professional and educational accomplishments are not recognized. Drivers license, credit history, certifications, and credentials—all need to be reestablished and reconfirmed. It often means also stepping down professionally and suffering economically.

Culturally, moving from one environment to another involves learning a new language, norms, social cues, and belief system and learning to live according to a new calendar, to enjoy different cultural events, and laugh at different jokes (sense of humor is culture dependent). The following incident in a recent conference is not atypical. In one of the presentations, a room packed with family therapists roared with laughter in response to a remark made by the speaker. A colleague who sat next to me whispered, "Did you understand what he said?" I nodded and she said, realizing that I wore a speaker's tag, "I am sorry, obviously you understand; I see you are speaking."

I said "Thank you. I appreciate it. I did understand."

"But you did not laugh."

"I did not think it was funny."

Emotionally, all the aforementioned changes create a lot of stress and confusion and may cause depression, lack of self-confidence and despair. Immigration may also mean the loss of a dream because of discrepancies between preimmigration expectations and the reality of life in the new country.

## PHASES IN THE IMMIGRATION PROCESS

Drachman and Shen-Ryan (1991) identified three phases in immigration: (1) departure—decision to emigrate and preparations, including separation from people, places, and possessions, with the prospect, in some countries, of never seeing them again; (2) transit—the actual move from the country of origin to the new country, characterized by temporality and uncertainty ("living in suitcases") and sometimes long waits in a refugee camp or a detention center for bureaucratic procedures to be completed; and (3) resettlement—relocation and adjustment to the rules and norms of the new culture (Stewart, 1986).

In initial phases, the uncertainty of the situation and major decisions that need to be made produce intense tensions that create emotional conflicts and increase familial discord (Halberstadt, 1992). During the third phase, resettlement in the new country, the need to address basic needs of survival such as getting a job, finding a place to live, and learning elementary rules and norms often keeps people so busy that they do not have the emotional freedom to recognize their losses or to mourn them. Therefore, the issues at this point are mostly instrumental. Later on, internal tensions in the diverse subsystems (marital, parental) are exacerbated because the pace of acculturation to the new social-cultural environment is different for all family members.

Children move through the immigration cycle (Landau-Stanton, 1985) and the stepfamily cycle (Papernow, 1993) at a very different developmental pace and rhythm than adults. Impressionistic data suggest also that women adjust faster than men. Consequently, individuals may be at different places on both the continuum of immigration and of step-relationship at different times, thus further broadening intergenerational and intergender gaps.

The extent of immigration-related issues for each family depends on several factors: (1) the degree of difference between their original culture and the new culture; (2) the availability of friends and kinsmen who have lived longer in the new culture, who are more familiar with the language and norms of the absorbing country and can serve as mediators and interpreters; (3) the extent and nature of problems, which depends on the family's history of coping with stresses (Baptiste, 1993; Berger, 1997).

## *PATHS TO BECOMING AN IMMIGRANT STEPFAMILY*

All immigrant stepfamilies experience a different sequence of immigration and remarriage, but there are three basic paths to becoming an immigrant stepfamily.

### The Path of Divorce—Remarriage—Immigration

These families became stepfamilies before they immigrated to the new country. Both the dissolution of the first marriage and the creation of remarriage preceded immigration, and the relocation was done by the stepfamily as a whole. The phase of the step–life cycle in which immigration occurs is a crucial factor in determining the combined effects of the two processes. For families in initial phases of becoming a stepfamily, enduring the additional stress of immigration may be detrimental. At the same time, going together through a macrocrisis of immigration and struggling with its hardship may become a unifying and solidifying factor, as family members initially tend to cling to one another and become highly enmeshed (Baptiste, 1993).

### The Path of Divorce—Immigration—Remarriage

These are stepfamilies in which the divorced or widowed parent immigrated with their children and then remarried in the new country. When a noncustodial natural parent did not immigrate with the family, the pains caused by the original loss due to the divorce may be reactivated and intensified as children blame parents and parents feel guilty for the suffering they inflict on their children.

Two groups can be distinguished among these families: those in which the single parent remarries a compatriot and those that are culturally mixed. In the latter, additional tensions evolve that are related to the cultural differences between the cultures of origin of the spouses. However, if the stepparent comes from the absorbing culture, he/she may serve as a bridge to the new culture and help pave the way for an easier adjustment process.

### The Path of Immigration—Divorce—Remarriage

In these stepfamilies, the immigration preceded the end of the original marriage. In some of these families, immigration represented an effort to solve preexisting marital problems; other families functioned adequately prior to immigration but could not sustain and cope with immigration-related tensions so the marriage collapsed.

## COMBINED EFFECTS OF IMMIGRATION
## AND STEPFAMILY

When families are both step- and immigrant, issues due to immigration and those created in the stepfamily magnify each other and may create a pile up of stresses. A pile up of stresses is the concept that has been introduced by McCubbin and colleagues (1982) to describe accumulation of stresses with which families have to cope because of simultaneous multiple stressors. When several stressors occur at the same time and require the family to cope with all of them concurrently, stress accumulates and outpaces the family's ability to handle it adequately (Burr and Klein, 1994). This combination of conflicting coinciding demands on the immigrant stepfamilies often becomes overwhelming and leads to ambiguity of internal and external boundaries, lessening of parental authority, and changes in roles that cause frustration and a sense of losing mastery over one's life.

During immigration, the family culture may serve as a support, and in remarriage, the cultural context may do the same. However, when remarriage and immigration coincide, families lose the stability of their anchors and the stresses exacerbate each other.

For example, immigration is an additional link in the chain of losses that intensifies the already burdensome history of losses typical to all stepfamilies. As discussed previously, immigrants experience many losses, including an economic loss. Immigrants often are unemployed or have to accept jobs that are below their educational level. This is typical at least initially, but sometimes extends to months and even years. Several reasons contribute to this situation. First, credentials and certifications from their country of origin are often not recognized in the new country. They have to study for professional exams in a foreign language and achieve new professional certifications. In addition, there is sometimes an anti-immigrants social atmosphere that prevents immigrants from getting jobs commensurate with their professional education. The result is economic loss as well as loss of identity, self-worth, and self-confidence.

Remarriage also often involves intensified economic stress. Typically the new family cares for a large number of children, some who live in the family and some who visit. Expenses are higher while income is not. The child support that the wife should receive does not necessarily compare to the child support that the husband pays. This is especially true if the ex-wife of the husband did not remarry. In this situation the man may feel guilty that he is resettled while she is not and that he "left his children to raise other children." The ex-husband of the wife, on the other hand, develops an attitude of "now she has a new man . . . he raises my children so let him pay for them." This leads in many cases to lowering or stopping of payment of child support.

For immigrant stepfamilies, the two types of economic stress intensify each other. More noncustodial divorced fathers do not pay child support in immigrant stepfamilies than in their nonimmigrant counterparts (Berger, 1997). The law in most countries demands that divorced fathers pay child support. However, failure to comply with the divorce agreement is a common norm in many societies. In addition, when custodial mothers apply for immigration, they often are obliged to trade off the father's commitment to pay child support for his permission for the children to immigrate. Even if the natural father also immigrated to the United States, it is not always possible to enforce payment. Since many immigrants work off the books, there is no viable way to make them meet their financial obligations toward their children from a previous marriage. This puts additional economic burden on the already stressed stepfamily in which the children live.

In addition to multiple losses, immigrant stepfamilies struggle to develop a new sense of identity as a stepfamily and as residents of the new country. They also need to reconcile competing values of the culture of origin and the absorbing culture as well as competing norms from the previous marriages to shape a way to function in the new family and in the new culture.

How immigrant stepfamilies cope with the situation depends on their cultural background. A major factor in determining stepfamilies' coping is the range of difference between the culture of origin and the absorbing culture regarding stepfamilies as an alternative family configuration. This affects the degree of comfort the stepfamily experiences in the process of relocation and the degree of dissonance or consonance created by the similarity or difference between the cultures.

For example, a recent study compared American stepfamilies, Israeli stepfamilies, and Russian Jewish immigrant stepfamilies. In this study, none of the biological fathers in the immigrant families paid child support, compared to about a half of the Israeli and American families. Previous studies showed that the figures for American and Israeli fathers in this study are similar to what is typical about Western fathers: over half of them do not pay child support on a regular basis, but the rest do (Martin and Martin, 1992). In immigrant families, no biological father contributed to the expenses of raising his children either on a regular or irregular basis.

The absence of financial assistance from the biological father exacerbates the economic stress caused by immigration. Immigrants often have to settle for employment below their level of education and professional experience; the loss of child support further burdens the family financially.

The same study indicated also that although in all three cultures integrated, invented, and imported families were found, the breakdown into the three types was different. Among American and Israeli families, about 40 percent were integrated, over one-quarter were invented, and about one-third were imported. Among the Russian immigrants, the majority of the families were invented, some were imported, and only a few were integrated. Russian families tended to repress the past and focus on the present. Almost all children went by their stepfather's last name, and the focus was on re-inventing the family. These differences can be understood in light of cultural differences between the culture of origin of these families.

Israel is a Westernized and to a certain degree Americanized society that adopts American patterns and norms in various domains of life, such as the importance of self-actualization and of being in touch with feelings. Therefore, it is not surprising that patterns of stepfamilies are similar in these two cultures. The Soviet culture that dominated Russian life for seven decades represents the opposite pole. Living under the open eye of the KGB in a paternalistic and omnipotent regime that practiced cradle-to-grave control (Goldstein, 1984) taught people to deny the past and repress emotions as a survival skill. Divorce and remarriage were shameful (for example, in some towns the names of divorce applicants were routinely published in local newspapers), consequently causing people to hide them. They were expected to "follow the party line" rather than be noticed as different. This situation was even more extreme for Jews. In addition, the Russian family is characterized by a lot of attention focused on the child (Mirsky and Prawer, 1992). This background may explain the high frequency of invented stepfamilies among Russian immigrants. Since they come from a cultural background that minimizes the past, discourages individualistic differences, and underscores children, Russian Jewish immigrants tend to form invented stepfamilies that have a strong present orientation, deny differences from non-stepfamilies, and focus on children.

As this example illustrates, the culture of origin is a major aspect to consider in understanding stepfamilies. Some cultures accept remarriage and stepfamilies far more readily than others, and some do not accept them at all. Although in California stepfamilies are abundant—reflected in the caricature that shows one young boy saying to another, "Is X your Daddy today? He was my Daddy last summer"—in less liberal and more traditional countries such as Ireland and most of the Middle East, stepfamilies are looked upon less positively and are therefore less visible, since their members try to pass for non-stepfamilies.

Immigrant stepfamilies find themselves caught between two cultures that may have different views on stepfamilies. Consequently, they experience "a double immigration" and may need to cope with, in addition to the issues common to all immigrants, the changing position of stepfamilies in their culture of origin as opposed to the absorbing culture.

The effect that culture has on stepfamilies calls for culture-sensitive practice. It is of utmost importance to know how the culture of origin looks at and relates to divorce and remarriage in order to better understand and address issues of family members. Thus, for an immigrant from China to hide the fact that she grew up in a stepfamily may mean something totally different than for an American-born child. We cannot assume that knowing the facts about the family configuration means that we understand the experience of the family. It is important to learn from the family the significance of its situation in its specific culture and subculture to gain a better understanding of family members' experience and be better equipped to help them adjust.

The degree and extent to which the combination of immigration and stepfamily configuration affects family life varies between different family types. This in turn is affected and shaped by cultural norms about families in the specific culture from which each family emigrates.

## CASE ILLUSTRATION: THE KOVARSKY FAMILY

Marina and Alexander (Sasha) Kovarsky emigrated to the United States six months ago with Marina's parents, her son from a previous marriage, fifteen-year-old Igor, and Yelena, their four-and-a-half-year-old daughter. All six people are crowded in a one-bedroom apartment in Brighton Beach, a southwestern shorefront section of Brooklyn, which is nicknamed "Little Odessa" because it has been settled by thousands of refugees, most of them Jewish, from the former Soviet Union. The following genogram presents the family.

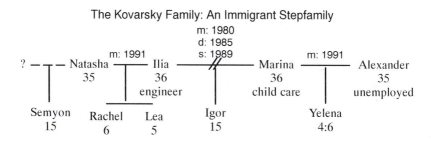

The Kovarsky Family: An Immigrant Stepfamily

Ilia and Marina, Igor's biological parents, lived in Moscow. They married when both of them were twenty, mostly because Marina became pregnant. The relationship was abusive from the start and they eventually divorced when Igor was five years old. However, they continued to live in the same apartment because of housing difficulties. Since both parents worked, Igor's maternal grandmother was the main parenting figure, a common practice in Soviet families.

When Igor was nine, his father moved in with another woman, Natasha, a single mother of Semyon, a boy the same age as Igor. They had together two daughters, married, and emigrated to the

United States, where Ilia secured a high-status engineering position and is financially very successful.

For five years, Igor had no contact with his biological father and his new family. Marina remarried to Alexander who had never been married before. Together they have Yelena. A year ago the family renewed the contact with Igor's biological father, who sponsored their immigration. Igor's stepfather has been unemployed for most of the last year, and Igor's mother works off the books in child care.

The family's focal subsystem is parental. Igor and Yelena are at the center of attention from both parents, and parenthood is perceived as the cornerstone of the family, as the following excerpt indicates:

> **Interviewer:** What, according to your experience, makes a good stepfamily?
>
> **Marina:** If you have a child you have to check what will be the relationship between your child and your husband. If they will be good it is a guarantee of success.
>
> **Alexander:** If the father does not think often about his stepson as a stepson, but as his own son. You have to consider all the children as your own and this will take care of all problems . . . for example, when we decided to marry we were very concerned how it will work with Igor. The future of the children was also a major consideration in our decision to emigrate.
>
> **Marina:** The children are to us very important. I would not have married my husband if I was not sure that he is going to be a good father for Igor and we would not have decided to emigrate if we were not sure that this is good for the future of the children.

The family tends to ignore any difference from non-stepfamilies and ignores the past to focus on the current family.

> **Alexander:** We never tell anybody that Igor was not born to me.
>
> **Igor:** Why? The family situation is nobody's business. This is the father who raises me and this is all that my friends need to know. They come here, they see a normal family: mother,

father, me and my sister, and this is all that matters. Not like the crazy American families: this family is without a father, the other one has two fathers . . .

**Alexander:** You see he is my son like Yelena is my daughter. What was—was. Now we are this family. This is better for everybody.

**Marina:** Nobody needs to know how our family developed. In Russia everybody minds their own business. It is better and safer this way. To be an unusual family or unusual anything was not good. Everybody does their own thing, so this family is our own thing.

The Kovarsky family is a typical example of a stepfamily that followed the path of divorce—remarriage—immigration. This path often means that one spouse, usually the father, not only moves to another house, another town, or another state, as in most stepfamilies, but also to another part of the world, leaving behind children who live with his ex-wife, whom he may not see again for many years or forever. This intensifies the sense of loss and puts additional burden on the new family, impeding the process of acculturation. The process is different for stepfamilies in which immigration preceded the remarriage because for them settling into a new family becomes part of the process of settling into the new culture, and these two processes reinforce each other. This is especially true when a remarriage to a veteran immigrant or a native of the absorbing culture occurs.

## *SUMMARY*

Immigrant stepfamilies experience simultaneously two major transitions: relocation and remarriage. Depending whether divorce and remarriage occurred prior, concurrent, or following immigration, diverse routes for becoming an immigrant stepfamily exist. The way in which an immigrant stepfamily copes with its unique situation depends on its culture of origin as well as on the type of stepfamily, according to the typology presented in Chapters 5 through 7 of this book. Among immigrant stepfamilies from traditional conservative cultural background, invented families tend to be overrepresented because their nature is compatible with major characteristics of these cultures. The relationship between culture and stepfamily life has not been explored. At the same time, the numbers of stepfamilies and of immigrant families are constantly growing. Consequently, intensive study of this area is of utmost importance.

# Chapter 9

# Black Stepfamilies

## *THE HISTORY OF BLACK STEPFAMILIES*

Black families come from various parts of the world and, therefore, have different cultures and histories. Despite differences within the black community, they share a distinct racial and ethnic experience that affects their unique strengths and issues (Boyd-Franklin, 1989). The history of slavery, segregation, and discrimination as well as African and West Indies legacies and cultural patterns have affected the nature and characteristics of black families (Logan, Freeman, and McRoy, 1990).

Stepfamilies are an integral part of the kinship patterns of black families. Slavery often caused the breakup of families when people were detached from spouses and children to be sold to different masters. Those who remained together developed substitute families. The black community adapted to the hardships imposed on families by the inhumane rules of the slave trade by expanding the definition of family to include nonblood-related family members and by developing a norm of residing in extended-family households. Many of the families that were created under these circumstances were stepfamilies.

The definition of family for African-American families refers to a network of kin that is wider than the nuclear unit (McGoldrick, Giordano, and Pearce, 1996). In the days of slavery, a tradition of "child keeping" developed wherein adult relatives took in children and cared for them. Later this tradition expanded to situations in which extended family members helped with medical, financial, and other types of circumstances. Parental divorce often led to such "informal adoptions." Because of these historical developments, multiparental families, the presence of nonnuclear adults within the household, reallocation of parental responsibilities, structural flexibility, and permeable boundaries are common to black families (Boyd-Franklin, 1989; Skolnick and Skolnick, 1992).

Manfra and Dykstra (1985) conducted a thorough survey and crossanalysis of documents of marriage termination and remarriages among blacks in the United States in the nineteenth century. They concluded that the period prior to the Civil War gave rise to alternative family compositions in addition to nuclear families, and one such common alternative is the stepfamily.

Many slave marriages were broken and followed by a second, third, or fourth marriage. By the end of the nineteenth century, about one-third of the black population lived in stepfamilies. Three-fifths of these families were stepfather families, about one-fifth were stepmother families, and the same percentage were complex stepfamilies into which both partners brought children from a previous marriage. The major reason for termination of marriages in the black population was forced separation through the selling of a spouse to another owner. Such separation preceded over one-third of the remarriages; about half of the stepfamilies followed the death of a spouse, and the rest resulted from mutual consent or desertion. Virtually all the people whose first marriages terminated were remarried irrespective of their ages and the reasons for the termination of their first marriage. Well over half of the remarriages included children from previous marriages, so that the remarriages created stepfamilies. This is not surprising given the lack of effective contraceptive devices and the normative patterns of reproduction at that time; voluntary childlessness was almost nonexistent.

Out of this history developed a tradition that accepts as valid a family configuration in which nonblood-related adults are an integral part of the household. They contribute to the family income and assume parental responsibilities. This tradition can serve as a very powerful model for modern black stepfamilies as well as offering helpful and empowering lessons to stepfamilies of other racial/ethnic background.

Modern black stepfamilies have been described as different from white stepfamilies in the way they are created. Black stepfamilies tend to include single mothers married to men who are not their child's father, and white stepfamilies tend to include divorced and subsequently remarried mothers. This difference is a result of two trends. First, blacks tend to divorce more than whites and to remarry less than whites. Second, the rate of single mothers is higher among blacks than among whites (Beer, 1992).

All the aforementioned factors in black history and demography caused black families to become a unique group with distinct characteristics. It is important to keep in mind that black stepfamilies share many of the characteristics and issues of nonblack stepfamilies. At the same time, black stepfamilies share with all black non-stepfamilies similar characteristics. These characteristics color the experience of black stepfamilies and make it both similar to and different from the experience of stepfamilies from other cultures.

Black stepfamilies bring with them a legacy of a communal-oriented philosophy, permeability of external boundaries, informal adoption, and role flexibility. In addition, they bring a history of experience with being different because of their color. This chapter will discuss those unique characteristics and underscore their relevance to stepfamily life. The discussion may appear tilted in the direction of focusing on uniqueness and neglecting commonalities. However, the reader should remember that together with their uniqueness, black stepfamilies share characteristics of all stepfamilies that have been discussed throughout this book; the current chapter focuses on highlighting what is unique to black stepfamilies in addition to what is typical to all stepfamilies across races and cultures.

## A BLACK COMMUNAL-ORIENTED PHILOSOPHY

Complex families, which include a complicated network of kin, not all of them blood-related, are common in the black community. Black heritage emphasizes and values family relations; therefore, kinship ties are central for black families and there is a strong relationship to the extended family group. Boyd-Franklin (1989) alludes to this in her book about black families: "Many black families function as extended families in which relatives with a variety of blood ties have been absorbed into a coherent network of mutual emotional and economic support" (p. 43). However, this sense of family is not limited to blood relationships and applies also to adults who are not blood-related: "Kinship network, not necessarily drawn along blood lines, remains a major mode for coping" (p. 8). It is not uncommon for black families to include relatives or people who are not blood-related but living with the family. Nieces, nephews, cousins, grandchildren, uncles, grandparents, and friends who reside in the same family are very common. Distinctive for black families is that individuals, couples with or without children, and even whole nuclear family units, which may or may not be related by blood ties, are involved in and function as part of the family.

The centrality of the extended family and the inclusion in the family of people who are not relatives by blood led black families to develop complex structures and intricate nets of relationships. While the typical model of white families is a clearly defined nuclear family, black inclusive families with more than two married adults and children who are related to each other in a variety of ways are common. The black community is receptive to such families and sees them as a legitimate family configuration. Blacks who live in nuclear families are also more familiar with the inclusive family type because they have seen such families in their environment, even if they did not grow up in one. This tradition has helped black families cope with diverse social and economic hardships throughout black history. It helps homeless families that share the homes of friends and relatives. It also helps stepfamilies, which share several characteristics of these families that are "put together."

As described in Chapter 3 of this book, complexity of structure and the need to develop within this complexity nets of relationships that transcend blood ties are typical in stepfamilies because of the diverse units and numerous relationships that are involved. Because of the commonness and legitimacy of inclusive family models in the black community, members of black stepfamilies most likely are familiar with raising nonblood-related children and sharing parental responsibilities with other adults within or outside of the family. Either they themselves experienced such an arrangement directly in their own family or they were exposed to such a model in their environment.

Coming from a culture that cultivates such complex cross–blood ties relationships, black stepfamilies' members bring with them familiarity and comfort with complex family models. This familiarity and comfort is relevant to their lives in the families that they create through remarriage. Furthermore, the black tradition of inclusive families provides black stepfamilies with role models and norms that are applicable to their situation.

The philosophy that emphasizes the group and mutual responsibility led to relatively high permeability of external boundaries within the immediate family unit and to the establishment of the practice of informal adoption. The next two sections of this chapter focus on these two characteristics and their relevance to stepfamily life.

## PERMEABILITY OF BOUNDARIES IN BLACK FAMILIES

As described earlier in this book, stepfamilies have unclear boundaries. Because of the existence of at least one parent who lives elsewhere and of children who travel between two households, external boundaries of stepfamilies are and should be more permeable than those of other types of families.

In a similar way, though for different reasons, black families traditionally also have permeable boundaries. Boyd-Franklin (1989) explains that the cultural norm for black families is to fall within what is defined as "enmeshed boundaries." When a family has enmeshed boundaries, it means that internal boundaries between subsystems and between individual family members as well as external boundaries between the nuclear family and its environment are relatively undifferentiated, permeable, and fluid.

As explained in the previous section, black families often include relatives and nonblood-related members who reside with the family. Three-generation families are very common in the black community. This is especially true regarding families that include single mothers, their own mothers, and their children. Consequently, maternal grandmothers serve as primary caretakers and important parental figures for many black children. Also, it is not uncommon among black families, both African American and Caribbean, to send their children to live for varying periods of time with their grandparents, uncles, or other relatives. This practice is not necessarily limited to times of crisis, but may occur on a regular basis. A three-year-old girl from New York may be sent for three months to live with her grandmother in Jamaica; a fourteen-year-old from New Jersey is sent to go to high school and to live with his paternal aunt in North Carolina, coming to visit during holidays, the summer vacation, and occasional weekends. Because of this tradition, children may belong to more than one household and call more than one place home. Adults regularly become active participants in parenting children who are not their own. This reality frequently makes both external and internal family boundaries more permeable.

This nature of family boundaries matches what is required by stepfamily configuration. Black stepfamilies bring with them a tradition of permeable boundaries concerning individuals, subsystems, and whole family units. This tradition is relevant to their reality because the situation of stepfamilies requires permeability of boundaries.

## INFORMAL ADOPTION AMONG BLACK FAMILIES

In the black tradition, when a child remained without parents because the parents had died or were sold into slavery without any consideration of family ties, it was common practice for informal adoption to take place. Children were often raised by adults who were neither their parents nor their legal guardians, and although these adults had no blood ties with the children, they still fulfilled parental roles. Later on, this tradition continued because formal adoption agencies did not cater to nonwhites. Black children whose parents could not raise them were left without an opportunity to be adopted (Hill, 1972). This required a different social solution; informal adoption offered such a solution. Although black children are currently being formally adopted across the United States, this tradition of informal adoption persists. Teen pregnancy and economic stress has led to the development of additional versions of informal adoption. Rather than assuming full parental obligations, nonparental adults assume parental roles for children who are not their natural or legally adopted children and for whom they have no formal obligation.

Informal adoptions occur not necessarily only in times of stress and crisis. As mentioned earlier, it is not unusual for children to live for extended periods with and be raised by their grandparents, uncles and aunts, cousins, and other relatives. This causes any number of adults to raise the same children "in installments."

Such informal adoption as well as a regular, noncontinuous parental role are very similar to parenting in stepfamilies. Members of black stepfamilies bring with them a cultural tradition that appreciates the practice of taking on parental responsibilities for children who are not their own and provides socially acceptable models for doing so. Black people who experienced or witnessed this practice enter the stepfamily life prepared to be involved in the roles of stepparent or stepchild.

## ROLE FLEXIBILITY OF BLACK FAMILIES

As indicated earlier in this book, stepfamilies include, on one hand, roles that do not exist in other families, such as stepparent, stepchild, step- and half-sibling, stepgrandparent, and so forth. On the other hand, traditional roles require changes and reshaping to adapt them to the realities of this type of family. For example, a father needs to learn how to father while living elsewhere; a mother needs to adapt her role to the fact that her children from a previous marriage may constantly leave and come back to the family for different lengths of time because they visit her ex-husband; a remarried couple needs to learn spousal roles that may include different degrees of presence of previous spouses. All this requires high role flexibility.

Role flexibility has been noted to be a typical characteristic of black families (Hill, 1972; Boyd-Franklin, 1989). Several historical and social facts contribute to black families' role flexibility. First, black families have lived under continuing stress for generations. This includes economic, social, and political stresses. Under stressful conditions, families have to develop changes in roles and rules to adapt to and cope with the stress (Burr and Klein, 1994). Family members are expected to take on commitments that other family members usually have. For example, when a mother becomes seriously ill, the father and probably older children may need to divide her roles among themselves to keep the family functioning. Because black families have historically experienced many stresses for long periods of time, they have developed considerable role flexibility.

A second cause for the development of role flexibility in black families has been economical necessity. Since black men have the highest rate of unemployment, many mothers and adolescents must work to support their families. Often parents have to work more than one job, put in long hours, and sometimes are required to work away from their family during the week and be available only on weekends (for example, in home care for the elderly, child care, and household management). To adapt to this reality, traditional role allocation had to be replaced by a more flexible one. Parents had to fulfill each other's roles and additional relatives, including aunts and uncles, grandparents, and cousins as well as other kin and nonkin adults, were needed to help so that families could survive severe economic hardships.

Finally, the communal-oriented philosophy and mutual responsibility that was discussed earlier in this chapter yielded families in which older siblings, grandparents, aunts, uncles, and cousins are often involved in raising black children in addition to or instead of the natural parents. Consequently, black people have learned to share and exchange roles. When they remarry and find themselves in a situation that requires such role flexibility, the model is not as unfamiliar to them as it may be to white people who grew up in intact nuclear families in which members were assigned distinct, exclusive, and well-defined roles.

## LIVING WITH THE EXPERIENCE
## OF BEING DIFFERENT

Families that include nonblood-related adults who parent other people's children and siblings who have different fathers are not uncommon and are acceptable in the black culture. Therefore, black stepfamilies share with black non-stepfamilies characteristics such as permeable boundaries, complex structure, flexible roles, many changes, multiple losses, and a complex history. Consequently, within their community, black stepfamilies feel comfortable. But in the white society around them, black stepfamilies experience discrimination.

As Boyd-Franklin (1989) points out, all black people live with a badge of difference because of their skin color. This discrimination is sometimes bold and clear and often it is more subtle, but it is almost always there.

As described in Chapter 4, all stepfamilies live with the experience of being different from the ideal type of family in Western culture. Since the world is slow to change, stepfamilies encounter discrimination in the different ways that have been discussed and illustrated throughout this book. This discrimination has legal, economic, social, and cultural components. It is sometimes more obvious and sometimes less clear, but all stepfamilies can report incidents in which they were made "to pay" for being a stepfamily.

Black stepfamilies live with a double badge of difference: that of their skin color and that of their family configuration. They are discriminated against for being black and for living in a stepfamily. Coming from a culture that fosters and appreciates those characteristics which promote their functioning as a stepfamily, black people bring with them considerable strengths as an aid to living in stepfamilies. However, in the wider society that is dominated by white values, they are often considered and treated as deviant.

## CASE ILLUSTRATION: THE WILSON FAMILY

Donnamae, thirty-eight, was remarried six years ago to Malcolm, thirty-five. Donnamae comes from a family of mixed background. Her maternal grandparents are Jamaican while her father's parents are from an African-American family in South Carolina. She had her first son Lorenzo when she was seventeen. She was never married to his father, who was a classmate of African-American origin. He later became a policeman and moved to another neighborhood, raised a family, and did not maintain any contacts with Donnamae or Lorenzo. After Lorenzo was born, Donnamae and Lorenzo lived with her parents, who helped her to raise him until she graduated nursing school and got a job in a hospital as a registered nurse. Lorenzo is now twenty-one and about to graduate college.

Malcolm is of African-American origin. He grew up in the deep South, where his family still lives. Malcolm's father was in two other relationships prior to marrying his mother and had a child in each of these relationships (Malcolm's half-brothers). One of Malcolm's half-brothers lived with Malcolm's parents for long periods of time during his adolescent years, while his own mother was hospitalized; she eventually died. Malcolm is the youngest of his parents' nine children. Malcolm is a physician and has been divorced for many years. His first marriage was short and childless. He and Donnamae met in the hospital where they both work. They have together two-year-old Sarah, and Donnamae was pregnant with their second child at the time of the interview. The following genogram presents the family.

The Wilson Family: A Black Stepfamily

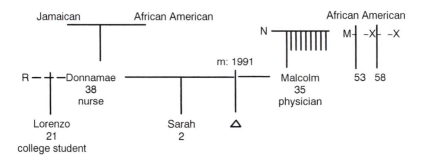

When Malcolm first dated and married Donnamae, Lorenzo was an adolescent and did not get along well with his stepfather. Having grown up without much contact with his biological father, he resisted Malcolm's effort to take charge and, after a few stormy months, moved to live with his maternal grandparents, who are warm and caring people in their late fifties. Later on, his relationships with Malcolm became more relaxed and he alternated between living with his mother's new family and his grandparents. Since the two families lived in the same neighborhood, this did not create a need to change schools or to be disconnected from friends.

Currently, Donnamae, Malcolm, and Sarah live in the hospital's houses for employees, and Lorenzo stays with them and with his grandparents when he comes home from college. The following excerpt from an interview with the remarriage couple illustrates some of the issues of black stepfamilies:

> **Interviewer:** Does living in a black stepfamily make your experience special in any way?
> **Donnamae:** It certainly does. Being black is difficult enough in this society. Being a stepfamily is not an easy experience either. Being both presents a serious challenge to your skills

of dealing with unpleasant reactions from teachers, physicians, and practically everybody else. It, excuse my cynical expression, may color one's life in black. Sometimes it takes a great deal of patience and humor to deal with all the ignorance and attitudes that you have to take.

**Malcolm:** Most of the occasions on which I feel the burden occur because of other people's reactions . . . mostly white people's reactions. Raising other people's kids is no big deal for me because this is not an unusual thing in my family. It is done all the time. When I was very young, my father was placed in Europe with the army and my mother joined him for a year, leaving me to live with my aunt and uncle. It was kind of fun growing up with all my cousins. Later on, when I was an adolescent, my older sister moved in with us because she got into some marital and psychological trouble, so in a way I helped raise my niece and nephews. Currently, all of them still live with my parents. So when Lorenzo came into my life it was not an unfamiliar experience . . . and it is pretty common in my community too.

**Donnamae:** This is certainly so on the overt level. We are used to it and there is no problem in raising other people's children, etc. . . . but deep down the story is more complicated . . . like there is this split . . . there are all those subtle ways in which the built-in split is expressed . . .

**Interviewer:** For example?

**Malcolm:** I do not feel this split . . . I really think that in black families raising children from all different relationships is pretty common and looked upon as normal.

**Donnamae:** This may be so as long as we are in the family. Once you are out there, it is a totally different story. In my job I see many people and I get all kinds of reactions from patients, from colleagues, from staff. . . . Sometimes I have a feeling that people who hear about me think, "You are black, you are a stepfamily . . . what else is wrong with you guys?" This is still very much a white-intact-nuclear-family society and people certainly let you know that you are way out of line being both black and remarried.

**Malcolm:** Whites react so much more than blacks. I think that for blacks this is more normal. We accept it. We are used to it. In black families there is always a gathering and food and a place for everybody.

**Donnamae:** But the cultural differences are not only between blacks and others. Even within our own family we have cultural differences that cause tension between us. In spite of being of mixed origin, I was educated mostly in the tradition of the Islands. This means that we had specific chores from a very early age; our parents had very high expectations of us; it was clear that certain things just had to be done and the whole atmosphere was strict and structured. In my husband's family the atmosphere is much more easygoing. Children are much less disciplined . . . this led to conflicts . . . he always teases me "you, the donkey riders . . ." referring to the agricultural and primitive nature of Jamaica.

## *SUMMARY*

The black community has a rich history of stepfamilies as well as additional family configurations that are compatible with stepfamily life. Slavery life caused the breaking up of families, and economic hardships required women to work long hours. Both those experiences necessitated recruitment of additional parental figures. In addition, the African-American and the Islands' traditions emphasize the importance of clan and extended family. These factors led the black community to be receptive of family configurations that have complex structures and include people of diverse kin relationships as well as nonblood-related members. The black community also has traditions of a communal-oriented philosophy, permeability of external boundaries, informal adoption, and role flexibility, as well as the experience of living with difference because of their color. This provides black stepfamilies with useful norms and models and with a cultural environment that accepts their configuration as legitimate. Concurrent with their uniqueness, black stepfamilies also share with all stepfamilies the characteristics, types, and issues that have been discussed throughout this book.

# Chapter 10

# Gay and Lesbian Stepfamilies

A growing number of gay and lesbian divorced parents are gaining custody of their children from previous marriages and are bringing them into their new family with a same-sex partner, thus creating a gay stepfamily, which is a unique subset of stepfamilies (Baptiste, 1987a, 1987b) that is often marginalized and neglected.

It is difficult to estimate the number of gay stepfamilies. Patterson (1992) indicated that no accurate answer is available regarding the number of children of gay and lesbian parents. Because of fear of discrimination, many gay parents conceal their lifestyles (Blumenfeld and Raymond, 1988). The estimation of gay stepfamilies is even more complicated because there are no data available for this information; therefore, we know very little about these families (Baptiste, 1987a, 1987b).

It is reasonable to assume that most gay men stepfamilies are noncustodial, while lesbian stepfamilies often have custody of children from previous marriages. Approximately 25 percent of gay men have previously been in heterosexual marriages, and some of them bring into their current relationships children from a previous marriage (Crosbie-Burnett and Helmbrecht, 1995). Most of these families are not stepfamilies in the legal sense because, in most cases, the gay couple cohabitates and is not formally married. Typically, they include a father who is living with his male spouse—the stepfather—and visiting children from a previous marriage who are in the custody of and live with their mother.

Gay women stepfamilies are often custodial, if the lesbian mother managed to overcome the prejudice-driven denial of custody because of the mother's homosexual lifestyle. Many lesbian stepfamilies include children of one or both partners, who became mothers within conventional marriages prior to their coming out to their families and social environment or even to themselves. They married and had children because that was "the right thing to do" or because they tried to fight their lesbian tendencies.

All gay stepfamilies struggle with issues of living in a stepfamily and with issues of being a gay parent concurrently.

## TRIPLE STIGMATIZATION OF GAY STEPFAMILIES

Given that they live within two minority groups, that of stepfamilies and that of gay people, members of gay stepfamilies experience social stigmatization of three types.

First, they are stigmatized for their homosexual lifestyle, which is perceived negatively and condemned; second, they are stigmatized for their family configuration because stepfamilies are negatively stereotyped; last, gay parenthood is often stigmatized by the nonparental homosexual community, especially by male homosexuals.

### The Stigma of Stepfamilies

As has been discussed earlier in this book, stepfamilies are still negatively viewed by many, as deficient by comparison to non-stepfamilies. Stepfamilies are treated, consciously or unconsciously, as a second-grade type of family. Therefore, invented and imported families hide from the world and try to pass for non-stepfamilies. Family members confide their family situation only to a number of close people whom they trust because they are afraid that the world will view them negatively (Martin and Martin, 1992).

### The Stigma of Gay Lifestyle

Gay people are stigmatized by the general heterosexual society for their lifestyle. Homosexuality is the subject of continuing and long-standing social hostility. Antihomosexual prejudice supports a picture of them as deviant, a threat to children, and agents of sexually transmitted diseases, especially AIDS (Strommen, 1989). Antigay prejudices are not limited to any specific educational, cultural, or social group. For example, gay people report prejudicial experiences with antigay physicians, lawyers, and employers in a wide variety of professions and occupations.

## The Stigma of Gay Parents

There is specific prejudice against gay parenthood both by the straight and the gay communities.

### Stigmatization of Gay Parents by Heterosexual Society

Social stereotypes and prejudices toward homosexuals create an image of homosexuality as incompatible with a family (Strommen, 1989). To many people, being gay and being a parent are contradictory. There is some recognition of the ability of gay people to parent, and there have been examples of openly gay people who were approved to become adoptive and foster parents. However, by the majority of the heterosexual community, gay families are not perceived as a legitimate family form. Gay people are perceived as unfit to be parents for fear that the children will imitate their lifestyle and that the children will be abused sexually and/or emotionally. These fears have not been supported by research.

Gottman Schwartz (1990) summarized empirical studies that examined the impact of being raised by a gay parent on children's gender identity, gender role, sexual orientation, and social adjustment. She also conducted her own research, which examined adult daughters of lesbian mothers, in order to identify long-term effects. She concludes that none of the studies confirm the prediction that living with a gay parent will harm a child's development. Patterson (1992) analyzed available information about children of gay/lesbian parents and concluded that, "There is no evidence to suggest that psychosocial development among children of gay men or lesbians is compromised in any respect relative to that among offspring of heterosexual parents . . . Not a single study has found children of gay or lesbian parents to be disadvantaged in any significant respect" (p. 1036).

Nevertheless, a parent's homosexual lifestyle is often enough to deny custody or visitation rights (McIntyre, 1994). In many cases, custody is awarded to the other parent or to a third party such as a relative or a foster parent because the parent who seeks custody is gay. It is automatically assumed that living in a gay family is detrimental to children. Those gay parents who do get custody of their children are in constant threat of losing it and therefore often try to conceal their lifestyle. Another reason to conceal this lifestyle is to protect children from embarrassment and confusion. Gay families are often afraid, undoubtedly justifiably, that the world will view them negatively. Furthermore, children of gay parents also go through the process of their parents' coming out, and in our antigay society, this is a painful process that exposes them to peer pressure. They are often affected by the stigmatization of their parents. Therefore, some gay parents tend to remain closeted, living in two worlds: the world of the gay community and the heterosexual world in which the children live. They hide from the world and try to pass for straight families. Others trust only a limited number of close friends with their family situation. Carina is a thirty-two-year-old graduate student. She has been living for the last four years with forty-six-year-old Stacy and Stacy's two adolescent daughters from a previous marriage. When the four attend a social or public event, Carina is introduced as the girls' aunt, Stacy's cousin, or a roommate, depending on the specific circumstances.

To protect secrecy, the family engages in a self-imposed isolation. The gay stepfamily prefers to limit its social contacts to conceal their family situation. Such secrecy and isolation adds to the already heavy burden on the family and may have devastating effects on family members. In one case, Baptiste (1995) reported that a nine-year-old daughter of a lesbian family developed elective mutism for fear of violating the parental injunction not to tell anyone about the parents' lifestyle. Not until the girl was released by the mothers from the imposed vow of secrecy did her mutism end. Gay parents often feel that they are untrue to themselves by maintaining this secrecy and that they indirectly confirm that being gay is negative and therefore needs to be hidden. On the other hand, when gay parents are open about their lifestyle, their children may be ridiculed and consequently experience isolation that is socially imposed rather than self-imposed.

Suspicion and prejudice lead heterosexual parents to fear that their children will be sexually abused or will witness inappropriate behaviors if in the company of members of gay families. Because they maintain the perception of AIDS as a "gay people sickness," these parents are scared that their children will be exposed to it via eating in gay people's houses or by having with them and their children any physical contact such as hugs, kisses, or the sharing of toys. Therefore, nongay parents often prevent their children from becoming friends and fostering close relationships with the children of gay parents. Gay parents who come out often experience guilt, as expressed by Julie, a lesbian mother of an adolescent girl: "We debate endlessly if we did right to come out . . . maybe we should have waited . . . maybe we did her an injustice."

## Stigmatization of Gay Parenthood by the Homosexual Community

Gay families often suffer stigmatization by the gay community because parenthood is often condemned by the nonparental homo-sexual community as much as homosexuality is rejected by the nongay parental community (Crosbie-Burnett and Helmbrecht, 1993). The gay culture tends to emphasize primacy of the couple relationship. This creates pressure to form a marital focal subsystem and "sharpens" loyalty issues. A nonparent gay often expects priority of the couple relationship, perceives a child as a potential threat to this priority, and is less receptive to the parent gay part-ner's commitment to children because the gay culture is still not geared toward gay parenting.

## The Combined Stigma of Gay Stepfamilies

Families who are both gay and step get "the worst of both worlds." Gay stepfamilies are not perceived as a legitimate family form and therefore they are even less culturally defined than the heterosexual stepfamily. Parental and marital issues typical to all stepfamilies are further complicated by the fact that both spouses are of the same sex.

Rosa is thirty-two. She is a social worker and she lives with thirty-three-year-old Inez. Both women are Puerto Rican. They share an apartment, have a domestic partnership registration, and raise fourteen-year-old Julian, Inez's son of a previous heterosexual relationship. Inez says, "Some people in our neighborhood would not speak to us and deliberately avoid any contact with us." One day, Julian, then nine, came home and told his mother that she is going to burn in hell. When asked to explain his statement, Julian reported that one of his friends is the son of a minister who gained custody of his son after his wife came out and divorced him to live with her same-sex partner. The child's father explained to his son that being lesbian is a terrible sin for which his mother will burn in hell. The child, with whom Julian openly shared his own family situation, told Julian that since Inez is also a lesbian she is probably doomed to the same destiny.

## TYPICAL ISSUES
## OF GAY AND LESBIAN STEPFAMILIES

Gay stepfamilies share with all other stepfamilies the same issues that have been discussed and illustrated throughout this book. However, being a gay stepfamily intensifies these issues. The issues of gay stepfamilies often vary by the gender of the same-sex partners and the children that they are raising.

### Issues of Legal Status

As explained previously, traditional remarriage creates a legal status between the adults but not between the stepparent and stepchild, unless adoption occurs (see Chapter 3). However, this situation is in the process of change. The constantly growing number of stepfamilies is forcing legislation to adjust to the new reality. Federal and state regulations are being changed to create routes and mechanisms for anchoring step-relationships in laws to regulate and institute them (Fine and Fine, 1992). Such changes are reviewed and discussed in Chapter 13.

Gay stepfamilies cannot legalize their status because marriage of gays and lesbian is not legal in most countries and states. Thus, their issues of legitimacy are more complicated, and the role of stepparent is even more vague than that of other types of stepfamilies.

In gay stepfamilies, the stepparent remains forever not included, since there are no blood ties and there are no venues for creating legal relationships.

### Lack of Reference Concepts

As described earlier in this book, all stepfamilies struggle with the absence of appropriate step-terms with which stepfamily members can refer to and introduce one another (see Chapters 2 and 4). In gay stepfamilies, the question of reference concepts is even more complicated than in other stepfamilies because the awkwardness in reference terms for gay families exacerbates the awkwardness of reference terms for stepfamilies. How does someone introduce his/her same-sex partner? Even though terms such as lover, significant other, and partner are being used, well-established concepts for roles in gay families have yet to be developed. The same shortage of concepts exists regarding relationships with children of the same-sex partner: "I am the child's second mother"; "I am the additional father"; or "I am the lover of the child's parent". Ten-year-old Alisa is living with her mother and stepmother on the East Coast. Her father is remarried and lives with his new wife and young sons from the second marriage on the West Coast. The two households have an amicable and cooperative relationship, and Alisa moves comfortably between the two families, albeit the geographical distance limits her visits to summer vacations and school breaks. When her mother, who teaches art in a private high school, was on an educational tour in Europe with her senior class students, Alisa became very ill. When her stepmother took her to the hospital, her efforts to explain openly who she was in relation to the child met with such difficulties that she ended up saying that she was the girl's aunt.

For children, the question is how to introduce the same-sex spouse of their parent. What do they say to their friends? Children and adolescents may feel very uncomfortable announcing their parents' lifestyle to their social environment by the way of introduction.

### Unbalanced Exposure to Sex Models

Children learn how to be a man or a woman by observing, imitating, and interacting with adults in their environment. Children in gay and lesbian stepfamilies experience unbalanced exposure to sex role models of masculinity and femininity. For these children, there are two sex role models for the same sex and limited or no sex role model for the other sex. A child who lives with a mother and stepfather has at least one consistent role model for each sex role plus an additional model of one sex role via the biological parent with whom the child does not reside. If that parent is also remarried, the child will be exposed to additional sex role models. In contrast, the child who resides with two same-sex adults experiences two same-sex adults. They may be similar, different, or even competitive and conflictual. At the same time, the exposure of the child to the other sex role model is much more limited and fragmented. Even if the child has regular contact with the noncustodial parent of the opposite sex, it does not balance the intensity of daily experience with the same-sex partners with whom the child lives.

### Lack of Acceptable Norms

As noted earlier in this book, there are no clear socially acceptable norms concerning roles and behaviors, nor are there rituals for occasions unique to stepfamilies. Although such norms are being developed, there is yet a long way to go. For gay stepfamilies, the situation is far worse than for the nongay stepfamilies. As these families are often socially invisible, there has been hardly any attempt to form a normative perspective for them. For example, how should same-sex spouses deal with behavioral expressions of affection? Is it OK for them to kiss and embrace in front of their children? Although it is clear that sexual expressions should be kept private in all families, step and non-step, gay and straight, the question of affection is much less clear regarding gay families.

It is generally acceptable for spouses to express tenderness openly. This sends a positive message about the loving atmosphere, educates children about the importance of expressing emotions, and models for them interpersonal relatedness. Norms regarding showing affection between spouses in stepfamilies are less clear. Children, especially as they approach adolescence, often feel uncomfortable watching their parents hug, kiss, and touch "a stranger." The question of such affectionate gestures between gay spouses is even more emotionally loaded and less obvious. Should a gay couple dance together at a family gathering? What is the place of a gay stepparent in ceremonies? Should a gay stepparent be an active part of the wedding ceremony of the child whom they have been parenting with their gay partner? These questions and many others lack any normative guidelines and cause confusion and uneasiness for members of gay stepfamilies.

### Imposed Losses

Although all stepfamilies are born of loss, experience multiple losses, and live with a "built-in" experience of loss, gay and lesbian stepfamilies are threatened by additional losses. Losing custody battles on the basis of the parent's sexual orientation is not uncommon. Both Nancy and Karen are fifty-year-old women of Anglo-Saxon origin. They have been living together for thirteen years and have a domestic partnership registration. Both women left heterosexual marriages following their coming out. Nancy was in a childless marriage and Karen was a stepmother of her ex-husband's four children from his first marriage. She also has a twenty-year-old daughter who lived with her father and his current wife until she entered adolescence and requested to come to live with Karen and Nancy. Karen's ex-husband gained custody of their then six-year-old daughter solely on the grounds of Karen's lesbianism. Even though she regained custody about seven years later, following a wearisome legal battle that she and Nancy carried out on the girl's request, these years were, for all three women, a tremendous loss of irreplaceable mutual experiences.

## CASE ILLUSTRATION:
## THE ROTH-JOHNSTON FAMILY

Evelyn, thirty-eight, and Jessica, twenty-eight, have been living together for six years. They share an apartment, bank accounts, and a car, and have a domestic partnership agreement. Jessica, a short, beautiful, dark-haired accountant, has been aware of her sexual orientation since her adolescent years. Her parents and two older brothers were very supportive and accepting when she came out to them. Jessica was always welcome to bring her same-sex friends to family gatherings. This attitude helped her in coming out to society. When she went to college, Jessica was active in the gay and lesbian caucus, and after graduation, she became openly involved in social and public activities in the gay community.

Evelyn, a tall, slim, and fair aerobic instructor was married for six years to Bob, a successful architect. During her thirties, she came out, and a short time after her divorce, she met Jessica and moved in with her. The couple purchased an apartment together in a progressive neighborhood in Brooklyn, New York.

Evelyn has one daughter, twelve-year-old Debra, who lived with her father, her stepmother, Gail, and her four-year-old half-sister, Cathy, by mutual agreement of Evelyn and her ex-husband. Two years ago, Evelyn's ex-husband and his new family moved to Europe for several years because of his job. Debra was reluctant to go and preferred to move in with her mother and her spouse. The following genogram presents the Roth-Johnston family.

The Roth-Johnston Family: A Gay Stepfamily

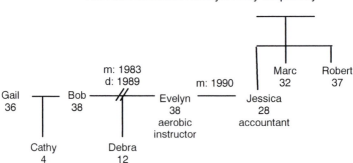

When Debra first entered fifth grade in her new school, she was received very warmly. Since she is a bright, friendly, and outgoing girl, a good student, and an excellent athlete, she soon became popular. About a month later, she told one girl in her class about her family situation. The word spread in school like wildfire and Debra started to experience social isolation. Girls who used to call her started to distance themselves, invitations for parties stopped coming, an invisible wall was built around her during breaks, and students refused to work on group projects with her. Debra told Evelyn and Jessica that when she passed groups of girls, they would start to whisper and point at her, and she often heard words such as dyke. Several parents anonymously complained to school authorities about her presence in class and expressed concern that she may have negative influence on their children. Jessica and Evelyn encouraged Debra to be honest about the family configuration, but not to "volunteer" information if she does not consider it necessary and does not feel comfortable.

> **Interviewer:** Can you tell me a little bit about how you present your family?
>
> **Jessica:** We need to be careful. It is better that people around you do not know about you. They start to think about you all kinds of nonsense . . . that you are not reliable, many do not want to work with you . . . some adopt that seemingly liberal attitude of "some of my best friends are gay."
>
> **Evelyn:** We need to be especially careful regarding Debra. Even though we do not make a top secret of our family, we try to play it down so Debra will not have a hard time. For example, Jessica would not come with me to parent-teacher meetings, to class parties, and so forth. I am not the only mother who shows up alone in these circumstances; this is acceptable, but I would have been the only mother to show up with her same-sex spouse.
>
> **Jessica:** We are out of the closet, yet we are to some degree in the closet . . . it is not that we choose to; circumstances make us behave so or else we will cause Debra tremendous difficulties.
>
> **Evelyn:** We do not hide information if asked directly but we often give vague answers that can be interpreted in either way . . . children are so cruel, and if they are not, their parents certainly are. We mostly do it to prevent Debra from feeling awkward and uncomfortable because people do not really accept gay families. We do not care what people say but we have a daughter to consider.
>
> **Jessica:** This is one thing about families like ours; every simple thing that you do naturally in other families without thinking twice, we have to think and rethink a million times . . . how

will this be seen? What will be the impact? We are constantly scrutinized. When we get ready to go to a parent-teacher meeting we need to think carefully what to wear . . . each step we take is looked at and judged. We have to remember on each step that it is not only us. We must take into consideration Debra's situation and how it affects her.

**Interviewer:** How do you see your situation compared to other families with children?

**Evelyn:** Even though we feel like usual parents the world would not let us feel this way. Our society is very much against gay families, let alone gay stepfamilies. For example, Jessica has much better health benefits than I. After a lot of effort we got me on her benefits. This involves unpleasant questioning every time I go to use it, but after a while you learn to live with it and when challenged you just stand there and say that you live in a domestic partnership. However, while all stepparents can have their dependent stepchild on their health plan, we had a very hard time to have Debra on Jessica's plan. When we tried to challenge it legally, it was even harder to find a lawyer who was willing to represent us, and this is only one example.

## *SUMMARY*

Gay and lesbian stepfamilies are a small group, neglected by the public and by professionals. They are stigmatized by the heterosexual community because of their homosexual lifestyle and their family configuration and by parts of the gay community because of their commitment to parenthood. A major dilemma that these families face is whether to come out or to keep their lifestyle secret. Both coming out and maintaining secrecy have social and emotional repercussions for the gay parent and stepparent and for the children. Gay stepfamilies share the problems of all other stepfamilies, but these problems are exacerbated by the parent and stepparent's sexual preference.

# PART IV:
# HELPING STEPFAMILIES
# OF DIVERSE TYPES—
# IMPLICATIONS FOR PRACTICE

Because of the growing number of stepfamilies, more and more professionals in the field of mental health are likely to meet them in their practices. Stepfamilies seek help for preventive purposes, for short-term consultations regarding step-related issues, or for help with more complex clinical problems.

Most of the professional literature about working with stepfamilies focuses on a developmental model and discusses clinical issues, strategies, and techniques that are suitable for each phase of the step–life cycle. Although this is a valuable and valid approach, a complementary way to address stepfamily issues is the differential approach. This approach assumes that there are different types of stepfamilies and looks at issues specifically in the context of each type. This is not to disregard the developmental stages of the stepfamily, but to expand the perspectives from which the family practitioner understands the stepfamily and addresses its issues.

The multiplicity and diversity of stepfamilies presents us with two challenges. One is the challenge of tailoring an intervention plan that will help the family to achieve a functional modus operandi and, at the same time, respect the basic pattern for which the family opted; either integrated, invented, or imported. The second challenge is that of promoting social changes to create a more stepfamily-friendly environment.

To meet these challenges, four aspects relating to stepfamilies need to be addressed. First, issues regarding differential assessment of stepfamilies require consideration; second, decisions about with whom to work on which issues need to be made; third, principles of direct practice with stepfamilies need be discussed; last, directions for working on behalf of stepfamilies in society at large have to be developed. The following chapters address these aspects of working with stepfamilies and on their behalf.

# Chapter 11

# Assessing Stepfamilies

To render stepfamilies services in the most effective way, a differential approach needs to be adopted and a type-specific practice developed for each group of stepfamilies. This requires assessing stepfamilies in order to understand their dynamics, issues, and mechanisms of coping with these issues and strengths.

In assessing families in general, a wide variety of conceptual frameworks is used. Models for assessing and diagnosing families have been discussed in detail (Hartman and Laird, 1983; Nichols and Schwartz, 1995; Kaslow, 1996) and are beyond the scope of this book. All these models for assessing families can be applied to assessing stepfamilies. However, in assessing a stepfamily, one needs to be aware of two kinds of differences. First, it is important to be aware of the differences between stepfamilies and non-stepfamilies. Human service providers need to educate themselves, their clients, social and educational institutions and professionals, and society at large regarding what is normative and what is pathological for stepfamilies. Given that stepfamilies are unlike first-time families, they need to be understood vis-à-vis other stepfamilies rather than vis-à-vis nuclear families.

Second, it is important to be aware of the differences among distinctive types of stepfamilies and the norms for each type of stepfamily. What works for imported families is different from what is right for invented families and so forth. Practitioners need to recognize and acknowledge type-specific dynamics and issues.

In light of these differences, three major questions need to be addressed in assessing stepfamilies:

1. What family patterns are remarriage specific as opposed to those that are pathological?
2. What patterns are specific to various types of stepfamilies?

3. What methods enable us to understand stepfamilies, identify their strengths, and comprehend their difficulties?

The following three sections of this chapter will deal with these questions.

## *DIFFERENTIAL EVALUATION*
## *OF NORMATIVE STEPFAMILY ISSUES*
## *VERSUS DYSFUNCTIONAL PATTERNS*

Since stepfamilies are different from intact nuclear families, they need to be assessed on their own terms and not by applying first-marriage families' criteria. "For these families the temptation to fall back on the traditional model is great and almost always self-defeating" (Morrison and Stollman, 1996, p. 169). Despite differences within stepfamilies, all of them share certain characteristics, dynamics, and issues. Generally, organizing all the relevant information and assessing stepfamilies is a challenging task because of the large number of family members and their relational complexities. This section of the chapter will focus on assessing stepfamilies vis-à-vis non-stepfamilies.

In assessing stepfamilies, several aspects require special attention. They are the permeability of external boundaries, parental effectiveness, family cohesion, flexibility and creativity, communication and decision making, and the phase in the step–life cycle.

### *Permeability of External Boundaries*

Permeability of the external boundaries of the family is a crucial dimension in stepfamily assessment because children often belong to two households, requiring adults to co-parent across the immediate family's boundaries. To allow children to move comfortably between the households of their custodial and noncustodial parents, stepfamilies need to allow more permeable boundaries than other families. External boundaries that would be considered functional for a non-stepfamily may prove to be too rigid for a stepfamily, while a level of strictness that would be considered rigid for a first-marriage family may be detrimental for a stepfamily. On the other hand, to establish and protect the new unit, clear boundaries are important. Balancing between these conflicting familial demands is a crucial task of stepfamilies, and it is important to assess how compatible the external boundaries are with everybody's needs and how they are maintained and adjusted according to changing needs in the developmental phases of family members. For example, how does a stepfamily allow more flexibility to enable adolescents to accommodate their visits with the noncustodial parent with their social activities and school demands? Such changes in visitation may impact on the schedule of the stepfamily in which that adolescent resides permanently.

### Parental Effectiveness

While in non-stepfamilies it is clear who the parental figures are and the "natural" authority of the parental figures is developed over the years, in stepfamilies this is less clear. In assessing stepfamilies, it is crucial to understand who is involved in the parental coalitions, how parental responsibilities are allocated, and how the two sets of parents complement, support, or sabotage each other.

Sometimes during the single-parent phase, an older child holds a parental role over younger siblings, and when the parent remarries, these responsibilities and power do not simply disappear. The older children are often reluctant to give up their parental roles. Their younger siblings may resist the reallocation of parental authority because accepting the stepparent as an authority may make them feel that they are betraying their noncustodial parent. Examining the complex nature of the stepparent-stepchild relationship, the mutual significance for each other and the different styles of parenting toward various children are important in understanding the dynamics and functioning of stepfamilies.

### Family Cohesion

Cohesion is another family aspect that needs to be assessed differentially in stepfamilies. Cohesion is a concept that has been developed by Olson and colleagues (1979) to reflect emotional bonding among family members. The level of cohesion changes during the family life cycle according to the changing tasks of the family and the needs of its members.

The normative level of cohesion is one of the family dimensions that is different for stepfamilies and non-stepfamilies. Typically, stepfamilies are less cohesive than non-stepfamilies. For example, Pill (1990) studied stepfamilies and found that they were less cohesive than nuclear families in similar stages of the life cycle. She also pointed out that stepfamilies that were moderately or modestly cohesive were more satisfied with their lives than other stepfamilies. In another study, Mathews (1989) compared stepfamilies' perception of their cohesion vis-à-vis nuclear families and found that stepfamilies considered themselves less cohesive than non-stepfamilies.

The importance of a more limited level of cohesion in stepfamilies is easily understood by their structure. Stepfamilies include two subsystems that represent a shared lifelong history between the children and the natural parent. Other subsystems of the remarried couple and stepparent-stepchildren have had a much shorter history, whereas in non-stepfamilies all subsystems are lifelong. Consequently, stepfamilies are less cohesive than other families, as has been shown empirically and clinically (Visher and Visher, 1996).

The lower level of cohesiveness is functional for stepfamilies because they need to maintain the balance between openness, to allow crossfamily access to the nonresidential parent, and closure, to achieve a sense of a cohesive stepfamily.

## *Flexibility and Creativity*

Achieving an adequate familial functional balance requires that stepfamilies have a high degree of flexibility and creativity. Because the situation that stepfamilies face and the dilemmas that they have to deal with are not only different than for non-stepfamilies but also are often different than those of other stepfamilies, they must sometimes develop unusual and original strategies. In assessing stepfamilies, it is of utmost importance to evaluate how open they are to exploring new ways that are different from what they knew in their families of origin and their previous family lives. How capable and willing are they to experiment with ways of doing things? How flexible or strict are they in changing rules and patterns? And, how willing are they to try unusual approaches that are nonconventional?

## Communication and Decision Making

The quality of communication and the nature of decision making are of utmost importance in stepfamilies. In the absence of clear established norms regarding roles, boundaries, and expectations, stepfamilies need to develop their own rules and norms. They need innovative solutions to everyday problems to maintain their functioning and well-being. This requires them to be involved in detailed negotiation, decision making, and problem solving in relation to issues that for non-stepfamilies are often guided by social norms. Therefore, it is not surprising that a study done by Mathews (1989) indicated that stepfamilies had clearer communication than non-stepfamilies. Since so much of their lives depends on having good communication, stepfamilies put a special emphasise on developing it.

Communication is difficult in all families because members may conceptualize, think, and express their thoughts and feelings in different ways. This may create ambiguity and mutual misunderstanding and misinterpretation of messages. In stepfamilies the issue of ambiguous communication may be even more complicated. Stepfamily members come from two separate first families with different styles of communication. Larry, a father of three remarried to Leha, a mother of two, explains the difference in communication style of stepfamily members:

> In my previous family expression of emotions was not acceptable. The motto was that everyone should be controlled and keep their feelings and thoughts to themselves. Sharing of emotions was totally inappropriate. My second wife had the opposite experience. It was OK for everybody to tell the others how they felt. What we dared to express in my previous family during a whole month, in Leha's first family they would say between the appetizer and the main dish at dinner.

The new unit needs to develop its own modus operandi. This is not an easy task because style of communication is a deeply rooted feature that takes years to develop and may take years to change.

The stepfamily may adopt the style that was typical of the previous family of one of the spouses. This often happens if members from that previous family heavily outnumber other members of the stepfamily. For example, Ruth and Martin raise Ruth's four daughters from a previous marriage while Martin's two sons live with their mother. Ruth and her daughters create such a powerful subsystem in the stepfamily that they set the tone of communication and decision making in the new unit.

Other stepfamilies choose to have a communication style that is deliberately different from their previous experiences. Harold and Marina, each a divorced parent of two, describe the following situation:

> We knew what happens when everyone swallows and swallows and never expresses their dissatisfaction regarding how things are going. Each of us decided that in our next relationship we are not going to allow the same thing to happen. We wanted to be able to be open, to get things out of our system and not "cook" with anger. The result is that in our family now it is OK for everybody to say anything. It is sometimes unpleasant but we prefer it to the alternative. We know the price of not being open.

Some families may try to merge cultural components from both previous families. Stephanie describes how this occurs in her current family:

> We create a blend of the way Peter [her husband] and his first wife used to communicate and the way I did with Marc [her previous husband]. Peter's family was "heavy" in decision making. Everything had to go through endless deliberations and careful discussions. Marc and I had a much more spontaneous style. We would say whatever was on our mind at the moment. Sometimes we would say things before they were on our mind without thinking . . . this caused us to say things that might have been better not said or said in a different way, at a different time. Peter and I live with a mix. Sometimes a lot of preaction discussion took place until somebody would say, "We had enough of the parliament; let's just do it." In the beginning it was very confusing for us and for the children.

Now we are used to this. I believe that we all feel more or less comfortable with it.

## Phase of the Step-Life Cycle

Building a stepfamily is a developmental process. In this process, families face different tasks and deal with different issues each step of the way, as was described earlier (see especially Chapter 2). Part of the assessment relates to the phase of the step–life cycle. This will give the practitioner a framework within which to judge whether the issues of the family are typical to stepfamilies in that phase or whether the family is "stuck" in dealing with issues that should have been resolved earlier.

For example, Mr. and Mrs. King married seven years ago. Mrs. King's youngest son from a previous marriage was six at the time. Mr. King and his stepson are still learning to ralate to each other. They are not yet comfortable with their mutual relationship, they do not know how to refer to each other on various occasions, and the whole situation still makes everybody feel that they are "walking on eggshells," according to Mrs. King. This kind of situation is typical of a much earlier phase of the step–life cycle. It seems that the King family did not move along the normative step–life cycle and is struggling with issues that in most stepfamilies are resolved in an earlier phase. Chronologically, this family should have been in the life cycle phase characterized by a developed stepparent-stepchild relationship and some degree of family stability. However, developmentally, this family experiences issues typical to much earlier phases such as the phase of awareness, when splits along biological lines and related difficulties are recognized and acknowledged, or the phase of mobilization, which is characterized by clashes between the diverse needs of individuals and subsystems.

In contrast, the Jurano family has been together for four years. Each partner brought to the stepfamily one daughter from a previous marriage. Both girls are currently in their early adolescence. While in the beginning each of the spouses was very busy parenting his/her own daughter, currently they work more as a couple and support each other in parenting and disciplining both girls. The girls often create a coalition to question their parents' demands and challenge boundaries such as curfew time and limitations on social activity. This family is in the action phase, which is characterized by the solidifying of the couple in responding to the needs of the children. Their issues are similar to those experienced by many stepfamilies in this phase and therefore should be assessed as normative phase-related issues.

The next section deals with differential assessment of various types within stepfamilies.

## DIFFERENTIAL ASSESSMENT
## OF DIVERSE TYPES OF STEPFAMILIES

As discussed in the previous section of this chapter, all stepfamilies need to be assessed according to their unique norms and not by norms of nuclear families. In addition, each type of stepfamily needs to be assessed by type-specific norms. That is, integrated stepfamilies should be evaluated by norms of integrated families and invented families need to be assessed in view of what is typical to invented stepfamilies in general and so forth.

Three components determine the stepfamily type: past orientation, acceptance/rejection of difference from non-stepfamilies, and focal subsystem. Different combinations of these components produce diverse family types. Families with high past orientation, a high level of acceptance of difference, and predominance of a marital subsystem are classified as integrated; families with low past orientation, low acceptance of difference, and a dominant parental subsystem, as invented; and families with low past orientation, low acceptance of difference, and a dominant marital subsystem, as imported.

The three components that define the type of stepfamily require careful in-depth evaluation in the assessment process. To assess the type of a stepfamily we need to know: (1) the level of orientation toward the past, (2) the degree of self-perception vis-à-vis non-stepfamilies, and (3) the dominant focal subsystem. On the basis of this information, we can define the type of the stepfamily and assess how it compares to other families of the same type. This section discusses assessment of the three components that determine each of the stepfamily types.

## Past Orientation

Integrated stepfamilies are characterized by high past orientation while invented stepfamilies and imported stepfamilies have a low past orientation. To determine stepfamily type, it is important to assess the time orientation of the family and evaluate whether patterns of behavior and interaction represent efforts to resolve unfinished business from the past or are relevant to the present. In the assessment of the past orientation of the family, several aspects need to be taken into consideration. First, the amount of space that the past is given in the current life of the family must be estimated. Is reference to events that happened in the previous family permitted? Are they encouraged? Are they prohibited? For example, does a stepparent ask a child, "How do you think that your father would like this?" Does a mother say to a child, "When I was married to Dad . . . "? Do spouses feel free to relate to their ex-spouses? Is there an uncomfortable silence in the room when someone mentions an event that happened in a previous family or involves past spouses?

Second, the way in which family members refer to the past is indicative of the past orientation of the family. Is it always with negative connotation? Is it OK for a child to tell something nice he/she recalls from the previous family? When a child refers to life in the previous family constellation does an adult immediately change the topic, not react, or respond with disapproval, such as "This happened a long time ago," "This is not important anymore," "I really wish you would not talk about it," etc.

Third, it is important to assess who monitors references to the past and how they do it. Are only adults allowed to speak about the past? Do children initiate the conversation?

Fourth, the purposes for which the past is used is worth exploring. Does a child constantly refer to the past to preserve the place of a noncustodial parent within the family? Do stepparents refer to the past to maintain distance from stepchildren? Does the couple talk negatively about the past as a means to cement their marital bond? Are ex-spouses used as a target for displacing anger and dissatisfaction with the current relationship? Is the past used as a criterion to measure the present?

Finally, it is important to assess the impact of the past orientation on the family. What effects does referring to the past have on the current life? How does it affect individuals, the couple, parental relationships, and siblings, stepsiblings, and half-siblings?

Knowledge about the time orientation of the family guides the development of strategies for intervention. For example, in integrated families, which have a high past orientation, it is reasonable to develop strategies to draw from past experience in handling problematic situations in the present, whereas working with imported and invented stepfamilies requires developing strategies that focus more on the "here and now" to resolve their issues because they are present oriented.

### Acceptance/Rejection of Difference

In the assessment of diverse types of stepfamilies, the degree to which the stepfamily perceives itself as similar or different from non-stepfamilies must be determined. Integrated stepfamilies are characterized by a high level of acceptance of difference, and invented and imported stepfamilies, by a low level of acceptance of difference.

To assess family self-perception, it is important to know if family members think that there are differences in daily life between step- and non-stepfamilies? Who thinks so? What are the differences? Do they see such differences, if they exist, as limited to certain domains of family life? Do these differences color the whole life of the family? Are they specific to certain occasions? Are they inclusive? What is their significance? Do family members see stepfamilies as better than nuclear families, inherently inferior to non-stepfamilies, or do they acknowledge differences without making value judgments on the differences?

The degree to which a family sees stepfamilies as different from non-stepfamilies can be assessed by exploring the belief system of family members and their expectations regarding social attitudes toward them. To what degree is living in a stepfamily perceived by its members as significant in shaping their lives? Is it common in the family to relate patterns of behavior and problems of members to the family configuration? Do family members think that stepfamilies should have special privileges, be recognized as special, or have special services? Does the family reject any "special atti-tude"?

Shawn, the intelligent thirteen-year-old son of Maira and stepson of Reuben, recently started to act out at home, his grades have deteriorated, and he talks back, is angry, and behaves disrespectful-ly most of the time. His mother and stepfather see their living in a stepfamily as a major source of his behavior. This family sees stepfamilies as greatly different from nuclear families and relates typical adolescent behavior to their being a stepfamily. A family who rejects the difference of stepfamilies would take the opposite position: Shawn's behavior would be perceived as having little or nothing to do with the family configuration, and problems would be explained primarily by non-stepfamily-specific circumstances.

### Focal Subsystem

One way of assessing the dominant focal subsystem is through direct exploration with the family regarding the relationship that has priority in the family.

Some families do not know or choose not to identify openly the focal subsystem, or they do not define themselves in terms of a focal subsystem because their focus on the marital and parental subsystems is balanced. When families do not identify their focal subsystem in response to a direct question, a less direct approach may be helpful. One such approach may be introducing situations that have to do with conflict between parental and marital loyalty and asking the family to comment on them. For example, ask family members how they would advise a friend who has to decide be-tween attending a child's school event or a spouse's important busi-ness conference.

Another line of exploration that may be fruitful in judging the focal subsystem is asking general questions regarding life in the family and identifying the position from which responses are given. For example, the question "Which criteria would you suggest to use in order to judge the degree of success of a given stepfamily?" offers insight into the focal subsystem. Families with a marital focus tend to use mostly, or exclusively, criteria that pertain to the marriage, such as the degree of understanding between the spouses, the frequency and intensity of conflicts between husband and wife and how they end conflicts, the range and amount of time the couple spends together, the level of complementarity, and the emotional tone of the marriage. Families with parental focal subsystems focus on aspects that concern parent-child relationships. For instance, such families judge success of stepfamilies by the level of intimacy between stepparent and stepchild, how stepsiblings get along, how comfortable children from previous marriages feel in the remarriage family, and how much space and freedom of expression children are allowed to enable them to live in peace with the family in which they reside permanently as well as the family they visit.

Several additional questions yield useful information regarding the focal subsystem. To the question "Based on your experience, what would you advise people who consider remarriage and have children from a previous marriage?", families with a marital focal subsystem refer to aspects of the remarriage. For example, "We would advise people about to be remarried that in times of tension in the remarriage they should remind themselves about the first marriage." Families with a parental focal subsystem answer the same question with an emphasis on children. For instance, "We would advise people who consider remarriage to think how they are going to handle being torn between loyalty to their spouse and their children."

To the question "If you had to start all over again, what would you do the same? What would you do different?", families with a marital focal subsystem address spousal aspects such as "If we started all over we would have lived together a little longer before getting married," while families with a parental focal subsystem address parental issues such as "If we were to start all over again we would have made clear much earlier our responsibilities regarding each other's children."

### METHODS OF ASSESSING STEPFAMILIES: INTERVIEWS, GENOGRAMS, AND STANDARDIZED INSTRUMENTS

Professionals use a variety of approaches and techniques for assessing families. The most common methods are interviews, genograms, and standardized instruments.

## Assessing Stepfamilies by Means of Interviews

The most common way for assessing stepfamilies, as with all other types of families, is via interviews with family members. Interviews can be conducted with individuals, dyads, triads, larger subsystems, and the whole family. Individual family members can be interviewed to discuss their unique perspectives in a confidential way that allows them to openly express opinions and concerns that they may not feel comfortable sharing with the rest of the family. For example, a stepmother interviewed without her husband present may express anger that her husband is not as warm to her children as she would have expected or that her husband showers his children with presents and attention when they visit while being demanding of her child.

Family members can also be interviewed in dyads such as the remarried couple, natural parent with his/her natural child, a stepparent with his/her stepchild, or a natural and stepsibling. Other units of interview are triads such as the divorced natural parents and the stepparent. In addition, large family units can be seen. For example, the remarriage couple with their residing and visiting children, the natural parent, stepparent, and the children who live with them, all the adults who parent the children full-time or part-time with the children, and so forth.

In these interviews, the professional collects from the interviewees information to understand the dynamics of the remarriage couple, such as what brought and holds them together, and what are the overt and the unspoken marital contracts, and what were the mutual expectations prior to the remarriage and how well they are met in the marriage. Another venue in these interviews is seeking to understand the stepparent-stepchild relationship. The professional evaluates the nature of these relationships, the role that the stepparent fulfills in the life of the stepchild, and vice versa. For example, does the stepparent see the stepchildren as "a second chance" and expect them to make up for expectations not met by natural children? Does the stepparent see the stepchild as an opportunity to be "a model parent?" Does the stepparent see the stepchild as an unavoidable cost of the marriage? Assessing stepsiblings' relationships is also important.

### Assessing Stepfamilies by Means of Genogram

Another way to assess stepfamilies is by genograms. The genogram is an intergenerational map that the professional and the family put together. It presents a picture of who is in the family and what the family looks like in terms of gender distribution, ages, professions, crises, disease, geographical location, cultural-ethnic background, and interpersonal relationships. It enables visualization of the family system (Visher and Visher, 1996) and identification of patterns that are transferred within the family from generation to generation and of issues related to family structure and strengths.

Family genograms are often difficult to draw. With stepfamilies, genograms quickly become even more complicated because of the large number of individuals involved, the multiple marriages, and the cross-family parental relationships. At the same time, a genogram is especially helpful with stepfamilies because it helps organize their very complex matrix. It can serve as an eye-opener both for family members and professionals. It serves to locate where potential "hot spots" exist (Burt and Burt, 1996), "who is with whom and who is against whom," how the experience of diverse subsystems compares, and what are dominant issues. For example, not until the genogram was developed did the Merton family realize the enormous number of parental figures that exist in the family regarding the different children and the conflicting demands that these diverse "parenting partners" created in the new unit.

Genograms are useful in helping stepfamilies that adopted a low past orientation because they enable family members to examine and discuss aspects of the past and relate to them in a safe setting (Kaslow, 1993). In working with integrated and invented families' genograms, I realized that gathering and organizing past-related information via a diagram helped them to deal with the information in an effective way; the genogram served as a mediator and enabled them to relate to issues that they were otherwise reluctant to deal with, since "We put it behind our back and see it as irrelevant to who we are today." Working on a genogram often enables family members to tell one another about people whom they have never mentioned. The presence of the worker ensures a protective environment that helps neutralize deep-seated emotions, helping family members overcome the hesitance and difficulties associated with discussing certain events, issues, and people.

## Assessing Stepfamilies by Means of Standardized Instruments

Standardized instruments, specifically self-report questionnaires, offer us an additional means of understanding the dynamics and issues of stepfamilies.

Self-report questionnaires are valuable tools for understanding the stepfamily from the "insider's" perspective of people who experience the situation, as opposed to the "outsider's" perspective of an observer (Gurman and Kniskern, 1981; Touliatos, Perlmutter, and Strous, 1990). One criticism about such a perspective is that it presents "distorted," subjective information rather than an objective picture. Yet, the way that people perceive their lives, rather than an objective external view, is what predominantly guides their behavior. Therefore, getting a picture of how people view their "family reality" is important.

In working with stepfamilies, two types of instruments can be used. First, instruments used to assess aspects that exist in all families are of special significance when used in stepfamilies. For example, there are excellent norm-tested instruments that measure the level of emotional bonding among family members (family cohesion). Such instruments are used to evaluate the level of cohesion in different types of families and can be successfully applied to stepfamilies. The norms for cohesion in stepfamilies are usually lower than those for non-stepfamilies, but the instruments used to measure the cohesion can be the same.

Second, there is a need for instruments that are specific to stepfamilies. There are dimensions that exist either in stepfamilies and do not exist in other families or exist in stepfamilies in a way that is unique to them. For example, issues of orientation to the past exist in all families. However, these issues assume a special significance in stepfamilies because their members have to relate to three separate pasts: the past of their family of origin, the past of a previous family, and the past of the time between families.

Unfortunately, not many instruments to assess stepfamilies exist to date. One recently developed tool is the Stepfamily Time Orientation Scale (STOS) (Berger, 1993). This instrument measures how stepfamily members perceive the way that their family relates to the past, specifically to previous marriages. It includes fourteen statements. Each statement describes how a stepfamily deals with people, memories, and issues that have to do with the pre-remarriage past, such as how family members react when they look at photo albums from a previous marriage, the nature of relationships with relatives from the previous marriage, and so forth. The person who fills out the questionnaire indicates to what degree the situation that is presented in the statement describes the reality in his/her own family. The way in which different family members perceive the family's way of handling past-related issues reveals how the family functions, which family members agree and differ in their picture of the family, and the place of the past in the family. Understanding these family aspects can help design an appropriate strategy for helping a family. For example, as invented families appear to function better with a low past orientation, the challenge is to help them make enough room for the past while maintaining their basic preference.

### Assessing Stepfamilies via a Combination of Methods

In assessing a stepfamily, one may choose to combine a variety of methods. Such a combination can yield a rich and comprehensive picture of family dynamics and how families cope with typical issues. Information achieved via one measure can shed light on aspects that remained unclear when assessed through another means and fill in gaps and complement aspects that were not fully assessed. At the same time, differences in information secured through different methods can raise questions and bring to attention inconsistencies, disagreements, and discrepancies. Evaluating such disparities and understanding their significance and sources contributes to a clearer picture of the family and hence to developing more effective ways to help stepfamilies create desirable changes.

### SUMMARY

This chapter addressed issues of assessing stepfamilies. The process of assessment involves awareness of the differences between stepfamilies and non-stepfamilies and recognition of the differences among various types of stepfamilies. To assess stepfamilies vis-à-vis non-stepfamilies it is important to examine the permeability of external boundaries, parental effectiveness, family cohesion, flexibility and creativity, communication and decision making, and the phase in the step–life cycle. To assess stepfamilies by type, their past orientation, acceptance/rejection of difference, and focal subsystem need to be explored. These assessments can be done by means of interviews, genograms, or standardized instruments, or a combination of these methods. The assessment of a given stepfamily enables the human service provider to develop a plan for helping the family. Chapter 13 deals with direct practice with stepfamilies of various types and Chapter 14, with issues of working on behalf of stepfamilies.

Chapter 12

# Partners and Focus: Choosing with Whom to Work on Which Issues

Recently, stepfamilies have become of increased interest to mental health professionals because we meet them more and more among our clients. Although it is true that there are no "quick fixes," many stepfamilies can and do find ways of succeeding without therapy, while others can use a brief solution-focused counseling process to negotiate resolutions appropriate for their situations and then go on with their lives. Conveying that living in a stepfamily by definition requires therapy may be pathologizing and professionals need to take special caution to avoid such a message. Sometimes it is useful to encourage a stepfamily to work on the issues on its own and thus empower the family with the ability to deal with its own issues.

However, sometimes stepfamilies need help in dealing with their unique issues. In working with stepfamilies, the various models used for working with families in general can be applied. These models include structural, contextual, Bowenian, psychoanalytic, experiential, behavioral, strategic, Milan, and other models of family therapy. These models have been described and discussed extensively in family therapy literature (Nichols and Schwartz, 1995; Goldenberg and Goldenberg, 1996).

In working with stepfamilies, the professional needs to decide with *whom* to work, on *which* issues to work, and *how* to work at each phase of the step–life cycle. The answers to these questions differ by the stepfamily type. Irrespective of the type of family that a remarriage couple decides to establish, the process of negotiating the marital and parental contract according to their belief system requires space, privacy, and time. Clinicians need to help remarriage couples in the beginning phases create the necessary conditions for struggling with the kind of stepfamily they want to be, evaluate the pros and cons of their choice, discuss compromises, and develop a strategy to promote their agenda.

Although considerations for identifying which family members to involve in therapy, prioritizing topics to address, and choosing strategies for interventions have been discussed in the literature (see Sager et al., 1983; Visher and Visher, 1988, 1990, 1996), tailoring treatment plans for diverse types of stepfamilies has not. In Chapters 5, 6, and 7, readers were introduced to three types of stepfamilies: integrated, invented and imported. These diverse types of stepfamilies call for different treatment plans. For example, the need to normalize stepfamilies' experiences that are different from non-stepfamilies has been emphasized recently by researchers and clinicians (Papernow, 1993; Burt and Burt, 1996; Visher and Visher, 1996). However, what needs to be normalized is different for all types of stepfamilies. The experience of integrated stepfamilies, for example, includes mostly a built-in sense of a constant process of merging, while the experience of invented families is that of a new unit. Chapter 12 discusses the questions with whom and on what to work in servicing stepfamilies, and Chapter 13 focuses on how to work with them.

## *DECIDING WITH WHOM TO WORK*

The human service professional has to make a decision about whom to see at each phase of the intervention. The complexity of stepfamilies offers a variety of possibilities. Possible options include: (1) the remarriage couple; (2) the parent-child sub-systems, including the custodial and noncustodial natural parents, the stepparents, and children of the couple from the current and previous marriages; (3) the natural, half-, and stepsiblings subsystems; and (4) the metafamily, which includes members of the extended families of current and previous marriages such as stepgrandparents, previous spouses and their new families, and so forth.

Several experts in the field advocate, when possible, for working with the whole stepfamily as a unit and including all the relevant suprafamily members—biological parents, stepparents, siblings, half-

and stepsiblings, and all types of grandparents—in the treatment as soon as possible (see Sager et al., 1983; Martin and Martin, 1992).

However, certain reservations apply to this recommendation. In integrated families, engaging as many members as soon as possible is often appropriate and effective because these families are amenable to working with a variety of combinations within the suprafamily. In invented and imported stepfamilies, it may prove less than optimal to work with many members, at least in the initial phases. In some invented and imported families, it may be difficult or not feasible to work with members who do not live within the stepfamily. These families allow their past a limited space in their current lives and tend to exclude past-related people and relationships from their definition of who belongs to the family. They may interpret the preference of the service provider to work with the whole family unit as an expression of disapproval of their self-definition and refrain from cooperation in defense of their self-perception. Most invented and imported families cooperate better when the professional respects the self-definition of the family and works with the remarriage family as the primary unit.

In most cases, the self-definition of a family as invented is chosen by the remarried couple rather than by the children. Insisting on a wider definition of the family—for example, to include the non-custodial natural parent—may create or intensify resistance to the point that the adults will force the family to drop out of treatment. Therefore, introducing ideas regarding unique aspects related to the family configuration needs to be done cautiously and in a very sensitive way. This is not to say that issues that have to do with the remarriage in invented families or issues that pertain to parenthood in imported families should not be addressed. Neither does it imply that the therapist cannot or should not see the noncustodial parent and additional members of the extended family. If this is necessary, it can be done later in the process, after the family members trust the therapist to respect their definition of themselves. Additional members of the suprafamily need to be involved under conditions and in roles that are acceptable to the stepfamily.

Visher and Visher (1996) comment that until the couple has had time to learn to work together as a team, seeing the children and adults together in therapy can split the group even further apart.

Focusing on the marital subsystem suits integrated and imported stepfamilies because the couple is their focal subsystem. In invented families, it is more effective to approach the couple in their parental role since this is the nucleus of the stepfamily.

A major consideration in choosing with whom to work is the question of who is willing to work. Some biological and stepparents may be motivated to work on issues more than others. A remarried father who is involved with his new family may have a limited degree of willingness to recognize problems of a child who lives with his/her mother and her new husband and refuse to cooperate. Sometimes one remarried biological parent and his/her spouse are willing to work with a professional but the other remarried parent and his/her spouse refuse. Sometimes a non-remarried mother may refuse to work together with her remarried ex-husband and his new wife because she feels outnumbered or inferior to the new couple because of her status as a single parent. A remarried father and his new wife may define issues regarding children from a previous marriage as "their biological custodial mother's problem and responsibility." On other occasions, it is the new spouse who does not want to get involved with their spouse's ex-partner because "it is up to them to deal with these issues."

In integrated families, it is often possible to convince all adults to get involved. When invented and imported families agree to work on step-related issues, it is typically the custodial biological parent and his/her spouse who are the primary cooperative partners. As a rule, it is better to start with whoever is willing to work and later decide whether to include additional figures. Sometimes it is impossible to include other significant figures because they live elsewhere or are not willing to participate or because some people cannot be in the same room with each other without creating enormous tension. In these cases, the party that is cooperative needs to learn to tolerate the other party as an unpleasant but unchangeable reality, at least to a certain point (snowstorms are also inconvenient and destructive but we learn to cope with them).

The question with whom to work depends also on the issues at hand. If the stepfamily struggles with an issue that relates to parenthood, it makes more sense to involve extrafamilial parental figures than if the issue concerns mostly the remarriage. Unfortunately, most of the time such clear distinctions are not self-evident. Issues are interwoven and mutually affect one another, making it impossible to sort out a given situation as a parental as opposed to a marital issue. Even though each stepfamily that comes for help has its specific issues, clinical experience and empirical research indicate several typical issues that require attention in working with stepfamilies. These issues are discussed in the next section of this chapter.

## DECIDING WHAT TO WORK ON

Although not all stepfamilies need help in the same areas of their lives, most of them require some work in establishing boundaries, clarifying roles, developing skills of communication, negotiation, and conflict resolution, and developing parental coalitions. The specific nature of these issues needs to be determined according to the type and circumstances of each family.

### Establishing Boundaries

Establishing and maintaining appropriate boundaries is a typical issue in stepfamilies of all types. Clear boundaries bring more clarity as to who belongs where and contribute to diminishing ambiguity and consequent confusion, thus enabling family members to function better and feel more comfortable. Clear boundaries need to be drawn both around the new marriage and between the stepfamily and its environment.

### Boundaries Around the New Couple

Establishing clear boundaries around the couple and strengthening its bond emerge in stepfamily literature as the single most important factor in building family stability (Visher and Visher, 1996). The task of combining and establishing an environmental and emotional foundation for the spousal relationship is especially important in the initial phases of the remarriage (Kaslow, 1993).

The recommendation to focus on the couple is not surprising, considering that most of our knowledge is based on families in therapy. Integrated families seem to seek therapy more frequently than other types of families and are therefore the families about which we know the most. Because in these families the marital subsystem is dominant, focusing on this subsystem is a common practice. However, Zucker-Anderson and White (1986) found that the quality of the remarital relationship is not necessarily associated with how well the stepfamily functions as a whole. This means that in some stepfamilies the spousal relationship is strong and stable and focusing on it would be "fixing something that is not broken."

In integrated families, it is effective to focus on the couple relationship as the raison d'être of these families is the marital subsystem. Typical issues of these families relate to recoupling, since most partners have been in a previous marriage and the task is to build the current spousal subsystem as free as possible of "spillover" from previous relationships.

In invented families, much of the work has to do with taking on diverse roles simultaneously and building a marital relationship concurrent with building a parental relationship. Given that the parental subsystem is the focus in these families, it is more useful to first help the family develop a clear boundary around the couple as parental figures and from this position extend it to the boundary around them in their marital role. For example, start with coaching the parent and stepparent to work as a team and support each other regarding educational issues. Help the natural parent support limit setting by the stepparent rather than "jumping" to rescue the child or empathizing with the child's complaints about "the wicked stepparent." This working together as a parental subsystem builds mutual trust and allows partners to draw around themselves a clear boundary as a couple.

In imported families, as in integrated families, building a clear boundary around the couple is compatible with their marital focus. However, a major issue is adapting the styles that the spouses experienced in their previous marriages to the current family. A lion's share of the work with these families includes negotiating a level of boundary permeability that is acceptable to both spouses.

## Boundaries Around the Stepfamily

In addition to establishing clear boundaries around the new couple within the stepfamily, it is also important to help families to establish boundaries around the stepfamily as a whole. Of special importance are boundaries between the past and present families.

This includes boundaries between the stepfamily and the family of the noncustodial parent and boundaries between the stepfamily and the extended family.

*Boundaries between the stepfamily and the family of the noncustodial parent.* The boundaries between the stepfamily and the family of the "other" parent need to be well defined but permeable for children to maintain a comfortable relationship with both households. It is believed that if boundaries are too loose, children get confused, and if boundaries are too strict and limit access of children to the noncustodial parent, children tend to build unrealistic fantasies about that parent.

In integrated families, establishing clear and permeable boundaries around the family often works rather smoothly because it fits their high past orientation and self-perception as different from non-stepfamilies.

In invented and imported families, establishing appropriate boundaries that meet the needs of all family members is more complicated. These families feel comfortable with boundaries with limited permeability between the households of the remarried parents. Therefore, they tend to establish solid boundaries around the new unit. Unlike integrated families, these families see the current unit as *the* "real family," consequently creating around it boundaries that make it difficult or even impossible for the nonresiding parent to gain access. Sometimes this is done in a very decisive way by using inappropriate language, negative labeling, and overt attacks or subtle devaluation of ex-spouses. Other families simply do not speak about the past and the noncustodial parent. As children are very sensitive to unspoken expectations of adults, they quickly learn that in their family it is not okay to mention their family situation, especially with positive connotations.

A major task in working with these families is to help them negotiate boundaries that will not block children from access to the "other parent" and his/her kin, without challenging or jeopardizing the profile that the adults choose to adopt. The practitioner needs to help the couple recognize their inability to "get rid" of the natural parent who lives elsewhere. Exceptions may be a parent who is endangering the welfare of the child. Other exceptions may include a chronically mentally ill and hospitalized parent, a parent who became an extreme cult member or joined an extreme segregated religious group, or a parent who is incarcerated for a long time in a high security prison or in another state. A compromise needs to be found between the desire of the couple, and sometimes of the children, to reinvent the family and the reality of the existence of this parent. This delicate task calls for caution and creativity on the part of the professional who works with the family.

One effective way to deal with this issue is to encourage the family to develop its own history together rather than to "destroy" previous history. The faster the new family develops its sense of belonging, the less there will be a need to "eliminate" the past, and consequently, the stress will diminish. Therefore, it is very important to encourage invented families to have vacations, "fun time," and positive experiences together. The Hudson family has been together for three years and is still split along biological lines. Mrs. Hudson would spend special time alone with her son, then ten, and even though the family would spend special occasions with Jay, Mr. Hudson's twenty-eight-year-old son, family members "lived by each other's side." At this point, they were encouraged to take a family vacation, and they went to Mexico for a week. Prior to leaving they spent a lot of time planning the trip in detail, carefully negotiating where to go (Mrs. Hudson was interested in archaeology, her husband and her son in sailing, and her stepson was not much interested in going), where to stay (the parents preferred modest accommodations, the sons wanted a fancy hotel), etc. When they came back, they reported that they had had a wonderful time and that this week had brought them closer together.

In some invented and imported families, the children from a previous marriage wish to adopt the family's agenda of disconnecting from the past. In these families, the task of the therapist is to help the family find the best ways of accomplishing its agenda. Helen, sixteen, insisted on referring to her stepfather as "Dad," preferred to call her natural father by his given name, and tried to keep her contacts with him to a minimum. She did not like his new wife and did not like spending time with him. She constantly complained about feeling exceptional in her warm and cohesive stepfamily. The therapist helped the family go through an adoption procedure. This involved presenting the idea to the natural father in a way that was acceptable to him, developing with the girl and all adults a plan for future contacts with her original father, and informing them individually as well as together what this change would mean for all. When the girl and her three parents left the court after the process had been completed, she kissed each of them, smiled, and told everybody (including her natural father) how grateful she felt for their allowing her to become "a real full member of my family. Now I am like everybody."

However, some families feel more comfortable with less clear boundaries than others. Ruth remarried to Simon, following her divorce from Harry, who remarried to Pat after her divorce from Brian. Ruth and Simon raise her daughter from her first marriage and three-year-old Gail born in the remarriage. Pat and Harry raise Pat's twins by her first husband and three-year-old Lily born in the remarriage. The two families live in a two-family house. Their toddlers go to the same school and spend a lot of time together. Ruth and Pat share car pool responsibilities, baby-sit for each other, and are close friends. All children eat, sleep, do their homework, and perform chores in both households. Both adults and children expressed satisfaction with this arrangement, which they describe as, "we live in a clan-like family but this works for us."

*Boundaries between the stepfamily and the extended family.* As with many issues, boundaries between the family and the extended family are a more complicated topic in stepfamilies than in non-stepfamilies. Living in a stepfamily requires adjustment not only of spouses, ex-spouses, and children, but also of grandparents, uncles, aunts, cousins, and other relatives. Some experts suggest including members of the extended family in therapy (see Sager et al., 1983). This enables all parties involved to cooperate in developing an appropriate boundary between the stepfamily and its extended family.

However, this suggestion has several drawbacks. First, it is not always feasible. Members of the extended family may live in different parts of the country, their schedules may not be readily coordinated, and some of them may feel too resentful and hurt to attend a meeting together. Second, having only members of the stepfamily in a meeting builds a boundary around the stepfamily; including members of the extended family may dilute these boundaries. My clinical experience shows that in most cases it is advisable to help stepfamilies develop strategies for handling their extended families rather than involve the extended families directly in therapy. Kathy was thirty-two when she married Brian, who was twenty-five years older than she. Within the first two years of their marriage, the couple had two children. Brian had been married before and had two adult children from his previous marriage. His daughter, Lynda, is Kathy's age and has two school-age children of her own. Lynda was very happy that her father remarried, since he had lived alone for many years following her parents' divorce. She used to visit her father's new family often and offer Kathy advice regarding child rearing. Kathy liked Lynda and thought that they had a lot in common. However, four years into the remarriage, she desccribed Lynda as intrusive and overstepping the boundaries of her father's new family. Kathy did not want to hurt either Lynda's or Brian's feelings, but wished to establish a clear boundary around her and Brian's family. In a consultation meeting, both Brian and Kathy expressed reluctance to involve Brian's daughter and son-in-law because they felt that this would jeopardize the generation boundaries between Brian and Lynda. In a short consultation with the couple, the therapist directed them to be assertive and to set clear boundaries around their family in a friendly way rather than bringing Lynda and her husband to a meeting to discuss the issue.

### Clarifying Roles

Clarifying roles, expectations, and myths often needs to be addressed in all types of stepfamilies. The lack of normative definitions for roles in stepfamilies has been discussed in Chapter 3. In the absence of clear norms for step-roles, each stepfamily needs to negotiate its own norms. A central goal in working with families that are current or potential remarriages is to discuss in detail mutual expectations and perceptions regarding family members' roles. The importance of this goal is recognized by many stepfamilies. For example, Martha and David, who were described in Chapter 5, define a good stepfamily as "a family with realistic expectations of each other and as few illusions as possible."

A number of families indicate that if they had an opportunity to start all over again they would have better-clarified, mutual role expectations. Mr. and Mrs. Drucker have been married for four years. They raise Mrs. Drucker's teenage daughter from a previous marriage and their mutual ten-year-old son. They state, "If we started then with what we know now, we would have entered the remarriage with a clearer mutual understanding of our rights and obligations as a parent and a stepparent." The wife says, "I would not have compromised my position as the sole natural parent in this house so easily and would not expect my husband to be involved as if he were the natural parent." The husband concurs, saying, "I would have been more clear about what I wish and do and what I do not wish to be and do for my stepdaughter." In a similar way, Mrs. Dragon, a remarried mother of two, says, "I would have negotiated and clarified more than I did both the expectation my husband and I had regarding our marriage and my husband's expectations regarding my boys."

Since there is a wide variety of potential roles for each spouse toward his/her partner's children, clarification of expectations is complicated. The role of the stepparent (who is most often the stepfather) needs to be specifically negotiated and agreed upon by all parties involved. Developing such an understanding is a long and sometimes bumpy road.

The contracting of roles should involve not only the spouses but also adolescent and sometimes younger children from previous marriages (depending on the maturity level of the specific child). Such discussions may help stepfamily members develop a clear understanding of what is expected of them by their new family, what they expect of themselves, and how to compromise between the different sets of expectations. However, it is better first to reach some level of understanding and agreement between the spouses before the children are brought into the discussion. This will enable the couple to agree upon "red lines" regarding issues that are nonnegotiable for each of them and to define the space for negotiation to accommodate children's expectations in a way that will help them to adjust rather than to feel guilt toward any of the parental figures in their lives.

Although clarification of roles is a task common to all stepfamilies, the specific agreement each family will reach regarding the role of the stepparent will depend to a great degree upon the type to which it belongs. In integrated families, it is clear that a parental figure, the noncustodial parent, exists outside of the family and that the stepparent does not replace him/her. This leaves families with the need to negotiate what indeed are the roles of each parent, within the stepfamily. For these families, it is most useful to follow the traditional recommendation, according to which the biological parent, at least initially and with older children, assumes the primary disciplinarian role (Keshet, 1987; Visher and Visher, 1988; Fine, 1996).

Clarifying parental roles is a major task for invented families. In these families, adults come together to establish a new family and a clear role definition regarding the step-relationship is of utmost importance, as this is the core of the new unit. These families often wish to assign the stepparent a full parental role, as if this parent is the real parent and there is no additional natural parent. This is done predominantly by the adults and by children who do not wish to be exceptional in their social environment. A major task for therapists is to help these families negotiate an arrangement that is compatible with the wish of family members to assign a full parental role to the stepparent and yet not exclude the children's accessibility to their natural parent who resides outside of the family.

In imported families, clarification of parental roles and parental style are related to the way these roles have been shaped and fulfilled in the previous marriages of the spouses because these families carry over patterns from their previous marriages into the remarriage. The function of the professional is to help the stepfamily identify and shape the family pattern that is most compatible with its specific situation and to help them find ways to live in peace with this choice.

Families can be helped to turn the situation of the stepparent as an outsider, often alluded to as a disadvantage, into an advantage. Many families assign the stepparent a role as mediator. The stepparent is not part of the history and is not associated with painful memories of separation and divorce (except when the now second spouse was in a relationship with the remarried parent prior to the divorce) and is therefore in a more neutral position. The stepparent can become a mediator between his/her stepchildren and their natural parent and between the divorced natural parents. Lily is married to Tony, who has never been married before. They raise Lily's seven-year-old daughter from a previous marriage and one-year-old Eric, who was born in the remarriage. Lily and her ex-husband had numerous conflicts regarding child support payment (a typical battlefield for stepfamilies). These conflicts often escalated to verbal aggression over the phone, mutual bad-mouthing, and threats by the father and stepmother to open legal procedures to transfer the custody from the mother to the father. The girl started to tell lies in both households, became withdrawn in school, and had several incidents of bed-wetting. At this point, the stepfather asked the natural father to meet with him without the presence of either the mother or the stepmother. In this meeting he conveyed to the father his belief that all four adults care for the little girl and are responsible for her well-being. He also expressed his concern that the tense situation between the two couples is detrimental for her. The two men managed to work out an agreement for a "cease fire." The stepfather was an objective moderator between his wife and her ex-husband because he did not carry grudges from the past.

Needless to say, a stepparent can only fulfill the role of a mediator when he/she is capable of maintaining a neutral view and does not automatically side with his/her spouse. Some remarried couples use animosity toward an ex-spouse to cement their relationship, as against an external "enemy." In these families, the unification around an "anti-ex" position needs to be evaluated and dismantled before a mediation role can be negotiated for the stepparent.

For the stepparent to acquire a parental role, the natural parent of the children needs to be able to accept it. Often parents express the wish for their new spouses to develop a good relationship with their children, but at the same time knowingly or unknowingly sabotage these relationships. This may happen because natural parents may be afraid to lose the exclusivity of their own relationship with their children, are jealous and overdefensive regarding their children's relationship with the stepparent, or are reluctant to give up their powerful position. Parents need to learn to "step aside" and allow their children and new spouse to develop their own relationships.

In addition to clarifying stepparent role, elucidation of expectations of the extended family, neighbors, and friends is also a crucial issue. Invented families see themselves as not different from non-stepfamilies. This perception may not be matched by their environment and may require helping the family to clarify these different expectations.

The Vish family was upset about the attitude of Mr. Vish's family of origin toward his stepdaughter. Mr. Vish was a bachelor when he married a divorced mother with a daughter. The couple has two sons together. The Vishs are an invented family. They minimize the presence of the past in their life, tend to deny any difference between their family and non-stepfamilies, and focus on raising "our children." Mr. Vish's family accepted his wife and stepdaughter in a friendly yet remote manner. When the children were born in the remarriage, the difference in attitude toward the stepdaughter and the boys became very clear. Mr. Vish's grandmother would come to visit and bring larger presents for his natural children than for his stepdaughter, his parents displayed only their natural grandchildren's pictures, and in social circumstances, family members would make a point of emphasizing that the Vishes have "two sons but Mrs. Vish also has a daughter." At this point, Mr. and Mrs. Vish sought help in handling this situation, which was unacceptable to them.

The family attended four sessions. In the first session, the couple clarified their mutual perceptions of their family. They clearly preferred solidifying the family unit, allowing no splits along biological lines. As Mrs. Vish's first husband has been hospitalized in another country because of a chronic mental disease since the daughter was three months old, the girl had no contact with him. The social worker raised questions regarding the reactions of the children to the invented profile preferred by the adults. A family session was set to address these questions. In this session, each child was seen separately and then the whole family met together. Alternative possibilities for being a stepfamily were discussed. Children were encouraged to express their views of the family. It became evident that all three children felt comfortable with the invented profile of the family. In a subsequent meeting, the family discussed strategies they can use to change the attitude of members of the extended family. They anticipated scenarios and negotiated appropriate responses. For example, they decided that when the husband's grandmother brought huge packages of candies for the boys and one candy for the girl, instead leaving the room in anger as before, Mr. Vish would bring a container to put all the candies together and calmly tell his grandmother that it is most important for him and his wife that each child receive a fair share, as they are all children of the family. In a follow-up meeting several weeks later, the family reported the beginning of a change in attitude of the extended family, which they felt was satisfactory.

One path for helping the family to clarify and agree upon everybody's role is by means of a discussion of reference concepts. The concepts that family members use to refer to each other within the family and within their social environment reveal their perception of mutual expectations of each other. It is important for the human service provider to refer to family members by the same concepts that they use for one another, thus showing respect for the way they wish to think about themselves. For example, the McDougal family was seen by a young social worker in the hospital following the diagnosis of juvenile diabetes of their youngest child. The family included Mr. McDougal, who was a childless widower when he remarried to Mrs. McDougal, a mother of three girls. The couple had together two boys, ages eight and four. The father of the girls maintained little contact with them, more in the role of a "good uncle" than in a parental capacity, while Mr. McDougal acted as a parental figure, to everybody's satisfaction. In the first meeting, the girls constantly referred to Mr. McDougal as Dad, while the social worker talked about their natural father as "Your Dad" and referred to Mr. McDougal by his given name when: "How does it make you feel when Fred tells you to do home chores?" and "Did you explain to Fred how you feel about this?" The family did not show up for the following appointment and avoided scheduling additional appointments. Contact with Mrs. MacDougal by the supervisor of the worker revealed that family members agreed that if the worker cannot understand how they see each other, he/she will not be able to help them.

## Developing Skills of Communication, Negotiation, and Conflict Resolution

Communication is an additional issue that needs to be addressed in stepfamilies. The combination of scarcity of norms for stepfamilies and the abundance of decisions these families need to make requires well-developed negotiation and conflict resolution skills. These skills are needed both for communication within the stepfamily and between the stepfamily and the family of the noncustodial or joint custodial parent.

## Communication Within the Stepfamily

In stepfamilies, everybody comes with different ways of doing things. These different ways need to be molded into the stepfamily's way of doing things (Visher and Visher, 1996). To do so successfully, family members need to talk, negotiate, and communicate with one another. This is particularly true in integrated families with high past orientation in which past experience is openly allowed to affect the current family.

Negotiations in stepfamilies are carried out both openly and covertly. One issue that is negotiated early in the life of the stepfamily is the type of stepfamily to establish. Although this is to a large degree governed by the adults, children do influence the decision, especially when they are adolescents.

Communication within the stepfamily is necessary at all life cycle phases to reach decisions regarding almost every aspect of family life. For example, in early phases, stepfamilies have to decide how stepchildren should address stepparents at home and in public. Some imported and invented families demand that children use the concept "Dad" or "Mom." Children may feel awkward regarding this demand because they interpret it as a betrayal of their natural parent or they do not feel close enough to the stepparent or ready for the degree of intimacy this concept implies. Dorothy, a twenty-seven-year-old stepdaughter, was twelve when her father remarried following the divorce of her parents, who had been separated since she was nine. Her mother went to live abroad, and Dorothy hardly saw her or heard from her. She recounts:

> Not until I reached my early twenties did I find a way of addressing my stepmother that felt comfortable for her and me. I would use all kinds of verbal manipulations to ask questions without addressing anybody specifically, like what is for dinner, or I would wait until someone else asked what I wanted

to know . . . just not to have to directly address her. I could not figure out how.

Stepfamilies have to deal with questions concerning celebrating holidays. Holidays are "a family thing." Even though non-stepfamilies often argue about how to spend holidays, for stepfamilies, the season between September to December is particularly difficult. This holiday season, from the Jewish Rosh Hashana through Thanksgiving and up to Christmas, Hanukkah, and New Year's Eve, poses a challenge to stepfamilies. They need to decide who will celebrate with whom which part of each holiday, which rituals to adopt for celebrating, which food to cook, and so forth. All these are sensitive and complicated issues that at times take a heavy emotional toll on family members. They require careful negotiation and decision making.

Transitional phases are also critical for negotiation and decision making in all families. In stepfamilies, transitions require communication about delicate, complex, and often painful issues. When a stepchild is attending a bar mitzvah, being baptized, or celebrating a confirmation, issues concern who should sign the formal invitation and welcome the guests. When a stepdaughter is getting married, who will walk her down the aisle and stand with her under the huppa (Jewish marital canopy under which traditionally the marrying couple and their parents stand during the marriage ceremony)? When a family member celebrates a significant birthday, who should be invited?

Integrated families tend to allow and expect the natural divorced parents to perform rituals regarding their children because they are open to including past-related people in their current lives and their focus is more on the marriage than on the children (therefore, where the stepchild spends the holiday is "not such a big deal"). Invented and imported families may require more negotiation and communication to develop satisfactory solutions. The practitioner has to be careful to help family members develop a solution that is compatible with their self-perception rather than promote a solution "from the book" that is inconsistent with the family's self-definition.

An important aspect of communication that is crucial for stepfamilies is conflict resolution. All families experience conflicts between spouses, between parents and children, and between siblings. In stepfamilies, conflicts are embedded structurally, there are more people with whom to be in conflict, more competition that paves the way to conflicts, and an absence of clear norms that regulate relationships.

It is important to help stepfamilies view conflicts not as negative events but as opportunities to develop their own agendas. Such a positive reframing is often difficult because being involved in endless conflicts is an exhausting experience. However, negotiations to address a conflict is part of developing intimacy while maintaining independence. The main task for stepfamilies is to discuss not how to avoid conflicts, but how to deal with them effectively. The mere reassuring of a family that conflicts are inevitable and they are useful can bring relief.

## Communication Between the Two Households

Children in stepfamilies typically belong to two households—the natural father's and the natural mother's. There is an agreement in the field that these households should be able to communicate appropriately when necessary (Burt and Burt, 1996). However, what is appropriate for diverse types of stepfamilies is still an open question. What is appropriate for imported families may be different from what is appropriate for integrated families. A major task of the professional who works with stepfamilies is to help each family develop what is an appropriate mode of communication that feels comfortable and serves the needs of adults and children effectively for that specific family.

Integrated stepfamilies typically feel more comfortable with communication between the two households. Danielle and Roger raise together her three children and his three children from previous marriages. Both noncustodial parents and their current spouses are welcome to call their children at any time and pop in to visit them whenever they are in the neighborhood. Whenever there is a question regarding the children, the adults call each other to negotiate the issue directly. This open communication is often expanded to issues that are not directly related to children. For example, Danielle would trust her husband's ex-wife, who is a nurse, regarding medical issues and seek her advice.

Invented stepfamilies may require more structured ways of communicating to maintain their feeling of safety and level of comfort. In the absence of clear, organized, and predictable patterns of communication, such families may develop hostile patterns as a means to maintain the distance they need. Therefore, it is important to help invented families develop clear and structured ways of communicating between households. This will validate the self-perception of the family and enable a relaxed and effective exchange of information and collaborative decision making regarding the children and their interests.

Imported families may have difficulty developing effective routes of communication with the children's other household because the mere existence of that household conflicts with the self-definition of such families. This requires a high level of caution and sensitivity on the part of the human service provider who works with the family. It is important to keep the communication between the two households focused on specific and concrete issues that pertain to children and to prevent rivalry between the current and previous carrier of the same role. It is helpful for the adults in the family to develop familiarity with each other "as people." This will enable them to communicate with each other in a more neutral way than when they cling to seeing each other in their respective roles such as "my husband's ex-wife" and "my ex-wife's new husband."

### Building Parental Coalitions: The Custodial Parent, the Stepparent, and the Noncustodial Natural Parent and Stepparent

As shown in previous chapters, stepfamilies have a larger and more complex parental subsystem than the nuclear intact family. A major question for clinicians who work with stepfamilies is how to help them develop parental coalitions that address their unique issues effectively. Each stepfamily contains several parental subsystems. First, there is the subsystem of the natural parents. This subsystem transcends the boundaries of the stepfamily and includes the previously married parents of the children from the first marriage. Second, there is a parental subsystem within the stepfamily. This subsystem includes the natural parent and the stepparent with whom children reside. In addition to these principal sets of parents, there are the subsystems that include a natural parent and stepparent of the same gender (for example, natural father and stepfather; natural mother and stepmother). In complex stepfamilies and multimarriage families (that is, when one or both spouses have been remarried more than once), the possibilities multiply dramatically.

The decision with which parental subsystem to work in each phase is affected by the type of the stepfamily. In integrated stepfamilies, a major task involves helping the family to develop clear roles for each parental figure. Of utmost importance is negotiating the roles of the natural parent and the stepparent of the same gender in a way that diminishes competition and enhances complementarity. Robin Ford, in her forties, remarried to Richard, who is four years younger than she. Robin is divorced from Mitch, the father of her son, Ethan, who is a senior in a prestigious high school. Her current husband has never been married before, and the couple adopted together four-year-old Dorine. All three parents attend parent-teacher conferences and school events and celebrate holidays together. Ethan introduces both men as fathers, referring to them as "my father Mitch" and "my father Richard." His mother has full custody, but the family maintains an "open-door policy" regarding Ethan's visits with his natural father. Robin is the principal disciplinary figure for Ethan, while she shares Dorine's discipline with Richard in a more equal manner.

Invented families and imported families pose for clinicians a delicate task regarding parental subsystems. While clinical literature underscores the necessity to negotiate and build a stepparent role that neither competes nor usurps that of the noncustodial natural parent of the same gender (see Robinson, 1992), the remarriage couple in these types of families wishes to see themselves as the central, if not exclusive, parental subsystem. At the same time, there may exist a noncustodial parent who wishes to practice a parental role to some degree. The expectations of children also may vary from adopting the perspective of the parent-stepparent to overtly or covertly desiring inclusion of natural and stepparents to some extent. This depends on the age of the children, their experience with and feelings toward all parental figures, and influences from extended family from previous and current marriages.

The family needs to be helped to "tailor" a unique settlement that respects the family's self-definition without compromising any party's legitimate wishes. This requires sensitivity. Special caution is needed when a child shares the stepfamily's "invented" perspective, while the noncustodial parent wishes to maintain the relationship. If no consensus is achieved, the situation may require working separately with the stepfamily and the noncustodial natural parent to develop a niche for the latter without unbalancing the self-perspective of the family. In the Dole family, both remarriage partners were only children, and they raise their twin girls and Mel, Mrs. Dole's son from a previous marriage. They see themselves as an intact normal family and minimize the place of the past in their current life. Mel, who was nine when the remarriage took place, calls his stepfather Daddy and sees him as his "full-time" father in all respects. Although Mrs. Dole's first husband considers this arrangement best for his son because his own life is very unstable, he wishes to maintain a relationship with Mel. With the help of a therapist, a role has been negotiated for him to be the "good uncle" of all the children of the family. They call him by his given name (including his own son); he joins the family to celebrate holidays, spends vacations with them, and functions as the uncle the children could never have because their parents did not have siblings.

## *SUMMARY*

This chapter discussed two aspects of providing counseling services to stepfamilies: deciding with which family members to work and on which issues to focus. Whether the human service provider works with the remarriage couple or the current stepfamily, with or without family members from the previous marriage, depends on the issues, the family self-perception, and the phase of the counseling process. Typical issues with which many stepfamilies need help are establishing boundaries, clarifying roles, developing skills of communication, negotiation, and conflict resolution, and developing parental coalitions. Once the decision is made concerning with whom to work on which issues, strategies and techniques for intervention need to be chosen. The next chapter deals with methods for working with stepfamilies to achieve desirable goals.

# Chapter 13

# Strategies and Techniques
# for Working with Stepfamilies

Effective interventions with stepfamilies involve normalizing stepfamily experience, supplying psychoeducational information regarding the realities of step-life, negotiating flexibility and promoting creativity, and using collaborative conversational approaches. These aspects of serving stepfamilies will be discussed in this chapter.

## NORMALIZING THE STEPFAMILY EXPERIENCE

Normalizing the step-experience is a major issue to address in stepfamilies. Because day-to-day life of stepfamilies is characterized by pervasive stress, especially in complex stepfamilies, it is important to normalize the stresses of their situation and help them recognize their strengths. Stepfamilies, and professionals who work with them, should become aware of the fact that they are not necessarily problematic families. In an in-depth study, nonclinical stepfamilies were found to be satisfied and well-functioning, unlike the common negative stereotype (Berger, 1993). Stepfamilies are an alternative family configuration rather than a defective variation of the nuclear family and need to be acknowledged as such by the families, professionals, and their communities. The importance of normalizing the experience of stepfamilies has been confirmed in a recent study conducted by Visher and Visher (1996). Stepfamilies who have been in therapy and were asked to identify interventions that they experienced as helpful named validating and normalizing their experience as especially beneficial.

Helping stepfamilies to view their issues in the context of normal remarriage issues rather than as problematic helps them become "unstuck," alleviates their anxiety, and enables them to use their strengths effectively. Visher and Visher (1996) indicate that normalizing the experience of stepfamilies and validating their feelings help to reduce helplessness and increase their autonomy, thus improving the functioning and well-being of the families and their individual members.

The importance of normalizing the experience of stepfamilies became real to me during a recent conversation with a friend. She is a forty-five-year-old highly intelligent journalist. She brought to the remarriage her adolescent daughter by her first husband, and her second husband brought his two adolescent sons from his first marriage. Together they have a son in the remarriage. My friend confessed to me that she does not love her husband's sons and experiences difficulty accepting them as her own. When asked why she thinks she is expected to love the boys, she looked at me in astonishment, "You mean that it's OK for me not to love them? Are not stepmothers supposed to love their stepchildren? After all, they are my husband's kids." She was extremely surprised to hear from me that her feelings are perfectly common and normal for people in her situation. Several days later, she called to thank me for helping her to alleviate the tremendous guilt she had felt and was embarrassed to share with anybody.

In addition to normalizing the step-experience, it is important to normalize diversity of stepfamilies. To help stepfamilies find "their own voice," it is important to validate diverse ways of struggling with step-issues rather than glorifying a singular model as desirable. Many stepfamilies shared with me their concerns: "Things in our family are not like they say in the book and advice in the psychological column in magazines. What is wrong with us?" A psychoeducational message that validates the normality of diverse types of stepfamilies is of utmost importance. Normalizing diversity alleviates pressure and enables families to find a way that works for them.

## *PROVIDING PSYCHOEDUCATION*

Educating stepfamily members about characteristics and processes that are typical to families similar to their own is of great importance. This provides families with a realistic perspective regarding their situation and helps them to be less anxious and to feel more confident and competent to master their lives. Psychoeducation for stepfamilies should include three components. First, stepfamilies need to be educated regarding what is unique to step- as opposed to non-stepfamilies; second, they need to be educated about the diversity of stepfamilies and the unique characteristics of their type of family; and last, some aspects of psychoeducation need to be type specific.

## Psychoeducation About the Uniqueness of Stepfamilies

Acquiring knowledge about stepfamilies and how they differ from non-stepfamilies helps build realistic and reachable expectations and a better sense of achievement when these expectations are accomplished. For example, if a stepfamily learns that stepfamilies tend to have ambiguity of roles as a normative characteristic, they will feel more comfortable and less frustrated with their lower level of role clarity. Members would not struggle to achieve the same level of clarity that they see in non-stepfamilies around them or that they remember having in their own non-stepfamily. After attending a psychoeducational session, one stepfamily said:

> Well, if you say that this is the way it is in stepfamilies, let it be. If we know that this is what is reasonable, so be it. We were concerned because we were convinced that we are doing something wrong and that if we did something different, things would be better. But, now that you told us that this is the way things are in many stepfamilies we are less troubled.

Visher and Visher (1996) suggest that psychoeducation for stepfamilies should include information about stepparent roles, remarried parent roles, and the need for dyadic relationships within the family. It is important to help families understand that a stepparent does not and should not replace a noncustodial (or even deceased) parent because the original parent continues to exist in the real or psychological life of the stepfamily. Rather, stepparents need to have their own roles in the family. This role depends on the type of the stepfamily and will be discussed later on in this section.

Providing psychoeducation about the importance of establishing boundaries as well as using special rituals to do so may be very beneficial for families. For example, getting a plate with double last names for the children from a previous marriage to put on their door or their desk was for one family a very concrete way to acknowledge the fact that these children belong to two households and need freedom to comfortably move between them.

### Psychoeducation About Diversity and Types of Stepfamilies

Developing awareness of the diversity of stepfamilies and gaining familiarity with the different types of stepfamilies are central in psychoeducation for stepfamilies. Learning that stepfamilies are different from non-stepfamilies is not enough. It is important for stepfamilies to learn that not all stepfamilies are made from one mold and that there is more than one way to be a functional and satisfied stepfamily. Very often, introducing to a stepfamily the idea of different types of stepfamilies and teaching them about the various types is met with reactions of relief:

> It is a comfort to know that not only do we not have to compare ourselves to our neighbors next door who live in a first marriage, but it is also okay for us not to be like the other neighbors across the street who are in a remarriage, but that they are another type of a stepfamily.

### Type-Specific Psychoeducation

As mentioned previously, some psychoeducation needs to be geared toward and tailored for a specific type of stepfamily. A major issue in providing psychoeducation is how to respect the family's decision and still guide them. For example, as a relatively high past orientation is functional for integrated families, working with them requires educating them about appropriate ways of combining the past and present in the life of the family. With such families, it is useful to adopt Visher's and Visher's (1996) recommendation to relate past experience to current situations. At the same time, it is important to help these families to remember that stepchildren cannot and should not "correct" mistakes done by the children from the previous marriage or replicate their successes. This was the issue in the Raid family. Both spouses had been married before and each had a son in the previous marriage. Edward, the thirty-year-old son of Mr. Raid, dropped out of college and has worked in low-paying, unstable jobs. When Mrs. Raid's thirteen-year-old son underachieved in school, his stepfather was furious with him: "I have seen this happening before with my son and I now know better than to let you go the same route."

However, imported or invented stepfamilies, which have a low past orientation and deny difference from non-stepfamilies, pose a challenge. The family must learn to enable children from previous marriages to maintain the connections with the past that are necessary for their well-being while accepting the basic present-oriented and difference-minimizing nature of the family perspective. A therapist may suggest to the family to develop the "not-different-from-other-families" attitude in domains that are not detrimental to the welfare of family members, such as having a shared bank account and allowing children to refer to their noncustodial parent.

Psychoeducation about the role of a stepparent also depends on the type of stepfamily. In integrated stepfamilies, stepparents' roles are mostly those of an adult friend, a confidante, or a mentor, while the major role of parenting stays with the natural parent. However, in imported and invented families, stepparents share with the natural parents more traditional parental roles, including nourishing, limit setting, and authority. This is especially true regarding invented families because of their parental focal subsystem. Telling these families that research and clinical observation show that it is better for the natural parent to take a leading parental role may not be helpful, since, by definition, they see the stepparent as a central parental figure. Therefore, psychoeducation will focus more on the authority a stepparent can take and how to develop it without threatening the children's bond with their natural parent.

It has proven helpful to teach stepparents to enter an authority role through the "soft side" of authority, as the giver. Control over resources and authority to allocate them are part of parental authority; a stepparent can start to establish parental authority through being in charge of allocating resources such as allowance and help in homework. Paul was thirteen when his mother, Janet, remarried to Herb. Paul was very rebellious and automatically refused any request that came from his stepfather. The preference of Janet and Herb to "forget the past and focus on our future" was supported by the fact the Paul's natural father barely kept any contact with him. Both felt comfortable with the model of the paternal figure as the main authority, which they had experienced in their previous families and wished to preserve in their new family. The marital subsystem was clearly the focus of this family. Therefore, the family was assessed as belonging to the imported type. The question was how to help Janet and Herb to address Paul's behavior in an effective way while respecting their wish to live in an imported family. In a consultation, the parents were advised about the two sides of authority: the demanding and the giving. Herb was guided to acquire his parental authority via the soft side of authority. Paul started to see his stepfather as an ally and to turn to him for help in his confrontations with his mother. Soon, Paul started to direct requests and ask permission from Herb, thus recognizing also the disciplinarian authority of his stepfather.

## NEGOTIATING FLEXIBILITY
## AND PROMOTING CREATIVITY

In the absence of clear norms, stepfamilies as well as human service providers who work with them, must develop creative solutions to their situations. Creativity arises out of the unknown (Lax, 1994), and in stepfamilies, much is unknown. There are no clear normative expectations regarding the "right" way to be a stepfather, appropriate boundaries, and so forth. At the same time, stepfamily counseling is a relatively new field, and knowledge about effective proven strategies and techniques is available only to a limited degree. Consequently, the stepfamilies, as well as the professionals who work with them, have to invent new ways of thinking and problem solving.

Rather than creating something out of nothing, creativity is the ability to uncover, select, reshuffle, redefine, combine, and synthesize already existing facts, ideas, faculties, and skills (Koestler, 1975). It is the ability to figure out "other" ways, to change patterns when necessary, to be original, and to go beyond the learned and self-evident and see new connections within existing circumstances. Creativity requires flexibility (as opposed to rigidity) in the approach to situations, redefining of circumstances, looking for ways that have never been tried before, and exploring the "unthinkable."

Families usually look for social guidelines and judge themselves vis-à-vis other families, but creativity requires the willingness to take risks and pursue freedom from the usual conditioning and social rigidities. One way to help stepfamilies is by educating them about the importance of inventing new ways, validating their efforts to try uncommon solutions, and encouraging them to take "un-paved roads" without being anxious about the social reaction and the judgment of their cultural environment.

For example, some invented families persistently struggle to include everybody in doing things together to demonstrate solidarity and prevent anybody from feeling angry, hurt, or deprived. This may cause difficulties in orchestrating family outings and celebrations. Helping these families to learn to take risks and "keep an open mind" will promote their ability to develop alternative scenarios with different "casting," loosen up the atmosphere, and enable them to enjoy themselves guilt-free.

Another technique that helps to develop creativity is by teaching stepfamilies the principles of creative processes and offering opportunities to develop their skills in generating creativity within the family. This can be achieved by guiding families to look at a given problem in a completely different way, reframing uncertainty as creative efforts, asking about things that they never did as a family and about the "craziest" thing they did, and inviting them to describe their experiences and expectations by means of metaphors.

It is also helpful for stepfamilies to control and reduce their anxiety because studies have shown that when people are anxious they are more rigid and less creative (Smith and Carlsson, 1990).

An important aspect of helping promote stepfamilies' creativity is by working with them to develop rituals that pertain to their special needs. Rituals are at the core of human experience and are an important part of all cultures. Because special rituals for stepfamilies are absent, they need to be encouraged and guided to develop their own culture and rituals. This can be done in family sessions as well as in groups in which families can share rituals that work for them.

Some approaches to working with families focus on generating new ideas as their main goal. These approaches emphasize creating conditions for the emergence of "inventions" and are therefore especially helpful in servicing stepfamilies. Two of these approaches will be discussed in the next section.

## USING COLLABORATIVE CONVERSATIONAL APPROACHES

As mentioned at the beginning of this chapter, all the current models of family therapy are applicable to serving stepfamilies. However, the evolving collaborative conversational approaches offer a special goodness of fit for working with stepfamilies. One prominent approach is the reflecting team model.

The reflecting team approach has been evolving since the late 1980s and during the 1990s with the advent of postmodernism (Andersen, 1991). Rather than a method, it is a way of thinking. This way of thinking is based on the philosophy of Heidegger; it is based on the hermeneutic tradition that assumes that all knowledge is context dependent. When we encounter a phenomenon, a person, or a system, our understanding of it depends on prior assumptions and beliefs that we bring to the situation from past experience. These assumptions are our preunderstanding. The preunderstanding will determine how we select and interpret the information we take in. At the same time, in such an encounter, we may be exposed to new information that may change our preunderstanding. This creates the hermeneutic cycle in which preunderstanding and understanding mutually affect each other.

Constructivism provides the conceptual underpinning for this approach. According to constructivism, individuals and families construct their own reality, and their experience depends on and is shaped by the way they construct their world, perceive it, and think about it.

The reflecting team approach adopted three basic assumptions of constructivism. First, objectivity is impossible; second, any observation and understanding needs to be in the context of the observed phenomenon; and, third, the observers bring to the observation their own biases that affect the way they see, hear, understand, and express what they experience.

Based on these assumptions, the reflecting team approach entertains the idea that each family member constructs his/her own description and meaning of a given situation. Rather than *an* absolute truth within each family, there are various constructions of reality created by different family members—multiversa, creating "multiple realities." The meaning that each person assigns to a given event or concept is valid for that person. Therefore, understanding the narrative metaphors that families hold about themselves is the key to understanding families and helping them to change.

A family with a problem is a family that is "stuck" with its perspective of its situation. To get "unstuck" the family needs new ideas to broaden its perspectives and its premises regarding its context. Exposing the family to such new ideas is the leitmotiv of therapy.

In the reflecting team approach, the human service provider and the family work together as a team to create a context in which all parties collaborate in reflecting about the experience of the family and its significance. The goal of this reflection is to generate new ways that the family can adopt to think about its experience in order to make it more coherent. Because all family members, as well as the professional, come into the situation with their own biases— ways of understanding the world and meanings that they assign to words—the focus is on enabling people to understand themselves, their environment, and their relationships rather than on interpreting for them their situation or guiding them how to change their behavior. The worker aids the family in generating new ideas rather than serving as a provider of ideas.

Family members and the practitioner share with one another their constructions of reality and therefore have joint responsibility to promote desirable changes. This mutual sharing produces an "ecology of ideas" and creates a supportive and honest environment in which the family and professionals work together. The family can then accept input from other perspectives, hear and reevaluate different perceptions of the same reality, explore different perspectives on its issues, understand that there is no one correct solution to a situation, and make their choice reading the perception of reality that works for them. People can only consider new ideas if they are innovative and different enough from their usual ideas to appear alternative, while at the same time not extremely different from the people's usual ideas to the degree that they are overwhelming.

To enable families to evaluate the ideas offered by the practitioner and consider them as an alternative to their current perspective, these ideas need to be presented in a way that respects the integrity of the family because families, similar to all living systems, are "structurally determined" and can only operate in accordance with how they are built. Therefore, the exchange between any two living systems, such as a therapist and a family, must respect the needs of both to retain its pattern of relationships. Ideas that are too threatening cause the family to close up and block further exchange. Therefore, the human service provider should offer the new ideas carefully and slowly, allow the family opportunities to consider them and react to them, and be sensitive to verbal and nonverbal reactions of family members.

One way of introducing new ideas is by asking hypothetical questions about the future. Questions about what will be "if," call for fantasies, wishes, hopes, and opinions. Using hypothetical questions regarding the future, rather than factual questions about the past or present, frees family members to respond "outside" the boundaries prescribed by current rules, thus enabling them to create a new reality. Such questions also convey a message about the power of the family to create changes in its situation.

The reflecting team approach is particularly valuable in working with stepfamilies for several reasons. First, it has been recommended when the family system is very complex, with multiple outside systems involved, because of the approach's flexibility and multiple perspectives (Lax, 1991). As described in Chapter 3, stepfamilies are complex and involve multiple systems, including those which are external to the unit created by the remarriage such as nonresiding or cocustodial natural parents.

Second, the reflecting team approach is geared toward addressing differences in descriptions and recognizes the validity of diverse versions of the reality of the family that are held by different family members. Different constructions of shared experiences exist in all families. Various members have different perceptions and interpretations of the reality of the family, and this diversity often leads to conflicts and misunderstandings. In stepfamilies, the construction of reality by family members varies even more because experiences and perceptions of individuals and subsystems regarding crucial issues of the family differ considerably. Having different histories from the pre-remarriage phases of their life cycle, stepfamily members come with various backgrounds and many different viewpoints. Consequently, it is a complicated task to build and maintain a functioning, satisfied stepfamily unit. The reflecting team approach values these differences and offers a tactic to use them for the benefit of all family members. Rather than encouraging the blending of such differences, this approach highlights them and defines them as sources for growth, the promotion of mutual understanding, and the development of new perceptions that lead to new meanings and ultimately to new solutions.

Third, as discussed in Chapter 3, there are no clear norms regarding roles and rules for stepfamilies, consequently requiring these families to develop their own norms. The reflecting team approach focuses on the family as the generator of innovative solutions rather than on guiding families toward familiar and conventional routes.

Fourth, the understanding of the affect of preconceived ideas on the experience of a given situation makes the reflecting team approach especially valuable in serving stepfamilies. As mentioned in Chapter 3, there are abundant myths about stepfamilies. Therapists and stepfamily members bring these myths with them into counseling, and they affect the way they observe and understand the family and its issues. In the reflecting team approach, being in touch with these myths, which color our observations, and acknowledging their effects on the way we see things is an integral part of the counseling process. Practitioners need to be aware of their own biases regarding remarriage, stepfamilies, and stepparenting because these preconceived ideas will affect their perception of the family and their interpretation of its situation. For example, a therapist who believes that first-marriage families are superior to stepfamilies and sees divorce as a failure and stepfamilies as a compromise, will not be able to help a stepfamily develop an optimistic perspective regarding the potential advantages embodied in its situation.

Finally, in the reflecting team approach, hypothetical questions about the future are typical. Because the past often serves as an obstacle to change in stepfamilies, such future-oriented questions present new possibilities that can free the family from being "bound" by the past and help them to develop together new ways for the future.

Michael White (1989) shares some of the assumptions and principles of the reflecting team approach. However, his model has several unique aspects that are helpful in working with stepfamilies. One such aspect is his belief that some families often develop "problem-saturated descriptions" of their lives. All families have stories about themselves. These stories have been defined as family myths or family belief systems. These stories are told and retold, becoming part of the family legacy that serves to consolidate the sense of the family as a unit. The stories can be about an amusing incident, a word or sentence that one of the children said in a distorted way, or an opinion all family members have about somebody or something. These stories become an integral part of the family's culture and are referred to by a clue that makes no sense to outsiders but is perfectly clear to family members; for example, "Aunt Sonia's hat" may be a family reference to a snobbish attitude or an absurdity. The stories evolve from a variety of sources; two of which are life experiences and cultural role expectations. These stories that families develop about themselves create a perceptual lens through which subsequent life events are sorted and interpreted (Lax, 1994).

Some stepfamilies place the story of being a stepfamily always in the forefront, allowing it to "color" their whole perspective and blaming any unsatisfactory aspect of their lives on their family configuration. To help these families, the practitioner guides them by the use of narrative metaphors to develop alternative stories about their lives that offer a different sense of self and a different relationship to problems. The new story highlights families' mastery over their lives and problems, putting them in charge, rather than presenting them as being controlled by their problems. This new story empowers the family and frees it from the oppression of the problems.

To help families to successfully separate themselves from the old problem-focused story, the practitioner first externalizes the problem, helping family members see it as a distinct entity rather than an integral part of a family member or a given relationship. Then, the family is guided to identify examples of situations when it managed to be in charge of the problem. These examples are seen as "unique outcomes." This frees family members to work together to fight against the problem rather than blaming one another for the problem.

This model is very helpful for stepfamilies who adopt "step-relationship-saturated descriptions" of their lives. These families view themselves mostly or exclusively through the lens of being a stepfamily, seeing themselves as totally different from non-stepfamilies. Therefore, they view any problem that family members experience as related to the family configuration. Families who attribute all their issues to their family configuration feel helplessness and become easy prey for problems.

In working with such stepfamilies, following White's model, the focus is on helping them to differentiate aspects of their issues that are related to their being a stepfamily from other aspects that are related to normative developmental phases of all families, temporary circumstances, or social, economic, or other factors. This will enable families to gain better mastery over their problems.

## SUMMARY

This chapter presented guidelines for serving stepfamilies directly. The major questions that a human service provider needs to address in planning to help a stepfamily are with whom to work, on what to work, and how to work. Decisions regarding these questions depend on the type of the stepfamily and the phase in the step–life cycle. This chapter offered guidelines for these decisions and introduced strategies and techniques that have proven to be helpful with stepfamilies. Although all models of family therapy are applicable and useful in working with stepfamilies, the principles and advantages of two contemporary models of practice—reflecting team and Michael White's approach—were discussed.

However, servicing stepfamilies directly is only one aspect of helping this type of family. An equally important aspect is working on behalf of stepfamilies to bring about social and legal changes in a way that will address the needs of stepfamilies. The next chapter deals with this issue.

# Chapter 14

# Changing Social Context:
# Working on Behalf of Stepfamilies

This chapter deals with macroaspects of stepfamilies. While some stepfamilies need direct clinical help to cope with their situations, most stepfamilies' issues require also social, cultural, and legal changes. Society needs to adjust to the reality of stepfamilies as a major family type.

Institutionalizing stepfamilies involves establishing clear legal definitions, codified as well as uncodified rules, and acceptable mutual expectations and commitments among family members. Developing such a set of rules and norms requires a long and complicated process. However, it is the responsibility of professionals in the fields of mental health, family therapy, psychology, social work, and sociology to raise awareness of the need to mainstream stepfamilies and to initiate social and legal processes that will eventually produce the necessary changes. The first step toward creating these changes is that relevant professional groups recognize the need. This can be done by bringing the issues of mainstreaming stepfamilies into the open by discussing them in professional conferences, raising them in stepfamilies' organizations, writing about them in professional journals and popular magazines, speaking about them in the media, and so forth.

Once this core of interested individuals and organizations acknowledges stepfamilies as normative, the recognition that such a development is of utmost importance should be extended to policymakers, legislative bodies, social organizations, the media, and the public. The promotion of changes regarding stepfamilies is of utmost importance but takes time. Some of the necessary cultural, social, and legal changes are discussed in this chapter.

### DEVELOPING A STEP-RELATIONSHIPS LANGUAGE

One means of institutionalizing a given family configuration as legitimate is to provide concepts to define it. As noted in previous chapters, the absence of adequate neutral terms of address and reference suitable for stepfamilies necessitates using awkward language and causes difficulties for stepfamily members and for those within their social environment. Available terms are inaccurate and bear negative connotations. The time has come to develop an appropriate terminology of stepfamilies and step-relationships. Concepts are necessary to describe such families, their variations, and the relationships among their members. An example of a step in this direction was the coining of the term "binuclear family" by Ahrons (1980) to refer to postdivorce families. One concept that can serve this purpose is re-family. This concept is emotionally neutral and conveys the fact that this is a family, yet it reflects the existence of recurrent-repetitive components. A collaborative effort of stepfamily members and social scientists should be undertaken to generate concepts for stepfamilies. Such concepts need to be clear and value free, and stepfamily members need to feel comfortable using them.

Creating changes in the use of language seems at first glance to pose insurmountable difficulties. However, recent history teaches us otherwise. A good example is the change from using the term negro to using the term black. Once it became clear that the latter is politically correct and the former is offensive and unacceptable, "black" became the predominant word used. The media and education played a major role in this cultural shift, which occurred relatively fast. A similar process should be initiated regarding stepfamilies.

### CHALLENGING THE BRADY BUNCH STEREOTYPE: DEVELOPING REALISTIC RECOGNITION OF STEPFAMILIES, THEIR UNIQUENESS, AND DIVERSITY

Clinical experience and research indicate lack of awareness of stepfamily issues by educational and social institutions. Eve, a five-year-old daughter of a remarried father, came home crying one day. Eve has a half-brother from her father's first marriage. The boy lives with his remarried mother in a nearby town and visits often with his father's new family. Questioned about her crying, Eve shared her experience in school. The children were directed to draw their family and explain their drawing. Eve, who is very proud of her half-brother and perceives him as part of her family, included him in her drawing. When she reported that this is her brother and he lives in another town, the teacher corrected her, saying, "This is not a brother. This is a cousin." The girl insisted that this is her brother, but the teacher would not accept it because "brothers and sisters live in the same house." Such incidents are not uncommon.

We need to promote the idea that stepfamilies are a different species and need therefore to be judged by their own criteria rather than in comparison to first-marriage families. Insisting on the comparison to intact nuclear families perpetuates the negative stereotype of remarriage. A recent incident illustrated to me how far behind our schools are in recognizing stepfamilies. My husband and I went with my son from a previous marriage to register him in a new school. The secretary handed us a standard form, which included space for information about the name, address, occupation, and telephone number of the father and of the mother. I asked the secretary whether to include the details of my son's father who lives across the ocean or of his stepfather who actively participates in raising him. The secretary thought for a minute and, based on administrative considerations (who will be responsible for paying the tuition), made her judgment that the stepfather should be indicated with an explanation about his role. Then she shrugged her shoulder and commented, "These days I guess we should re-edit our forms, so many children come from stepfamilies." This secretary was right. Given that about a third of children live in stepfamilies, standard forms should stop being blind to this social reality and have spaces titled, "father, stepfather (if applicable), mother, stepmother (if applicable)." Such wording would reflect nonjudgmental recognition of stepfamilies and save their members from embarrassing moments of elaborate explanations and from feeling apologetic and defensive. Unfortunately, such incidents are common in educational, medical, and social human services, and we clearly need to prevent them.

Stepparents comment on the need for the educational system to be more sensitive to the experience of their children. For example, schools should offer an adequate number of invitations to include stepparents in graduations, school performances, etc.; teachers should create opportunities for preparing cards to natural and step-parents for Mother's Day and Father's Day; and be receptive to children's drawings and compositions that reflect stepfamily real-ities (Berger, 1993).

Even though it is recognized that stepfamilies are different and require specific knowledge, many teachers, school administrators, therapists, and counselors are not aware of this gap in knowledge. Martin and Martin (1992) summarized studies that showed clear evidence that these professionals see stepfamily members in a nega-tive stereotypical way and do not recognize the need to have specif-ic knowledge about stepfamilies and their unique issues to work with them effectively.

Stepfamilies need to be recognized, and their unique characteris-tics also need to be acknowledged. Stepfamilies are not only differ-ent from first-marriage families; they are also different from one another, as there are various types of stepfamilies. Clinging to a singular model of *the* functional stepfamily contributes to limiting the recognition of diversity within the population of stepfamilies.

Social recognition of stepfamilies has been growing. In Michi-gan, the first Sunday of the year was made Stepparent Day. Califor-nia, Florida, and Nebraska also designated a special day for steppar-ents. The national board of the Stepparent Association of America has been lobbying congress and senators to add to current Mother's Day and Father's Day a legal holiday for nationwide recognition of stepparents. The process of recognizing the existence of stepfami-lies as a legitimate type of family is in its initial phases. Much more needs to be done. Special greeting cards, bumper stickers, getting rid of idioms that convey perceiving stepfamilies as "second grade," favorable television shows, books, and movies, and much more are means for developing such recognition.

## DEVELOPING SPECIFIC SERVICES FOR STEPFAMILIES

A growing need exists for pre-remarriage and post-remarriage services to help prospective members of stepfamilies prepare for their new family configuration and provide them with a place to discuss ways to handle unique issues as they unfold during the step–life cycle. A wide variety of preventive, psychoeducational, and curative services should be offered to remarried couples, natural parents, stepparents, and children and adolescents who are members of stepfamilies as well as to their kin such as stepgrandparents. The need for such services has been expressed by many stepfamilies, especially those of the integrated type.

Currently, such opportunities have started to appear. Several nonprofit organizations offer services for stepfamilies. One example is the American Association of Stepfamilies, which offers a variety of services for stepfamilies and for professionals such as educators, therapists, and medical staff. Activities include psychoeducational meetings, mutual support and self-help groups, a bulletin, seminars, conferences, and literature for members of stepfamilies. The American Personnel and Guidance Association offers workshops on strengthening stepfamilies. In various cities local organizations exist. For instance, the Pittsburgh Center for Stepfamilies offers support groups, counseling, and seminars and publishes a newsletter. Some school districts offer workshops for stepparents and stepchildren. On the Internet, a site for stepfamilies enables interested people to share experiences, disseminate information, mutually consult with one another, seek and give advice regarding resolution of problems they face, and pose and discuss questions. There are also books for stepparents, remarriage families, stepchildren of all ages, therapists, counselors, and educators to help them deal with stepfamily issues.

Although it is of utmost importance to develop services for stepfamilies, it is also important to recognize that such services are often met with ambivalence and skepticism. This is especially true regarding invented and imported families, for whom reluctance to use services reflects their rejection of seeing themselves as different from non-stepfamilies. Therefore, creativity is required of service developers and providers to work with these families in innovative ways in addition to using traditional clinical and psychoeducational models. For example, two groups were offered concurrently for parents of adolescents. Both groups were offered under the same conditions regarding fee, schedule, location, and facilitator. One group was defined as specific for stepfamilies and the other was not qualified. Three stepparents enrolled in the specific group while six natural and stepparents from stepfamilies joined the general group. Sensitive to the message conveyed by the choice to attend the general group, the facilitator addressed issues relevant to stepfamilies without labeling them as such. The stepparents were then able to use these "threads" and be helped by the group to address their issues.

In addition to direct services to stepfamilies, schools, social services agencies, health services, and other service providers should be encouraged to educate themselves about the dynamics and needs of stepfamilies. For example, the National Council on Family Relations has a focus group on remarriage and stepfamilies to promote recognition of stepfamilies by professional circles.

All the aforementioned resources indicate a change in the right direction; however, they are still far from adequate to address the needs of diverse types of stepfamilies. A variety of such services needs to be further developed and provided across the nation.

## INSTITUTIONALIZING LEGAL ASPECTS OF STEPFAMILIES

Professionals who service stepfamilies need to understand their legal status because of its affects on their lives. Unfortunately, the legal status of step-relationships is unclear and inconsistent between states and within the same states between courts. This section briefly reviews the gaps in laws that apply to stepfamilies. A comprehensive discussion of stepfamilies and the law can be found in Mahoney (1994).

Law usually follows life. Although the social environment rapidly changed to make stepfamilies a common family form, legal aspects of step-relationships have yet to be institutionalized. The confusion regarding the legal status of stepfamilies exists on several levels.

First, legal commentators point out that current federal and state laws do not define clearly stepfamilies and the mutual responsibilities and rights of their members (Fine and Fine, 1992; Mahoney, 1987, 1994). Even when definitions of step-relationships exist, they are not specific enough. For instance, if a stepparent is an adult who lives permanently with children of his/her spouse and acts as a parental figure, many questions remain unanswered: How long do they have to live together before it is considered "permanent"? What does the adult need to do in order to be considered "acting as a parental figure"? What if an adult lives with the child and acts as parent but is not formally married to the biological parent? Cultural differences also may affect what "acting as a parent" means because not all cultures have the same expectations about parenting.

Also, when laws do refer to step-relationships, definitions are inconsistent and different criteria are used for eligibility on the basis of this relationship (Mahoney, 1994). For example, according to the Social Security Act, only stepchildren who live with and are supported by the stepparent are eligible, while according to the Immigration Act the fact that the natural parent is married to the stepparent, who is a U.S. citizen, is enough to make the stepchild eligible to be considered a relative of a U.S. citizen and granted immigration rights. Laws that deal with rights of family members to sue one another (such as abused children suing their abusive parents) and responsibility of parents for their children's actions are applicable to stepfamilies inconsistently and selectively (Mahoney, 1994).

In addition, issues of stepfamilies are treated differently in different states. For example, in about one-sixth of the states, state laws refer specifically to the authorization of visitation rights to stepparents, in another sixth of the states there is a broad reference to visitation rights of nonparents that can be applied to stepparents as well as to other adults, and in other states, there is no legal reference to the issue (Mahoney, 1994).

Because family laws in most states contain no clear and uniform doctrine regarding stepfamilies (Mahoney, 1987), states rely on common law (laws made by judges as opposed to statutory laws that are made by a legislative authority) to resolve step-relationship issues. The problem with leaving decisions mostly to state courts is that opposing conclusions have been reached in similar cases.

Major legal issues regarding stepfamilies pertain to support, custody and visitation, inheritance, and sexual abuse.

## *Support*

The major issues concerning support are whether stepparents should be legally obligated to support stepchildren, the scope of their obligation, how this obligation should be balanced with the obligation of the natural parents and with the obligation stepparents have toward their own natural children from previous marriages, and should the obligation to support a stepchild extend following a termination of the remarriage. Additional questions pertain to financial benefits from employers, welfare services, and so forth. For example, are stepchildren entitled to have their education or camp stays paid for if their stepparent is employed by a workplace that pays for these expenses for their employees' children? If so, does the entitlement differ for children who live with the stepparent from those who live alternately with the stepparent and with the other natural parent? Currently there are no clear legal answers to these questions due to the absence of statutes that directly address stepfamily members' support responsibilities. Ramsey (1986), Mahoney (1987, 1994), and Fine and Fine (1992) analyzed laws and policies embodied in federal and state regulations that affect stepfamilies and showed the gaps and inconsistencies that exist in this terrain.

Traditionally, the general principle is that stepparents' obligations to support stepchildren are mostly voluntary rather than anchored in law. For example, under the regulations of Aid to Families with Dependent Children (AFDC), a majority of states maintain that the income of a stepparent is available for support of a stepchild, but only fourteen states actually require stepparents to support stepchildren. This requirement is valid only as long as the remarriage exists, and only five of these states have statutes to impose it. No state requires stepparents to support stepchildren who do not live with them (Victor, Robbins, and Bassett, 1991). Nor does any state require a stepparent to support stepchildren if the remarriage ends, even in cases where support was required during the remarriage (Fine and Fine, 1992). However, in a number of cases, courts have required stepparents to support stepchildren even after they had divorced the natural parents of these children and did not live with the children or see them anymore (Redman, 1991). In several states, the income of the noncustodial stepparent is taken into consideration in deciding how much child support his/her spouse—the noncustodial natural parent—has to pay. This may create a situation in which a person is liable to support children with whom he/she may have hardly any contact.

The legal stand regarding the balance between obligations to natural and stepchildren is also inconsistent. According to AFDC regulations, natural children have priority over stepchildren in the allocation of the stepparent's income, but under the Social Security Act, stepchildren are equated with natural children and are eligible to similar benefits. In some states, stepchildren are considered "equitably adopted," which means that they have the same rights as adopted children. In nearly all the states, the obligation of a stepparent to support a stepchild is more limited than the obligation to natural children, but in certain cases, courts required stepparents to support stepchildren as they would natural children.

In dealing with the obligations of stepparents to support stepchildren, the courts used three principles: in loco parentis, contract, and equitable estoppel.

## In Loco Parentis

This term means "in place of a parent." According to this principle, an adult with effective control of a child can take a parental role and assume parental obligations. This principle has been applied to stepparents. It requires stepparents to see that a minor child is properly educated, housed, and fed (Redman, 1991). The status of in loco parentis is voluntary and depends on the wish of the stepparent, who can take this role and terminate it at any time. The intentions of stepparents to serve in loco parentis is deduced from what they say about their relationships with their stepchildren and from their behavior. This standard was adopted in some areas (workers' compensations) and not in others (inheritance rights). In loco parentis laws are enforceable only in some states and only as long as the parent and stepparent are married (Mahoney, 1994).

## Contract

Stepparents may be obliged to support stepchildren if they commit in a contract to do so. This contract can be in writing or verbal. However, precedents indicate that courts tend to enforce such contracts only when they are specific (as opposed to a general promise of a stepparent to treat stepchildren as his/her own) and supported by behavior that clearly implies the intention of the stepparent to be responsible for the stepchild (Mahoney, 1994).

## Equitable Estoppel

This principle applies when a person commits, verbally or in action, to certain obligations and another person relies on this commitment to choose a certain course of action. If the first person later decides to deny the original commitment and this denial has detrimental consequences for the other person, the latter is eligible to any claim that will prevent these consequences. For example, a remarried stepfather promises to support his stepchildren if his wife stays home to raise the children from previous marriages of both spouses, and therefore, she did not develop her career and earning potential. If the couple divorces, the lawyer of the wife may seek to hold the husband accountable for his original commitment on the basis of this principle. However, precedents show that courts seldom apply equitable estoppel and only if the behavior of the stepparent eliminated any possibility for the noncustodial natural parent to support the children.

## Custody and Visitation

Custody during and after the remarriage and visitation rights if the remarriage ends are also unclear. Should stepparents be recognized as having the legal rights of custodians when they participate in raising their stepchildren, such as giving consent to medical treatment of a stepchild or attending a parent-teacher meeting and being advised regarding the stepchildren's educational records? Can stepchildren assume the surname of the stepfather who raises them? Does a stepparent have the right to maintain contact with stepchildren if he/she divorces the natural parent of the child? Should stepparents have such rights, to what extent, and under which circumstances? Although currently there are more possibilities than in the past to maintain stepparent-stepchild relationships if the remarriage is terminated, there is still a void in the law, and the issue creates turmoil and hurt for both stepparents and their stepchildren.

In recent years, there has been a movement to repair this void, but the change has been slow (Fine and Fine, 1992). In many states, a person who is not a biological parent can seek custody of a child under certain conditions, such as the nature of the relationship with the child and the adult's ability to sufficiently address the needs of the child. This includes stepparents who have dissolved their marriage to the biological parent of the child (Victor, Robbins, and Bassett, 1991). Several states specify stepparents as eligible to seek such custody, whereas other states include stepparents among "third parties" such as grandparents (Fine and Fine, 1992; Mahoney, 1994).

However, it is extremely difficult and most unlikely for stepparents to be granted custody after the remarriage ends. This sometimes may create detrimental consequences for stepchildren and stepparents alike. For example, Elissa's mother was pregnant with her when she divorced Ed, who spent the next twelve years in Japan. During these years, he talked to Elissa on the phone two or three times a year, visited her four times, and did not write to her except to send her a birthday present and New Year's cards. George, whom Elissa's mother married when the girl was two months old, was the only father that Elissa ever knew. His large family accepted Elissa and her mother warmly, while no contact was maintained with Ed's extended family. When Elissa was twelve, her mother died in a car accident. Her natural father was granted custody on his demand and moved Elissa to live with him and his Japanese girlfriend in Japan. Elissa's and George's requests to grant custody to George, whom both of them considered "her real father," were denied. In Japan, Elissa became depressed, did not do well in school, and was socially withdrawn. A day after her eighteenth birthday, she flew back to live with George and his new wife and little boy despite Ed's protest.

Although custody is hard to achieve, in a considerable number of states, stepparents may be granted access to stepchildren even after the stepparent has divorced the natural parent. This is guided by considerations of the interest of the child rather than by rights of either the natural parent or the stepparent. However, these decisions are often made by courts rather than rooted in legislation.

It is also very difficult to change a stepchild's surname so that the stepchild carries the same surname as his/her remarried mother (if she changed her name following the remarriage) and half-siblings that are born in the remarriage. Sometimes children wish to have this change because they are the only ones in the family with a different name. Such a change cannot be done without the consent of the natural noncustodial father unless the father neglected the child constantly for a long time or was involved in serious misconduct.

## Inheritance

Rights of inheritance are an additional issue that pertains to step-relationships. Legal aspects of the relationship between the remarried couple are more clear than the relationships between step-kin. Yet, a death or redivorce of a remarried person may also raise questions of the eligibility of the new spouse to assets that have been acquired fully or partially during a previous marriage or the period between marriages. Experts in the field recommend that a prenuptial agreement and will be prepared to address such issues (Kaslow, 1993). The process of negotiating such an agreement may be different for diverse types of families, depending on their emphasis on the past and their focal subsystem.

Although generally step-kin do not inherit from each other, in some states, children can inherit from a stepparent if there are no other beneficiaries (Fine and Fine, 1992). Yet, step-kin face difficulties in establishing their right of inheritance, unless they are specifically named in a will.

## Sexual Abuse

As mentioned in Chapter 3, sexual abuse is a crucial issue in stepfamilies because the norms regarding sexual relationships between stepparents and stepchildren or stepsiblings are not as clear and absolute as those regarding blood or adoptive relatives.

Incest and sexual abuse are criminal. Unlike the strict ban on such situations in the past, currently most states allow close step-relatives to marry and do not include such relationships in the legal definition of incest. In nineteen states, step-relatives are included in laws that deal with criminal sexual activities, while other states take into consideration the age of the victim and the nature of the relationship with the abuser. In about a third of the states, incest laws do not regulate step-relatives at all (Mahoney, 1994). In many states, the legal protection of minor stepchildren against sexual abuse is via other laws rather than incest laws. There is no nationwide consensus on whether laws concerning sexual relationships apply to step-relatives as long the remarriage exists or even after the natural parent divorces the stepparent or dies.

Some of the social issues and emotional reactions involved in such relationships were illustrated in the public debate regarding the affair of movie director Woody Allen with actress Mia Farrow's adopted daughter.

In summary, with some exceptions, step-relationships are not recognized as a legal status (Mahoney, 1994). The absence of laws regarding stepfamilies both reflects and maintains their status as a marginalized group. In light of stepfamilies becoming a major family type in our society and the ambiguity and inconsistency of legal aspects of step-relationships, the time has come to clearly define legal responsibilities and rights of people involved in step-relationships and to establish mechanisms to enforce them. Calls for such initiatives have been intensified recently (see Mahoney, 1987, 1994; Redman, 1991; Fine and Fine, 1992). The American Bar Association Family Law Section dedicated its Spring 1991 issue of its professional journal to discussing issues of stepfamilies and established a standing committee on stepfamilies (Buser, 1991). This committee drafted a proposal for a Model Act Establishing Rights and Duties of Stepparents (Tenenbaum, 1991). Lawmakers must decide if a stepchild and stepparent have a legal relationship immediately after the remarriage or within a short time (several laws include stepchildren nine to twelve months after their natural parent remarried), if the stepparent and stepchild have to live together, if the rights of stepchildren and natural children are similar or different (in several laws, the obligations to stepchildren come after the obligations to natural children), and if the relationship remains if the parent and stepparent divorce or the parent dies.

Some scholars recommend that mutual rights and obligations of step-kin will depend on the nature of their relationship, the length of time they lived together, the child's age, and the role the stepparent has been playing in the child's life (see Mahoney, 1987; Buser, 1991). Others suggested adopting principles of the English Children

Act, which permits granting stepparents rights that are similar to those of biological parents (Fine and Fine, 1992). Whichever principles are adopted, it is clear that the current situation is unhealthy and that laws for stepfamilies need to be developed.

## *SUMMARY*

This chapter discusses changes that society at large needs to make to adapt to the new social reality, in which stepfamilies are becoming the most common type of family. Such changes include developing appropriate concepts and references that do not carry negative connotations and are relevant to stepfamilies. In addition, a more realistic picture of stepfamilies needs to be presented in the media. Special services to address their unique needs should be implemented. Finally, there is a need for a clear legal definition of stepfamilies and for legal regulations of mutual obligations and rights of step-kin on federal and state levels.

# Chapter 15

# Stepfamilies: The Future

Because the social phenomenon of stepfamilies is currently in the process of multiplying and developing, any effort to capture their complexity, describe their variety, and understand their experience at this point is a "work in progress." This book is no exception. We are currently developing a broad understanding of the uniqueness of these families, which are on their way to being the most common family in Western society. By the beginning of the new millennium, half of the married adults and over one-third of the children in the United States are expected to live in stepfamilies, and the rest of the world follows a similar pattern.

This book belongs to the "new generation" of stepfamily literature that focuses on in-depth understanding of the variations and subtleties of the step-experience. The first wave of literature regarding stepfamilies was characterized by viewing stepfamilies in comparison to non-stepfamilies, a perspective that yielded mostly pathologizing conclusions regarding stepfamilies. Stepfamilies were considered a less than ideal family configuration. The stepfamily was labeled an "incomplete institution" and was blamed for negative affects on the psychosocial well-being of its members.

The next wave of books and articles about stepfamilies underscored viewing them as a different species with unique characteristics and dynamics. This liberated stepfamily literature from the pathologizing perspective and opened the door for "familial diversity." As alternative family configurations multiplied and gained growing legitimacy, researchers, academics, and practitioners started to advocate for seeing stepfamilies as a normative family type. Despite this, negative stereotypes of stepfamilies still exist because myths and biases take a long time to disappear. The fact that the vast majority of books and articles are still based on studying families who were in counseling probably helped to perpetuate the "deficit" nature ascribed to stepfamilies.

We are currently in the midst of the third wave of research, which focuses on understanding nonclinical stepfamilies. This book joins the few that examine stepfamilies that "made it." In the spirit of learning from success, it makes a lot of sense to learn from stepfamilies that are functioning well and are satisfied with how they do it. Our best teachers about stepfamilies are stepfamilies themselves.

Successful stepfamilies are not made from one mold. They are a rather complex group that includes diverse types, each different from the others in their dynamic characteristics. Three distinctive types have been identified and discussed in depth. However, it is quite possible that additional types of well-functioning stepfamilies currently exist and/or will be born as the population of stepfamilies continues to grow. For example, given the number of children who grow up in stepfamilies today, many stepfamilies in the future will include adults who have had the experience as children of being stepchildren, stepgrandchildren, and step- and half-siblings. They will be able to provide their children with role models not available to most children who are currently growing up in stepfamilies. Also, it is reasonable to anticipate that the social atmosphere regarding stepfamilies will change. Growing numbers of stepfamilies in the future will live in a society that is more familiar with stepfamilies. This will hopefully lead to a cultural climate that is more favorable to stepfamilies.

To bring about such changes, a lot remains to be done. We need to conduct research to learn more about all types of stepfamilies. We need to know how the experience of growing up and living in different types of stepfamilies affects members, especially children, who have a limited say, if any, about the type of their stepfamily. We need to understand the "careers" of stepfamilies of diverse types and how they develop along their step–life cycle.

The whole field of ethnic and cross-cultural aspects of stepfamilies has hardly been explored. Is the experience similar in different social, racial, religious, and cultural environments? Is it different? How is it similar or different? Which types of stepfamilies are encouraged and discouraged in different cultures? How are these types compatible with particular cultures' values? How do different cultures shape their own version of the different types of stepfamilies?

Another set of questions to be studied deals with understanding coping and success of stepfamilies. What are ways of coping with the step-situation that prove useful? What are strengths of different types of stepfamilies? To be able to address all these and many other questions, considerable research needs to be done.

However, until such research is conducted, large-scale changes should be fostered, including changing the way society sees stepfamilies and the way stepfamilies perceive themselves. Further normalizing of stepfamily experience should be encouraged. Social mechanisms that promote the idea of stepfamilies as a legitimate family configuration in everyday reality need to be put into action.

Moving further away from the pathologizing perception of stepfamilies as a "deficit institution" to stepfamilies as an additional legitimate family configuration is only one much needed change. An additional change that we as a society should seek is understanding the diversity and richness of stepfamilies. New types of stepfamilies are constantly being born. A growing phenomenon is that of remarriage in old age. This creates a growing number of a new type of stepfamily in which adults become members of stepfamilies. Such families struggle with their own unique issues. For example, much has been written about the "sandwich" generation, people in their forties and fifties who cope with their children on one hand and elderly parents on the other. Recently, debates have begun about the place of the new spouse of the elderly parent in this picture. To what degree should an adult whose elderly parent remarried be committed to their new "stepparent?" Does such a commitment persist after their own parent perishes? A middle-aged participant in a recent workshop that I facilitated in a conference described his situation: "My mother died a number of years ago and my then eighty-five-year-old father remarried. Eighteen months later he passed away. Only now I realized that I was a member of a stepfamily for eighteen months." Another participant asked him, "Why do you say that you were a stepson? Is your stepmother dead?" A heated argument developed about whether the step-relationship in such instances outlives the life of the remarried natural parent. Such debates are expected to enter the social arena more and more as the number of old-age remarriages increases.

In conclusion, as the numbers and complexity of stepfamilies are growing, more and more needs to be done to understand them and develop for them an appropriate place in society as well as build relevant services to address their unique needs. This book is a modest contribution toward these ends.

# References

Ahrons, C.R. (1980). A crisis of family transition and change. *Family Relations,* 29, 533-540.

Ahrons, C.R. and Rodgers, R.H. (1987). *Divorced families: A multidisciplinary developmental view.* New York: W.W. Norton.

Amato, P.R. (1987). Family processes in one-parent, stepparent and intact families: The child's point-of-view. *Journal of Marriage and the Family,* 49(2), 327-337.

Andersen, T. (1991). *The reflecting team: Dialogues and dialogues about dialogues.* New York: W.W. Norton.

Atwood, J. D. and Zebersky, R. (1996). Using social construction therapy with the REM family. In C.A. Everett (Ed.), *Understanding stepfamilies: Their structure and dynamics.* Binghamton, NY: The Haworth Press, pp. 134-162.

Baer, J. (1972). *The second wife: How to live happily with a man who has been married before.* New York: Doubleday.

Baptiste, D.A. (1987a). The gay and lesbian stepparent family. In F. Bozett (Ed.), *Gay and lesbian parents.* New York: Praeger, pp. 112-137.

Baptiste, D.A. (1987b). Psychotherapy with gay/lesbian couples and their children in "stepfamilies": A challenge for marriage and family therapists. *Journal of Homosexuality,* 14(1-2), 223-238.

Baptiste, D.A. (1993). Immigrant families, adolescents and acculturation: Insights for therapists. In B.H. Settles, D.E. Hanks, and M.B. Sussman (Eds.), *Families on the move: Migration, immigration, emigration, and mobility.* Binghamton, NY: The Haworth Press, pp. 341-364.

Baptiste, D.A. (1995). Therapy with a lesbian stepfamily with an electively mute child: A case report. *Journal of Family Psychotherapy,* 6(1), 1-14.

Beer, W.R. (1992). *American stepfamilies.* New Brunswick, NJ: Transaction Publishers.

Benson von der Ohe, E. (1987). *First and second marriages.* New York: Praeger.

Berger, R. (1993). *Past orientation, acceptance/rejection of difference and focal sub-system in non-clinical stepfamilies.* Jerusalem: The Hebrew University of Jerusalem.

Berger, R. (1995). Three types of stepfamilies. *Journal of Divorce and Remarriage,* 24(1-2), 35-49.

Berger, R. (1997). Immigrant stepfamilies. *Contemporary Family Therapy,* 19(3), 361-370.

Blumenfeld, W.J. and Raymond, D. (1988). *Looking at gay and lesbian life.* Boston: Beacon.

Bogolub, E.B. (1995). *Helping families through divorce.* New York: Springer Publishing.

Bohannan, P. (1970). Divorce chains households of remarriage and multiple divorces. In P. Bohannan (Ed.), *Divorce and after.* New York: Doubleday, pp. 113-123.

Bohannon, P. (1975). *Stepfathers and the mental health of their children.* Final Report, Western Behavioral Sciences Institute, La Jolla, California.

Boss, P. and Greenberg, J. (1984). Family boundary ambiguity: A new variable in family stress theory. *Family Process,* 23(4), 535-546.

Boszormenyi-Nagy, I. and Spark, G. (1973). *Invisible loyalties.* New York: Harper & Row.

Bowen, M. (1978). *Family therapy in clinical practice.* Northvale, NJ: Jason Aronson.

Bowerman, C.E. and Irish, D.P. (1962). Some relationships of stepchildren to their parents. *Marriage and Family Living,* 24(2), 113-121.

Boyd-Franklin, N. (1989). *Black families in therapy.* New York: Guilford Press.

Bradt, J.O. and Bradt Moynihan, C. (1988). Resources for remarried families. In M.A. Karpel (Ed.), *Family resources.* New York: Guilford, pp. 272-304.

Bray, J.H., Berger, S.H., and Boethel, C.L. (1994). Role integration and marital adjustment in stepfather families. In K. Pasley and M. Ihinger-Tallman (Eds.), *Stepparenting: Issues in theory, research, and practice.* Westport, CT: Greenwood, pp. 69-86.

Bumpass, L., Sweet, J., and Martin, M.C. (1990). Changing patterns of remarriage. *Journal of Marriage and the Family,* 52(3), 747-756.

Burgoyne, J. and Clark, D. (1984). *Making a go of it: A study of stepfamilies in Sheffield.* Boston: Routledge and Kegan Paul.

Burr, W.R. and Klein, S.R. (1994). *Reexamining family stress.* Thousand Oaks, CA: Sage.

Burt, M.S. and Burt, R.B. (1996). *Stepfamilies: The step by step model of brief therapy.* New York: Brunner/Mazel.

Buser, P.J. (1991). Introduction: The first generation of stepchildren. *Family Law Quarterly,* 25(1), 1-18.

Carter, B. and McGoldrick, M. (Eds.) (1990). *The changing family life cycle.* Boston: Allyn and Bacon.

Chandler, J. (1991). *Women without husbands: An exploration of the margins of marriage.* New York: St. Martin's.

Cherlin, A. (1978). Remarriage as an incomplete institution. *American Journal of Sociology,* 84(3), 634-650.

Cherlin, A. (1992). *Marriage, divorce and remarriage.* Cambridge, MA: Harvard University Press.

Clingempeel, W.G. and Brand, E. (1985). Quasi-kin relationships, structural complexity and marital quality in stepfamilies: A replication, extension and clinical implications. *Family Relations,* 34(3), 401-409.

Clingempeel, W.G., Brand, E., and Segal, S. (1987). A multilevel-multivariable-developmental perspective for future research on stepfamilies. In K. Pasley and M. Ihinger-Tallman (Eds.), *Remarriage and stepparenting today: Current research and theory*. New York: Guilford, pp. 65-93.

Crosbie-Burnett, M. and Giles-Sims, J. (1989). Adolescent power in stepfamilies: A test of normative resource theory. *Journal of Marriage and the Family*, 51(4), 1065-1078.

Crosbie-Burnett, M. and Helmbrecht, L. (1993). A descriptive empirical study of gay male stepfamilies. *Family Relations*, 42(3), 256-262.

Drachman, D. and Shen-Ryan, A. (1991). Immigrants and refugees. In A. Gitterman (Ed.), *Social work practice with vulnerable populations*. New York: Columbia University Press, pp. 618-646.

Dreyfus, E.A. (1990, October). Antenuptial agreements revisited: Intimate negotiations. *Independent Practitioner*. Phoenix, AZ: APA Division #42, pp. 27-30.

Du Canto, J.N. (1991, March). Passing your wealth on to others: How to avoid financial pitfalls. *USA Today Magazine*, pp. 82-83.

Fast I. and Cain, A.C. (1966). The step-parent role: Potential for disturbances in family functioning. *American Journal of Orthopsychiatry*, 36(3), 485-491.

Fine, M.A. (1996). The clarity and content of the stepparent role: A review of the literature. In C.A. Everett (Ed.), *Understanding stepfamilies: Their structure and dynamics*. Binghamton, NY: The Haworth Press, pp. 19-34.

Fine, M.A. and Fine, D.R. (1992). Recent changes in laws affecting stepfamilies: Suggestions for legal reform. *Family relations*, 41(3), 334-340.

Finkelhor, D.M. (1984). *Child sexual abuse: New theory and research*. New York: Free Press.

Fishman, B. (1983). The economic behavior of stepfamilies. *Family Relations*, 32(3), 359-365.

Furstenberg, F.F. and Spanier, J.A. (1984). *Recycling the family: Remarriage after divorce*. Beverly Hills, CA: Sage.

Ganong, L.H. and Coleman, M. (1987). Effects of parental remarriage on children. In K. Pasley and M. Ihinger-Tallman (Eds.), *Remarriage and stepparenting*. New York: Guilford, pp. 94-140.

Ganong, L.H. and Coleman, M. (1994a). *Remarried family relationships*. Thousand Oaks, CA: Sage.

Ganong, L.H. and Coleman, M. (1994b). Adolescent stepchild-stepparent relationship: Changes over time. In K. Pasley and M. Ihinger-Tallman (Eds.), *Stepparenting: Issues in theory, research, and practice*. Westport, CT: Greenwood, pp. 87-104.

Garfinkel, P. (1990). The best man. *The New York Times*, October 14: 24, 56.

Giles-Sims, J. (1987). Social exchange in remarried families. In K. Pasley and M. Ihinger-Tallman (Eds.), *Remarriage and stepparenting*. New York: Guilford, pp. 141-163.

Glick, P.C. (1989). Remarried families, stepfamilies, and stepchildren: A brief demographic profile. *Family Relations*, 38(1), 24-27.

Goetting, A. (1983). The relative strength of the husband-wife and parent-child dyads in remarriage: A test of the Hsu model. *Journal of Comparative Family Studies*, Spring, 14(1), 117-128.

Goldenberg, I. and Goldenberg, H. (1996). *Family therapy: An overview.* Pacific Grove, CA: Brooks/Cole.

Goldner, V. (1982). Remarriage family: Structure, system, future. In J.C. Hansen and L. Messinger (Eds.), *Therapy with remarriage families.* Rockville, MD: Aspen Systems Corporation, pp. 187-206.

Goldstein, E. (1984). "Homo Sovieticus" in transition: Psychoanalysis and problems of social adjustment. *Journal of the American Academy of Psychoanalysis,* 12(1), 115-126.

Gottman Schwartz, J. (1990). Children of gay and lesbian parents. In F. Bozett and M.B. Sussman (Eds.), *Homosexuality and family relations.* Binghamton, NY: Harrington Park Press, pp. 177-196.

Gould, J. and Kolb, W.L. (Eds.) (1964). *A dictionary of the social sciences.* New York: Free Press.

Green, P. (1978). *A second mother for Martha.* New York: Human Sciences Press.

Groll-Barnes, J., Tompson, P., and Burchard, N. (1989). Stepfamilies in Britain. Paper presented at the First International Congress of Family Therapy, Dublin.

Gross, P.E. (1986). Defining post-divorce remarriage families: A typology based on the subjective perceptions of children. *Journal of Divorce,* 10(1-2), 205-217.

Gurman, A.S. and Kniskern, D.P. (1981). *Handbook of family therapy.* New York: Brunner/Mazel.

Halberstadt, A. (1992). The Soviet Jewish family: A cultural perspective. In L. Orenstein (Ed.), *Immigration and resettlement issues facing Jewish emigres from the former Soviet Union.* New York: The Board of Family and Children Services, pp. 2-12.

Hartin, N.W. (1990). Remarriage: Some issues for clients and therapists. *Australian and New Zealand Journal of Family Therapy,* 11(1), 36-42.

Hartman, A. and Laird, J. (1983). *Family centered social work practice.* New York: Free Press.

Hetherington, E.M. (1993). An overview of the Virginia longitudinal study of divorce and remarriage with a focus on early adolescence. *Journal of Family Psychology,* 7(1), 39-56.

Hetherington, M., Cox, M., and Cox, R. (1981). The aftermath of divorce. In E.M. Hetherington and R.D. Parke (Eds.), *Contemporary readings in child psychology.* New York: McGraw Hill, pp. 99-109.

Hill, R. (1972). *The strengths of black families.* New York: Emerson-Hall.

Hobart, C. (1989). Experiences of remarried families. *Journal of Divorce,* 13(2), 121-144.

Hodder, E. (1985). The stepfamily: An introduction to its problems. *Journal of the Royal Society of Medicine,* 78(Sup. 8), 28-31.

Hughes, C. (1991). *Stepparents: Wicked or wonderful?* Brookfield, VT: Gower.

Jacobson, D. (1996). Incomplete institution or culture shock: Institutional and processual models of stepfamily instability. In C.A. Everett (Ed.), *Understanding stepfamilies: Their structure and dynamics.* Binghamton, NY: The Haworth Press, 3-18.

Kalmuss, D. and Seltzer, J.A. (1986). Continuity of marital behavior in remarriage: The case of spouse abuse. *Journal of Marriage and the Family,* 48(1), 113-120.

Kaslow, F.W. (1988). Remarried couples: The architects of stepfamilies. In J.C. Hansen and F.W. Kaslow (Eds.), *Couples therapy in a family context.* Rockville, MD: Aspen, pp. 33-48.

Kaslow, F.W. (1991). Enter the prenuptial: A prelude to marriage and remarriage. *Behavioral Sciences and the Law,* 9(4), 377-386.

Kaslow, F.W. (1993). Understanding and treating the remarriage family. *Directions in marriage and family therapy,* 1(3) (November), 2-16.

Kaslow F.W. (1996). *Handbook of relational diagnosis.* New York: John Wiley and Sons.

Keshet, J.K. (1987). *Love and power in the stepfamily.* New York: McGraw-Hill.

Kirk, D. (1964). *Shared fate.* New York: Free Press.

Kirk, D. (1981). *Adoptive kinship.* Toronto: Butterworth.

Koestler, A. (1975). *The act of creation.* London: Picador.

Korittko, A. (1987). Family therapy for the family in transition. Paper presented at the International Conference of Family Therapy, Prague.

Kupisch, S. (1987). Children and stepfamilies. In A. Thomas and J. Grimes (Eds.), *Children's needs: Psychological perspectives.* Washington, DC: National Association of Psychologists, pp. 578-585.

Kurdek, L.A. (1989). Relationship quality for newly married husbands and wives: Marital history, stepchildren and individual difference predictors. *Journal of Marriage and the Family,* 51(4), 1047-1064.

Landau-Stanton, J. (1985). Adolescents, families, and cultural transitions: A treatment model. In A. Mirkin and S. Koman (Eds.), *Handbook of adolescents and family therapy.* New York: Gardner Press, pp. 363-381.

Langner, T.S. and Michael, S.T. (1963). *Life stress and mental health.* New York: Free Press.

Larson, J. (1992). Understanding stepfamilies. *American Demographics,* 14(7), 36-38.

Lax, W.D. (1991). The reflecting team and the initial consultation. In T. Andersen, *The reflecting team: Dialogues and dialogues about dialogues.* New York: W.W. Norton, 127-142.

Lax, W.D. (1994). Offering reflections. In S. Friedman (Ed.), *The reflecting team in action.* New York: Guilford Press, 145-166.

Logan, M.L., Freeman, E.M., and McRoy, R.G. (Eds) (1990). *Social work practice with black families.* New York: Longman.

MacDonald, W.L. and DeMaris, A. (1995). Remarriage, stepchildren and marital conflict: Challenges to the incomplete institutionalization hypothesis. *Journal of Marriage and the Family,* 57(2), 387-398.

Maddox, B. (1975). *The half parent: Living with other people's children.* New York: Signet.

Mahoney, M. (1987). Stepfamilies in the federal law. *University of Pittsburgh Law Review,* 48(1-2), 491-537.

Mahoney, M. (1994). *Stepfamilies and the law.* Ann Arbor, MI: University of Michigan Press.

Manfra, J.A. and Dykstra, R.R. (1985). Serial marriage and the origins of the black stepfamily: The Rowanty evidence. *Journal of American History,* 72(1), 18-44.

Martin, D. and Martin, M. (1992). *Stepfamilies in therapy.* San Francisco, CA: Jossey-Bass.

Martin, T.C. and Bumpass, L.L. (1989). Recent trends in marital disruption. *Demography,* 26(1), 37-51.

Mathews, B.L. (1989). *Systemic family functioning in nuclear families and stepfamilies.* PhD Dissertation, University of Texas.

McCubbin, H.I., Cauble, A.E., and Patterson, J.M. (1982). *Family stress, coping and social support.* Springfield, IL: Charles C Thomas.

McGoldrick, M. and Carter, B. (1989). Forming a remarried family. In B. Carter and M. McGoldrick (Eds.), *The changing family life cycle.* Boston: Allyn and Bacon, pp. 399-429.

McGoldrick, M., Giordano, J., and Pearce, J.K. (1996). *Ethnicity and family therapy.* New York: Guilford.

McIntyre, D.H. (1994). Gay parents and child custody: A struggle under the legal system. *Mediation Quarterly,* 12(2), 135-149.

Messinger, L. (1976). Remarriage between divorced people with children from previous marriage: A proposal for preparation for remarriage. *Journal of Marriage and Counseling,* 2(2), 193-200.

Meyers, G. (1992). Family therapy with divorcing and remarried families. In J.D. Atwood (Ed.), *Family therapy: A systemic approach.* Chicago: Nelson-Hall, pp. 159-172.

Mirsky, J. and Prawer, L. (1992). *To immigrate as an adolescent.* Jerusalem: Van Leer Institute and Elka.

Morrison, K. and Stollman, W. (1996). Stepfamily assessment: An integrated model. In C.A. Everett (Ed.), *Understanding stepfamilies: Their structure and dynamics.* Binghamton, NY: The Haworth Press, pp. 163-182.

Nelson, M. and Nelson, G.K. (1982). Problems of equity in the reconstituted family: A social exchange analysis. *Family Relations,* 31(2), 223-231.

Nichols, M.P. and Schwartz, R.C. (1995). *Family therapy: Concepts and methods.* Boston: Allyn and Bacon.

Noy, D. (1991). Wicked stepmothers in Roman society and imagination. *Journal of Family History,* 16(4), 345-361.

Olson D.H., Sprenkle, D.H., and Ruseii, C.S. (1979). Circumplex model of marital and family systems: I. Cohesion, adaptability dimensions, family types and clinical applications. *Family Process,* 18(1), 3-28.

Papernow, P. (1993). *Becoming a stepfamily: Patterns of development in remarried families.* San Francisco, CA: Jossey-Bass.

Parish, T.S. and Coopland, T.F. (1979). The relationship between self-concept and evaluation of parents and stepparents. *Journal of Psychology,* 10, 135-138.

Pasley, K., Dollahite, D., and Ihinger-Tallman, M. (1993). Bridging the gap: Clinical applications of research findings on the spouse and stepparent roles in remarriage. *Family Relations,* 42(3), 315-322.

Pasley, K. and Ihinger-Tallman, M. (1982). Remarried family life: Supports and constraints. In G. Rowe (Ed.), *Building family strengths 4.* Lincoln, NB: University of Nebraska Press, pp. 367-383.

Pasley, K. and Ihinger-Tallman, M. (Eds.) (1987). *Remarriage and stepfamilies: Current research and theory.* New York: Guilford.

Patterson, C.J. (1992). Children of lesbian and gay parents. *Child development,* 63(5), 1025-1042.

Perkins, R.F. and Kahan, J.P. (1979). An empirical comparison of natural father and stepfather family systems. *Family Process,* 18(2), 175-183.

Phipps, E. (1986). Sexual tensions in a remarried family. *Contemporary Family Therapy,* 8(3), 208-216.

Pill, C.J. (1990). Stepfamilies: Redefining the family. *Family Relations,* 39(2), 186-193.

Prosen, S.S. and Farmer, J.H. (1982). Understanding stepfamilies: Issues and implications for counselors. *The Personnel and Guidance Journal,* 60(7), 393-374.

Quick, D.S., Newman, B.M., and McKenry, P. (1996). Influences on the quality of the stepmother-adolescent relationship. In C.A. Everett (Ed.), *Understanding stepfamilies: Their structure and dynamics.* Binghamton, NY: The Haworth Press, pp. 99-116.

Ramsey, S.H. (1986). Stepparent support of stepchildren: The changing legal context and the need for empirical policy research. *Family Relations,* 35(3), 363-369.

Redman, R.M. (1991). The support of children in blended families: A call for change. *Family Law Quarterly,* 25(1), 83-94.

Robinson, M. (1991). *Family transformation through divorce and remarriage.* London: Tavistock.

Roosevelt, R. and Lofas, J. (1976). *Living in step.* New York: Stein and Day.

Rosenberg, B. and Hajal, F. (1985). Stepsiblings relationships in remarried families. *Social Casework,* 66(5), 287-292.

Rosenberg, M. (1965). *Society and the adolescent self-image.* Princeton, NJ: Princeton University Press.

Rosenfeld, J.M. (1989). *Emergence from extreme poverty.* Paris: Science et Service, Quotre Mond.

Russel, D.E.H. (1984). The prevalence and seriousness of incestuous abuse: Stepfathers versus biological fathers. *Child Abuse and Neglect,* 8(1), 15-22.

Sager, C.J., Brown, H.S., Crohn, H.M., and Engel, T. (1983). *Treating remarried families.* New York: Brunner/Mazel.

Saint-Jacques, M.C. (1996). Role strain prediction in stepfamilies. In C.A. Everett (Ed.), *Understanding stepfamilies: Their structure and dynamics.* Binghamton, NY: The Haworth Press, pp. 51-72.

Schulman, G. (1972). Myths that intrude on the adaptation of the stepfamily. *Social Casework,* 53(3), 131-139.

Schultz, N.C., Schultz, C.L., and Olson, D.H. (1991). Couple strengths and stressors in complex and simple stepfamilies in Australia. *Journal of Marriage and the Family,* 53(3), 555-564.

Skolnick, A.S. and Skolnick J.H. (1992). *The family in transition.* New York: HarperCollins.

Sluzki, C.E. (1983). Process, structure and world view: Towards an integrated view of systemic models in family therapy. *Family Process,* 22(4), 469-476.

Smith, J.W. and Carlsson, I.M. (1990). *The creative process: A functional model based on empirical studies from early childhood to middle age.* Madison, CT: International Universities Press.

Spruijt, A.P. (1996). Adolescents from stepfamilies, single-parent families and (in) stable intact families in the Netherlands. In C.A. Everett (Ed.), *Understanding stepfamilies: Their structure and dynamics.* Binghamton, NY: The Haworth Press, pp. 115-132.

Stacpoole, M. (1988). *Legal points for stepfamilies.* Cambridge, MA: National Stepfamily Association, # 6.

Stevenson, B. (1976). *The MacMillan book of proverbs, maxims and famous phrases.* New York: MacMillan.

Stewart, E.C.P. (1986). The surival stage of intercultural communication. *International Christian University Bulletin,* 1(1), 109-121.

Strommen, E.F. (1989). Hidden branches and growing pains: Homosexuality and the family tree. *Marriage and Family Review,* 14(3-4), 9-34.

Tenenbaum, J.D. (1991). Legislation for stepfamilies: The Family Law Standing Committee Report. *Family Law Quarterly,* 25(1), 137-141.

Touliatos, J., Perlmutter, B.F., and Strous, M.A. (Eds.) (1990). *Handbook of family measurement techniques.* Newbury Park, CA: Sage.

Victor, R. S., Robbins, M.A., and Bassett, S. (1991). Statutory review of third-party rights regarding custody, visitation, and support. *Family Law Quarterly,* 25(1), 19-57.

Visher, E.B. and Visher, J.S. (1988). *Old loyalties, new ties.* New York: Brunner/Mazel.

Visher, E.B. and Visher, J.S. (1990). Dynamics of successful stepfamilies. *Journal of Divorce and Remarriage,* 14(1), 3-12.

Visher, E.B. and Visher, J.S. (1996). *Therapy with stepfamilies.* New York: Brunner/Mazel.

Wald, E. (1981). *The remarried family: Challenge and promise.* New York: Family Service Association of America.

White, L.K. and Booth, A. (1985). The quality and stability of remarriage: The role of stepchildren. *American Sociological Review,* 50(5), 689-698.

White, M. (1989). *Selected papers.* Adelaide, Australia: Dulwich Center Publications.

Whiteside, M.F. (1982). Remarriage: A family development process. *Journal of Marital and Family Therapy,* 8(2), 59-68.

Whitsett, D. and Land, H. (1992). The development of a role strain index for stepparents. *Families in Society,* 73(1), 14-22.

Wilson, B.F. and Clarke, S.C. (1992). Remarriage: A demographic profile. *Journal of Family Issues,* 13(2), 123-141.

Wolpert-Lur, A. and Bross, A. (1982). The formation of the reconstituted family system: Processes, problems, and treatment goals. In A. Bross and P. Papp (Eds.), *Family Therapy.* New York: Methun, pp. 114-127.

Zucker-Anderson, J. and White, G.D. (1986). An empirical investigation of interaction and relationship patterns in functional and dysfunctional nuclear families and stepfamilies. *Family Process,* 25(3), 407-422.

# Index

# Order Your Own Copy of
# This Important Book for Your Personal Library!

## STEPFAMILIES
## A Multi-Dimensional Perspective

_____ in hardbound at $49.95 (ISBN: 0–7890–0280–9)

_____ in softbound at $29.95 (ISBN: 0–7890–0281–7)

| | |
|---|---|
| COST OF BOOKS _____ | ☐ **BILL ME LATER:** ($5 service charge will be added)<br>(Bill-me option is good on US/Canada/Mexico orders only;<br>not good to jobbers, wholesalers, or subscription agencies.) |
| OUTSIDE USA/CANADA/<br>MEXICO: ADD 20%_____ | |
| POSTAGE & HANDLING_____<br>(US: $3.00 for first book & $1.25<br>for each additional book)<br>Outside US: $4.75 for first book<br>& $1.75 for each additional book) | ☐ Check here if billing address is different from<br>shipping address and attach purchase order and<br>billing address information.<br><br>Signature _____ |
| SUBTOTAL_____ | ☐ **PAYMENT ENCLOSED: $**_____ |
| IN CANADA: ADD 7% GST_____ | ☐ **PLEASE CHARGE TO MY CREDIT CARD.** |
| STATE TAX_____<br>(NY, OH & MN residents, please<br>add appropriate local sales tax) | ☐ Visa   ☐ MasterCard   ☐ AmEx   ☐ Discover<br>☐ Diner's Club |
| **FINAL TOTAL**_____<br>(If paying in Canadian funds,<br>convert using the current<br>exchange rate. UNESCO<br>coupons welcome.) | Account # _____<br><br>Exp. Date _____<br><br>Signature _____ |

Prices in US dollars and subject to change without notice.

NAME _____

INSTITUTION _____

ADDRESS _____

CITY _____

STATE/ZIP _____

COUNTRY _____ COUNTY (NY residents only) _____

TEL _____ FAX _____

E-MAIL_____
May we use your e-mail address for confirmations and other types of information? ☐ Yes    ☐ No

Order From Your Local Bookstore or Directly From
**The Haworth Press, Inc.**
10 Alice Street, Binghamton, New York 13904-1580 • USA
TELEPHONE: 1-800-HAWORTH (1-800-429-6784) / Outside US/Canada: (607) 722-5857
FAX: 1-800-895-0582 / Outside US/Canada: (607) 772-6362
E-mail: getinfo@haworthpressinc.com
PLEASE PHOTOCOPY THIS FORM FOR YOUR PERSONAL USE.

BOF96